시사영어산책

이 종 호 저

남두도서

남두(南斗) : 남두육성(南斗六星)

은하의 중심인 사수자리에 있는 국자모양의 여섯 개의 별로서, 인간의 탄생을 결정하는 별로 알려져 있다.

| 개정판을 내면서 |

본서가 세상에 처음 나온 지 벌써 햇수로 3년의 세월이 흘렀다. 시사적인 지문을 제공해 줌으로써 학생들로 하여금 흥미 유발과 함께 영어 문장에 대한 거부감을 줄일 수 있도록 하는 데 일차적인 목표를 두었던 만큼, 이제 지문을 수정할 시점이 되었다고 판단하여 핵심적인 부분을 중심으로 재구성하게 되었다.

시사용어, 국내외 뉴스, Ann Landers(Abby), 독해문제, 유머영어 등의 코너에 수록된 지문을 상당부분 새로운 내용으로 교체하였다. 더 나아가 연습문제의 경우에는 각 단원마다 2~3개의 지문을 제시함으로써 학생들 스스로 해석해볼 수 있는 기회를 넓혀 주었다. 다양한 지문 선택을 위해 좀더 충분한 시간을 투자하지 못한 아쉬움이 있긴 하지만, 이번 개정판에 수록된 지문 역시 국내외적으로 세간의 관심을 끈 핫이슈들이 다수 포함돼 있어 학생들의 궁금증과 갈증은 어느 정도 해소시켜줄 수 있으리라 생각된다.

영어 학습에 왕도는 없는 법. 부디 본서가 영어 문장에 친숙하고자 하는 모든 분들에게 조그만 도움이 되기를 기대해 마지 않는다.

저 자 올림

| 차 례 |

제7장 Annan: No Death for Saddam

제8장 Quake Razes Jewel of Iranian Heritage

제9장 Duty over Freedom

제10장 Lifting Age Limits on Teachers Likely to Compound Youth Unemployment

제11장 Filipino Troops Leave Iraq to Save Hostage

제12장 N-E Asia History Body Proposed

제13장 Crimes Surge amid Economic Slump

제14장 Crude Hits 21-year High on Supply Fears

제15장 7 Former East-bloc Nations Join NATO

ANSWERS

제1장

130 Military Dodgers to Be Drafted Again

1 Warm-up

(1) In 1863 President Lincoln proclaimed all slaves to be free.

(2) The mine exploded, sending lethal fragments in all directions.

(3) The novice player is usually intimidated by the tennis champion's reputation.

(4) She enjoyed the lassitude of convalescence in which time, hurry and doing did not exist.

(5) Some reports suggested lowering blood cholesterol help prevent heart disease, but some others have been equivocal.

(6) An example of hyperbole is "I've told you a million times not to use that word."

(7) He wants to get his money's worth before the appliance becomes obsolete.

(8) His postwar policies brought criticism upon him which would have tarnished his popularity.

(9) A darkened sky in the daytime is usually an indication that a storm is imminent.

(10) In chemical factories, employees sometimes receive extra pay for doing hazardous work.

Note

1) pro(=forth)+claim : 여러 사람 앞에서 외치다 → 주창하다, 선언하다(declare)
2) lethal : 치명적인(causing death, fatal, deadly)
3) intimidate : 겁주다, 위협하다(make afraid, frighten, threaten)
4) lassitude : 나른함(weariness, languor)
5) equi(=equal)+voc(=call)+al : 양쪽에서 같은 소리로 부르는 → (어딘지) 불분명한, 모호한
6) hyperbole : 과장(법) → exaggeration
7) obsolete : 진부한, 안 쓰이는(=out-of-date)

Cf We have to get our money's worth. 「본전 뽑아야 해.」

⇒ Get one's money's worth : "본전 뽑다, 치른 돈만큼의 것을 획득하다"라는 의미로 투자한 만큼 얻어야 한다고 할 때 쓰는 표현이다. 비슷한 표현으로는 "We want what we paid for." "We expect a lot for our money." "We want a good return on our investment." 등이 있음.

8) tarnish : 더럽히다 → dimmed
9) imminent : 임박한 → about to take place
10) hazardous : 위험한 → dangerous

2 Current Terms

(1) Hot Money

But Korea will face a more serious problem if the won becomes the target of an attack from hot money as it did during the 1997-98 foreign currency crisis. The Korean economy, whose fundamentals were sound, collapsed when a sudden outflow of short-term funds created a liquidity squeeze. Some of the foreign funds recently invested in Korean stocks are reportedly hot money. (from The Korea Herald)

Note

hot money : 핫머니(투기성 외화자금) / foreign currency crisis : 외환위기 / fundamental : 펀더멘털(기초, 토대) / liquidity : 유동성 / squeeze : 곤경, 난관

(2) Global Warming

China is the second largest emitter of carbon dioxide-one of the principal factors contributing to global warming-accounting for 14 percent of the planet's total. And by 2020 it is expected to surpass the United States, emitting 18 percent of the world's total. According to the IEA, China's energy consumption will more than double in the next 20 years particularly since 77 percent of its energy consumption is provided by coal. The increasing number of vehicles in China is also a significant factor in the worsening pollution situation, according to World Watch, an American environmental research center. (from The Korea Herald)

3 Practical English

(1) Telephone English

A Hello, Kelly. How are my travel documents for the trip to Rome?

B Your documents are ready, sir. You're flying to Rome on a Cathay Pacific flight.

A What time will the flight be?

B At 12:30 p.m.

A What time do I arrive in Rome?

B At 5:30 p.m. sir, and Mr. Romano, the Naples branch office manager will pick you up at the airport.

A That's good. And what is my return schedule?

B You return on Wednesday the 5th and your flight number is 540 on Lufthansa.

A Kelly, can you change my ticket for Tuesday the 4th? I think I have to meet Mr. Reed from the Kowloon branch on Wednesday the 5th.

B But your meeting with Mr. Reed is on Thursday the 6th, isn't it?

A Yes, it is. But I have to meet him earlier to discuss Hang-seng Stock.

B All right, sir. So you'll have a meeting on Wednesday the 5th and your returning flight will be on Tuesday the 4th.

A That's right.

B Anything else, sir?

A Yes, is my seat in the smoking section?

B No, sir. Actually smoking is not allowed on all Cathay Pacific flights.

A You mean I have to stand 5 boring hours without cigarettes?

B Yes, sir. That's the new regulation.

A Okay. If that's the regulation.

B All right sir. Have a nice trip.

A Well, I hope so.

Note

travel documents : 출장서류 **cf** itinerary : 여행일정 / Cathay Pacific : '홍콩' 항공사 비행기 / be ready를 응용한 표현 : Everything is ready.(모든 준비완료) / reach : ~에 도착하다 **cf** 이 경우엔 전치사가 따로 필요없다. 즉 reach in Rome 이라고 쓰지 않음. / Naples : 나폴리 / pick you up at the airport : 공항에 마중 나오다 혹은 공항에 와서 당신을 모셔가다 / return ticket : 귀국행 비행기표 **cf** round-trip ticket : 왕복표 / How was your return trip? : 귀국하는 동안 어땠어? / on Wednesday the 5th : 날짜 앞에는 전치사 on을 씀. / flight number : 항공기의 번호 / change : 변경하다 **cf** Can you change my seat, please?(내 좌석을 다른 좌석으로 바꿔 주실래요?) / Have a nice trip : Bon voyage! 라는 표현도 쓴다. 이것의 의미는 Happy trip!임.

(2) Introduction of a Company 1

Well What does your company do?
Kwon We produce cotton buds and sell them all over the world.
Well Oh, I see. Where is the company located?
Kwon The company is in Kyonggido.
Well What are the annual sales of your company?
Kwon We have annual sales of $1million.
Well How many workers does your company currently employ?
Kwon 300 people are working for the company.

(3) Introduction of a Company 2

1) **A** If you don't mind, may I ask some questions?
B Why not?
A How many directors and managers are working in the Singapore branch?
B We have 2 directors and 4 managers.

2) **A** Mr. Stevenson, this is our new general manager, Mr. Krinston.
B Nice to meet you, Mr. Krinston.
A Nice to meet you, too, Mr. Stevenson.

3) **A** Who is the head of the Engineering Department?
B Mr. Jekinson is, but he is on leave now.
A When is he coming back?

4) **A** I've heard you have new regional manager for Southeast Asia, is that right?
B That's true, his name is John Randon.
A Where is he from?

(4) Answering machine

1) I'm not in my office at the moment.
2) Please leave your name, number and message when you hear the sound of the tone.
3) Could you call me at 567-1234 during office hours or 224-5634 after 6:30?
4) The office will be closed from 2:30 to 5:30 today and tomorrow.
5) If your call is an emergency, please dial 435-4567.
6) You're reached Mr. Adams office.
7) You can try again after 4:30.
8) This is a recorded message from Singapore Airlines.
9) Due to the bad weather, all flights to Guam are temporarily canceled.
10) All other flights are on service without any delay. Thank you.

Note

be not in~ : 부재중 / the sound of the tone : 삐 소리 / during office hours : 아홉시부터 다섯시까지(왜냐하면 미국에선 근무시간이 일반적으로 from nine to five이기 때문) / be closed : 병원이 '진료를 하지 않는다' / emergency call : 비상전화 **cf** emergency room : 응급실 / you're reached~ : (자동응답기로) '~입니다' / after : 이후 / due to the bad weather : 악천후 / delay : 연착 **cf** Our flight will be delayed for thirty minutes.(우리 비행기가 30분 연착할 겁니다.)

④ Domestic News

130 Military Dodgers to Be Drafted Again

JAbout 130 alleged military draft dodgers, including baseball players and TV celebrities, will be drafted by the end of November or face trial and probable prison terms, the military conscription office said yesterday. Among them, three TV celebrities, Song Seung-hun, Chang Hyuk and Han Jae-suk, have been barred from leaving the country since Oct. 14, with the cooperation of the Justice Ministry, and the remaining draft dodgers have faced that restriction since Tuesday, officials said. The Military Manpower Administration announced the steps after it received from police a list of the alleged draft violators who reportedly doctored urine tests to fake kidney ailments so they could gain exemption from the draft. The MMA said it retracted earlier orders that exempted 52 men from the service due to inadequate physical condition, and decided to call them for enlistment by the end of November. The men cannot be prosecuted under the criminal code due to expiration of the three-year statute of limitations, but they are still eligible for military duty. Korean men between the ages of 18 and 35 are subject to 24 months of military service unless they suffer from major physical or mental problems. In the case of 77 other men who also allegedly faked kidney ailments, the statute of limitations has not expired. Their exemptions also have been cancelled, and they face either prison or military service, a Military Manpower Administration spokesman said.

By law, draft dodgers face one to three years in prison. The conscription authorities have vowed to toughen the punishment so that anyone who dodgers enlistment will face three to five years in prison, instead. In addition, they propose to extend the statute of limitations for offenders to five years instead of three. The MMA decided to include two kidney-related cases in its intensive control lists. Patients on such a list get unexpected medical check-ups for an additional six months. Atopic dermatitis, scars caused by tattoos or self-inflicted wounds, high blood pressure, hepatitis, spinal or optical defects, and psychiatric problems are among 13 designations for which intensive checkups are required. (from The Korea Herald)

5 Ann Landers

Parents of sick child

Dear Ann Landers:

I hope my letter will help some of the caregivers of children who are frequently hospitalized. I have a child with long-term medical problems, and I spend three or four weeks in the hospital with him each year. My husband and I have worked out a system where at least one of us is at his side all day. I have met several other parents whose children are in the hospital for long stays, and we have a "wish list" for those who might want to give us a hand.

1. If the hospital allows it, please visit us. Our days start at 6 a.m., and we cannot leave our young children alone while they are awake. We would love having a

visitor to help break up the tedium and stress.

2. If our child knows you, can you stay with him or her for a few minutes while we grab a cup of coffee or a quick bite? I sometimes go for days without talking to my husband alone. Even a few minutes would be appreciated.
3. If you cannot visit us, ask if it is OK to call our child's hospital room to chat. It could be the highlight of our day. People often forget that parents of sick children need a break now and then. Helping us will also help our child, because it allows us to be calm and rested.

— Any Parent, Any Town

Dear Any Parent:

Thank you for a letter that could be a godsend for parents of sick children. I hope those who are blessed with healthy little ones will follow through some of these suggestions.

Note

break up : 분쇄하다 / tedium : 지루함 / grab a quick bite : 간단한 식사를 하다 / highlight : 가장 중요한 부분 / break : 쉬는 시간, 휴식 / godsend : 뜻밖의 행운 / follow through : 이행하다, 마무리하다

6 Reading Comprehension

I have to go out for a while now, but I'd like this fax to go out before eleven o'clock. And here's a list of files I'll need pulled. Just put them on my desk and I'll get to them later. If anybody calls, tell them I'll be back at around two-thirty. Thanks a lot.

(1) What request does the speaker make concerning the files?

ⓐ That they be faxed.
ⓑ That they be left on her desk.
ⓒ That her secretary put them on disk.
ⓓ That they be sorted according to importance.

(2) When will the speaker return?

ⓐ At around 2:30
ⓑ After about an hour
ⓒ In about a half-hour
ⓓ In just a few minutes

Note

go out : 외출하다, 전송되다 / for a while : 잠시(동안) / fax : 팩스, 팩스로 보내다 (=facsimile) / list : 목록 / file : 파일 / pull : (컴퓨터에서 자료를) 꺼내다 / put A on B : A를 B 위에 놓다 / get to : ~을 시작하다(착수하다) / call : 전화하다 / be back : 돌아오다 / around : ~경

⑦ Humour in English

(1) Unemployment

A man who in line to receive unemployment benefit suddenly became ill and collapsed. A crowd gathered around him, and it was apparent that no one knew what to do. "Is there a doctor in the room?" a young woman pleaed. A gruff voice from the back of the crowd spoke up. "Good Lord! Have you ever seen an unemployed doctor?"

Note

unemployment benefit : 실업수당 / collapse : 쓰러지다 / gruff : 목소리가 거친, 무뚝뚝한, 퉁명스러운

(2) This Indian is incredible

A film crew was on location deep in the desert. One day an old Indian went up to the director and said, "Tomorrow rain." The next day it rained. A week later, the Indian went up to the director and said, "Tomorrow storm." The next day there was a hailstorm. "This Indian is incredible" said the director. He told his secretary to hire the Indian to predict the weather. However, after several successful predictions, the old Indian didn't show up for two weeks. Finally the director sent for him. "I have to shoot a big scene tomorrow" said the director, "and I'm depending on you. What will the weather be like?" The Indian shrugged his shoulders. "Don't know" he said. "My computer is broken. I can't use Internet."

Exercise

(1) Yonsei University Sticks to 'Admission through Contribution'

One of the most prestigious universities in Korea, Yonsei took a stand for a new admission system based on contributions. It will allow entrance to students whose family have contributed to the university or the country.

Kim Woo-sik, the president of Yonsei University, has declared to pursue the new admission system. President Kim said, "I regret that the system has made such a big stir nationwide. But I will keep pushing for the admission system based on contributions. It is inevitable if the school is to remain competitive." He added that the general plan for the new admission system is already under way, and the committee for the evaluation of the contributions will be organized soon.

Meanwhile, the student council is strongly opposed to this new admission system. Students of Yonsei University held an open forum in front of the central library last week. "The admission system should be fair by all means. The new system will give a bad name to our school," said Kim Jang-il (22), a junior majoring in Physics.

The government's assistance to private schools in Japan and Taiwan reaches 19 percent of their budgets, but in Korea it is around four percent. As a result, many Korean universities are facing a serious financial crisis.

The government must take proper action to support schools so they can focus on education, not surviving. Otherwise, more schools may follow Yonsei and find other ways to support themselves. (from The Teen Times)

Note

prestigious : 유명한(일류의, 신망이 있는) / took a stand : 입장을 취하다 / stand for의 for : ~을 옹호(지지)하는 / admission system based on contributions : 기여입학제도 / contribute to : ~에 기여하다/ declare : ~을 선언(공포, 포고)하다(proclaim) / pursue : ~을 추적하다(따라 다니다, 계속 추구하다) / regret : ~을 후회하다(유감으로 여기다, 아쉬워하다, 애석하게 여기다) / make a big stir : 소란을 일으키다 / push : 추진하다 / inevitable : 피할 수 없는(논리적으로 당연한, 필연적인) / under way : 진행중인 / the committee for the evaluation of the contributions : 기여평가위원회 / organize : 구성하다 / meanwhile : 반면에 / the student council : 학생회 / oppose to : ~에 반대하다 / by all means : 반드시 / give a bad name : 오명을 가져다 줄 것이다 / government's assistance : 정부보조 / budget : 예산(안)(예산집행계획(안), 일정기간의 자금할당) / face a serious financial crisis : 심각한 경제위기를 맞다/ take proper action : 적당한 조치를 취하다 / otherwise : 그렇지 않으면

(2) Arroyo Re-elected in Philippines

After six weeks of counting votes, Gloria Arroyo was finally announced the Filipino president. She beat her opponent, film-star Fernando Poe Junior, by just over a million votes. "It was very difficult, but this is democracy," said Senate President Franklin Drilon. The controversy over the votes was started when Poe declared himself to be the winner, accusing Arroyo's party of buying votes and harassing voters. Lawmakers insisted that records from small villages be opened to be investigated for fraud. Police had to use force to keep back pro-Poe protestors, who marched in front of the presidential palace. Mrs. Arroyo's opponents accused her of returning to martial law, but the President defended her actions against the "agents of anarchy". President Gloria Arroyo first took rule in January 2001, during a popular revolt against Joseph Estrada. She has much more political experience than Poe, but many say she lacks charisma. Still, after a difficult six weeks, Arroyo was able to secure her seat as president. (from The Teen Times)

Note

opponent : 정적 / declare : 발표하다 / harass : 협박하다 / insist : 강요하다 / investigate : 조사하다 / fraud : 사기 / force : 강압, 완력 / protestor : 항의하는 사람 / accuse : 고발하다 / martial : 군인의 / anarchy : 무정부, 무질서 / revolt : 반란 / secure : 확보하다

제2장

Koizumi Visits Controversial Shrine

① Warm-up

(1) The criminal insinuated that he had been roughly treated by the arresting officer.

(2) The driver tried to avert the accident by bringing the car to a sudden stop.

(3) In many cultures, costumes are worn largely as adornment on social or religious occasion.

(4) All employees should familiarize themselves with the new company guidelines.

(5) No deposit can be refunded unless reservations are cancelled less than one week in advance.

(6) I was driving at a moderate speed, but the police said I drove over the speed limit.

(7) My favorite program was on another channel.

(8) All shipments entering the country must be accompanied by an official document from the government.

(9) Campfires should be thoroughly extinguished before campers leave the campsites.

(10) The service committee will provide participants with extra copies upon request.

Note

1) insinuate : 암시하다 → suggest indirectly
2) avert : 피하다, 막다(prevent, ward off), 어근 'vert'는 'turn'의 의미를 가지고 있다. avert는 '방향을 돌려 피하다'의 의미에서 '막다'의 의미를 갖게 되는 것이다.
   cf re(=back)+vert(=turn) : 되돌아가다 / intro(=within)+vert(=turn) : 성격이 안으로 돌아서는 사람 → 내성적인 사람
3) adornment : 장식(decoration, ornamentation) **cf** masquerade : 가장 무도회
4) 주어가 3인칭 복수이므로 재귀대명사도 이에 일치시켜야 함.
   familiarize oneself with : ~에 익숙해지다 / guideline : 방침
5) deposit : 보증금, 계약금 / refund : 환불하다 / in advance : 전에, 미리
6) moderate : 적당한, 알맞은 **cf** moderately : 적당하게 / moderator : 중재자
7) TV 채널에는 전치사 on이 사용됨.
8) official document : 공문서 / accompany : ~에 따르다, ~에 첨부되다
9) extinguish : (불을) 끄다
10) upon request : 요청에 따라

② Current Terms

(1) Casino

Barely a week has passed since Korea's first casino for locals opened in the former mining town of Chongsun, Kangwon Province, but a host of problems are already cropping up, officials and residents said yesterday. First of all, local residents as well as cash-laden customers from afar are swarming the gambling complex. The government originally allowed the construction of a casino to help the local government and residents make ends meet after closing the mines in the town, officials said. (from The Korea Herald)

(2) Wild Goose Father

Park's two children, now in grade eight and 10, have lived in the suburbs of Vancouver, Canada with their mother since 2000. Park and the ill-fated Sin represent a new class in Korean society called "wild goose" fathers, who pack their children and their mothers off to Canada, the United States, Australia, New Zealand and elsewhere while financing the move by continuing to live and work here alone. (from The Korea Herald)

Note

ill-fated : 불운한, 나쁜 운명의 / wild goose : 기러기 / pack : 짐을 꾸려 급히 나가다(off) / finance : 자금을 조달하다

3 Practical English

(1) It's my treat.

A Let's go out for lunch, it's my treat.
B What's up? Is it your birthday or something?
A Actually, I won some money in a lottery last weekend.
B Wow! How much did you win?

Note

treat : 누구누구를 ~로 취급하다 → They treated me as one of the family.(그들은 나를 가족의 한 사람으로 대해 주었다), ~를 대접하다 / go out for lunch : 점심식사하러 가다 **cf** Let's go out for dinner.(저녁 먹으러 가자.) / or something : 그와 비슷한 것 **cf** Is this a camera or something?(이거 사진기 같은 거야?) / lottery : 복권 또는 그런 종류 **cf** win a lottery(복권을 사서 돈을 벌다)

(2) What is the special tonight?

A Waiter, what is the special tonight?
B A T-bone steak with freshly baked potatoes.
A I had steak for lunch. Do you have a seafood special available?
B Yes, we do. It's 2 lbs of Canadian lobster.

Note

I had steak for lunch : have동사는 '~을 소유하다'라는 뜻 외에 뒤에 '음식'이 나오면 '그 음식을 먹다'라고 해석됨. **cf** I will have chicken for lunch.(난 점심으로 닭고기를 먹겠어요.), Did you have breakfast?(너 아침식사 했니?) → Did you eat breakfast?(밥 먹었어?) 보다 정중한 표현임(친구나 아랫사람에게 쓸 수 있는 표현).

(3) I've had enough!

A Come on, have some more potatoes!
B No thanks, I've had enough.
A Okay, what about dessert?
B Do you have strawberry ice-cream?

Note

I've had enough : 많이 먹었어요 **cf** Have some more!(더 드세요!) / 일반적으로 dessert로 나오는 음식은 ice-cream 또는 색깔이 검은 German chocolate cake이 있다. 물론 과일이 나오는 경우도 많다.

(4) At a restaurant

A Good evening, ma'am.
B A table for two, please.
A This way, please. Your waiter will serve you in a minute.
B Thank you.

*** A minute later**

A Good evening, ma'am. My name is Rich. I'll be your waiter for the evening.
B Hi, Rich.
A Are you ready to order?
B Yes, let me have a sirloin steak and baked potato.
A Very good choice. How would you like your steak?
B Well done, please.
A All right. Anything else?
B That's all.

*** The food is served.**

B Waiter!
A Yes, ma'am. Can I help you?
B Yes, I ordered a steak well done, and this is medium rare. Can you see the blood in it?
A Oh, I'm sorry, ma'am. The cook just started today. Let me get you another steak.
B Oh, I understand. Take your time. I'm not in a hurry.
A Thank you for your consideration.

4 International News

Koizumi Visits Controversial Shrine

Prime Minister Junichiro Koizumi marked the new year on Thursday by praying at a shrine honoring Japan's war dead, including convicted war criminals, drawing rebukes from China and South Korea and criticism from opposition lawmakers. Visits by Japanese leaders to Tokyo's Yasukuni Shrine generally outrage Asian countries that were invaded and brutally occupied by Japan before and during World War II. But Koizumi's visit Thursday came as Japan embarks on a mission to send troops to help the U.S.-led reconstruction of Iraq-its largest overseas military deployment in nearly 60 years-and could provoke a greater outcry from neighboring countries that have warily eyed Koizumi's efforts to broaden the Japanese military's role.

Koizumi arrived at Yasukuni shrine amid a throng of New Year's revelers. He was led into the shrine by a white-robed Shinto priest and offered a personal donation of 30,000 yen($280). Koizumi said he decided on the visit–his fourth since becoming prime minister in April 2001–to pray for "Japan's peace and prosperity." "Japan does not rest solely upon the efforts of people living now. Japan stands upon the sacrifices of others in the past," he told reporters. (from AP)

Note

controversial : 논쟁의 / shrine : 신사, 신전 / dedicate : 바치다, 헌신하다 / take office : 집권하다, 자리에 오르다 / rebuke : 비난, 질책 / opposition : 야당 / outrage : 화나게 하다, 격분하게 하다 / brutally : 잔혹하게 / embark : 시작하다(on), 승선하다 / deployment : 배치 / provoke : 화나게 하다, 일으키다 / angry outcry : 항의, 절규 / throng : 무리

5 Ann Landers

(1) A source of anxiety

Dear Ann Landers:

I am almost 17, and have never been kissed. I'm beginning to think something must be wrong with me. People say I'm pretty, and I'm comfortable with guys, so what's my problem? Please give me some pointers.

—A Cactus in Phoenix

Dear Phoenix:

Nothing is wrong with you. Be patient, and let time do its work.

P.S.: Don't let any guy kiss you unless you are sure he is sincere.

Note

pointer : 한마디의 충고 / cactus : 선인장

(2) Spanking a child

Dear Ann Landers:

Thank you for printing those letters about spanking and reiterating that there is never a good reason to hit a child. Many of those readers said, "My child learned better behavior in a hurry when I spanked him," or "I never spanked my child in anger." I say, "Baloney". There is never a time an adult hits a child when it is not in anger. I know, because I have done it myself. Whenever I have spanked or slapped my two children(and I am deeply ashamed to admit that I have done both), it was because I was frustrated and impatient and thought this was the way to get the message across pronto. These spankings produced unfortunate results. First, my daughter learned to fear me, and second, my son learned that hitting back was the way to respond to anger. I have worked long and hard to correct my own behavior so my children will not repeat my mistakes. Please, Ann, keep on advocating nonviolent forms of discipline.

—A Remorseful and Reformed Dad in Boston

Dear Reformed and Remorseful:

My congratulations for being both. This requires a lot of humility. I have been saying for years, when you hit a child, it is a sure sign that you are out of control. And while we are on this subject, I'd like to reiterate–belts, whips, straps, brushes and switches are OUT. No excuse is good enough to use any of the above.

6 Reading Comprehension

As you all know, our first quarter profits were not good. We need to make some major changes in the way we do business. Our prices are among the highest in the industry. We can't raise them and hope to remain competitive, and we can't cut them and hope to remain in business. Our only answer is to reduce manufacturing costs. I want the heads of all departments to come up with a list of suggestions to streamline our process. I suggest that you seriously consider eliminating any unnecessary positions. Please have your reports on my desk by 9 a.m. Wednesday.

(1) What does the manager say the company must do?

ⓐ Sell assets
ⓑ Raise prices
ⓒ Decrease costs
ⓓ Motivate employees

(2) What does the manager ask department heads to do?

ⓐ Cut the work force by 10%
ⓑ Encourage employees to work harder
ⓒ Make suggestions for increasing efficiency
ⓓ Recommend employees for special recognition

Note

first quarter : 1/4분기 / profit : 수익 / make a change : 수정(변경)하다 / major : 중대한 / do business : (사업체를) 경영하다 / price : 가격 / industry : 업계 / raise : 올리다, 인상하다 / remain : ~인 채로 남아 있다 / competitive : 경쟁력이 있는 / cut : (가격을) 내리다, 인하하다 / answer : 대안, 해결책 / reduce : 줄이다, 감소시키다 / manufacturing cost : 제조원가 / head : 장, 우두머리 / department : 부서 / come up with : ~을 강구해 내다(제안하다) / list : 목록 / suggestion : 제안 / streamline : 합리화(간소화)하다 / process : 공정, 여기서는 제조공정(manufacturing process)을 의미 / seriously : 진지하게 / consider : 고려하다 / eliminate : 없애다, 제거하다 / unnecessary : 불필요한 / position : 직책 / report : 보고서

7 Humour in English

(1) A Blonde

A blonde came home her first day commuting into the city. Her mother noticed she was looking a little haggard and asked, "Honey, are you feeling all right?" "Not really," the blonde replied. "I'm nauseous from sitting backward on the train." "Why didn't you ask the person sitting across from you to switch seats for a while?" "I couldn't," she replied, "there was no one there."

Note

commute : (정기권을 이용) 통근하다 / haggard : 초췌한 / nauseous : 메슥거리는 / blonde : 흔히 IQ가 낮은 사람으로 조롱거리가 됨.

(2) The Wrath of King

The king was angry with one of his lords and put him in jail. Wishing to keep him there, the king said he would only set him free if he could bring to the court a horse neither brown nor black-in short, no possible color a horse could be. The lord promised to get such a horse. As soon as he was set free the lord asked the king to set a day of the week that suited His Majesty for the horse to be brought to the court, but he begged it be any day but Monday, Tuesday, Wednesday, Thursday, Friday, Saturday and Sunday.

Note

lord : 영주, 귀족 / His Majesty : 폐하

Exercise

(1) Koreans Protest against Japan in 150 Cities around the World

"Korea had to be annexed to guarantee Japan's security and protect the interests of Manchuria. The U.S.A., Britain and Russia did not oppose Japan's annexation of Korea because they believed it would help stabilize East Asia."–from the approved junior high school history textbook in Japan

There will be a worldwide movement against distorted Japanese history textbooks on June 12. Korean residents in 70 different countries will gather in front of the Japanese embassy in 150 cities demanding Japan correct the history textbooks. They will issue an official manifesto, which says that Japan's distortion of history is not only a problem between Japan and Korea, but also a threat to world peace.

"We'll protest and make a strong appeal to Japan in the name ot conscience. Japan must correct their textbooks that are full of nonsense," said Cho Seong-young, President of Korean Associations in UK.

Tensions between Japan and Korea are at a peak because of the textbook issue. Japan decided to hold off Emperor Akihito's visit to Seoul next year because of security concerns, said the Yomiuri daily newspaper in Japan.

Korean President Kim Dae-jung sent a letter to Japanese Prime Minister Junichiro Koizumi at the end of last month urging him to settle the problem. In the letter, President Kim asked Prime Minister Koizumi to take positive and sincere steps to clear its history. (from The Teen Times)

Note

Manchuria : 만주 / President of Korean Associations in UK : 재영한인회 회장 / annex : 병합하다 / guarantee : 보장하다 / security : 안전 / interests : 이익 / oppose : 반대하다 / stabilize : 안정시키다 / approved : 승인된 / distorted : 왜곡된 / resident : 거주자 / gather : 모이다 /

embassy : 대사관 / correct : 고치다 / issue an official manifesto : 공식성명을 발표하다 / threat : 위협 / make a strong appeal : 강력하게 호소하다 / in the name of conscience : 양심의 이름으로 / nonsense : 헛소리 / tension : 긴장 / are at a peak : 최고조에 달하다 / hold off : 보류하다 / concerns : 관심사, 사건, 용무 / urge : 강요(요구)하다 / settle : 해결하다 / take positive and sincere steps : 긍정적이고 성실한 조치를 취하다

(2) Civic Groups Raise Their Voices against Sending Troops

Kim Sun-il, who was kidnapped by Iraqi militants, was killed sometime between 8:00 to 9:00 a.m.(Korean time) on June 22. Civic groups are raising their voices against sending troops to Iraq. 'Anti-dispatch' is the name for 365 civic groups that gathered at an urgent meeting on June 23. A press conference was held at 12:00 p.m. in Gwangwhamoon. At 7:00 p.m., a candlelight vigil was held in memory of Kim Sun-il. A nationwide candlelight vigil was held on June 26. Human rights groups, including Sarangbang Group for Human Rights, held a press conference in front of the National Human Rights Commission on the morning of that day. They strongly urged against sending troops to Iraq. Prior to this, 'Anti-dispatch' had gathered in front of Cheongwadae on June 18. In a statement they said, "How the Korean government collected public opinion is doubtful. The first decision of the government should not have gone against the will of the nation." (From The Junior Times)

Note

kidnap : 납치하다 / dispatch : (군대) 파병하다 / gather : 모으다 / militant : 투사 / urgent : 긴급한 / candlelight vigil : 촛불집회 / urge : 촉구하다

제3장

Roh at War with Dailies over Capital Relocation

1 Warm-up

(1) Role models for what one "ought to do" are important determining behavior in every walk of life.
(2) Ken swore he would get even with Terry one day.
(3) It is almost impossible for a successful politician to write a good memoir: the skills involved in the one area are antithetical to good prose.
(4) Nations are not to be judged by their size any more than individuals.
(5) It still remains the truth that one can no more jazz through education than one can jazz through life.
(6) Not that I was ever the sort of person to fall in love with a house in the best of circumstances.
(7) Today, divorce is no longer regarded as a disgrace, a tragedy, or even a failure.
(8) It was not till all was dark that the prince halted from pursuit.
(9) Life is too short to be interested in everything, but it is good to be interested in as many things as are necessary to fill our days.
(10) Not until his life was over did the seed which he had sown bear fruit.

Note

1) every walk of life : 각계 각층의 모든 사람들(all kinds of people)
2) get even with : 복수하다(take revenge on)
3) a good memoir = good prose
4) 「A가 ~아님은 B가 ~아님과 마찬가지이다」 라는 A no more ~ than B의 구문은 A not ~ any more than B의 형태로도 쓰인다.
be judged by ~ : ~에 의해 판단되다 / individual : 개인
5) 문장 제일 앞의 It는 가주어이고, that one can ~ 이하 끝까지가 이 문장의 진주어이다. that절 내의 문장은 A no more ~ than B의 구문이다.
remain : 남아 있다, 여전히 ~이다 / truth : 진리 / jazz through : 춤추며 지나가다, 춤추듯 보내다 / education : 교육 / life : 인생, 삶
6) to fall은 형용사적 용법으로 쓰인 부정사로서 to fall in love with a house는 person을 수식하는 형용사구이다. sort : 종류 / fall in love with : ~와 사랑에 빠지다, ~에 마음을 빼앗기다 / in the best of circumstances : 대단히 훌륭한 상태에 있는
7) 이 문장은 A is regarded as B(A는 B라고 여겨진다)라는 구문의 활용 형태이다.
divorce : 이혼 / no longer : 더 이상 ~아닌 / disgrace : 치욕, 창피 / tragedy : 비극 / failure : 실패
8) not ~ till… (~한 이후에라야 비로소 …하다)의 강조구문이므로 「It+be동사+not till ~ that…」의 형태가 되어야 한다. halt : 멈춰서다, 정지하다 / pursuit : 추적
9) but 앞부분의 문장은 too ~ to 구문이다. but 뒤의 문장에서는 it가 가주어이고, to be interested ~ 이하가 진주어이다. as many things as are ~에서 as는 주격 관계대명사로 쓰인 것이다. as many as ~의 구문으로 잘못 이해하면 문맥 파악이 불가능해진다.
be interested in ~ : ~에 관심이 있다 / necessary : 필요한 / fill : 채우다
10) 부정어 not과 부사절 until his life was over가 문장 앞으로 나온 도치구문이다. 따라서 주어와 동사의 어순이 바뀌어 「동사+주어」가 되어야 한다. which he had sown은 관계대명사절로서 주어인 the seed를 수식하고 있다. 이 문장의 골격만을 다시 써 보면 The seed did not bear fruit until his life was over가 된다. be over : 끝나다 / sown : sow(씨를 뿌리다)의 과거분사 / bear : (열매를) 맺다 / fruit : 열매, 과일 / seed : 씨(앗)

② Current Terms

(1) Road Map

As the first official dialogue between Pyongyang and Washington under the Bush administration, the Beijing talks will reportedly allow each side to sound out each other's position. Few expect the talks will lead to a viable conclusion anytime soon. Nonetheless, it is imperative that the participants draw out an agenda in the form of a "road map" with different phases leading toward a diplomatic conclusion. (from The Korea Herald)

Note

administration : 행정, 통치, 관리; 정부 내각 / sound out : 소리를 내다 / viable : 존립 가능한 / imperative : 꼭 해야 할, 필수적인 / road map : 도로지도, 이정표

(2) Local Referendums

In an attempt to upgrade local government, the Roh administration is planning to submit a bill on local referendums to the National Assembly during its regular session starting in September. If approved, the bill will allow the electorate to make decisions on local issues of magnitude. Permitting residents to decide on an important proposal affecting their lives will mark a great step forward in the nation's participatory democracy. (from The Korea Herald)

Note

upgrade : 향상시키다 / local referendums : 주민투표제 / the National Assembly : 국회 / electorate : 선거민 / magnitude : 중대, 중요함 / participatory democracy : 참여 민주주의

③ Practical English

(1-a) May I have your full name, please?

A May I have your full name, please?
B My name is Antonio E. Lopez.
A Is Lopez your family name?
B Yes, it is.

Note

생활영어는 "나와 타인간의 만남"에 필요한 도구이다. 그러므로 나를 상대방에게 정확히 알릴 필요가 있다. 우리나라에선 자신 또는 타인을 소개할 때 성(姓)만을 알리는 경우가 많다(예를 들면, 김 선생님, 강 여사 등). 하지만 원어민들은 full name을 자주 사용한다(예를 들면, This is Linda Kim. 등). Full name이란 말 그대로 "성(family name)과 이름(first name)"이다. 영어 이름은 일반적으로 "이름(first name)을 먼저 쓰고 성(family name)"을 나중에 쓴다. 그래서 Bill Clinton의 성(family name)은 Clinton인데, 뒤에 온다고 하여 종종 last name이라고도 한다.

(1-b) What is your middle name?

A Mr. Kim, what is your middle name?
B Koreans don't have middle names.
A Oh, I see.

Note

영어이름에서 우리에게 생소한 것 중의 하나가 바로 middle name이다. 일반적으로 엄마쪽 성씨의 initial을 많이 쓰거나 또는 자신이 존경하는 인물의 성씨 initial을 많이 쓴다. 일례로 유명한 미국의 35대 대통령의 이름(full name)은 John F. Kennedy이다. John은 first name이고, F는 Fitzgerald의 준말로 외가의 성씨(즉 외할아버지의 성)이며 Kennedy는 자신의 family name(친가)이다. 그래서 줄여서 JFK라고도 한다. 일반적으로 영어권의 여자들은 결혼을 하면 남편의 성씨를 따라간다. 예를 들면 "정 태욱"이라는 남자가 "박 순미"라는 여자와 결혼을 하면 호적에는 "박 순미"라는 분이 "정 순미"라고 기록된다. 만일 이 "정 순미"라는 분이 middle name을 만들려면 자신의 원래 성인 "박"을 쓰면 된다. 그럼, 영어로는 Soon-mi P. Chung이 될 것이다. 이때 Soon-mi는 first name이 되고, P는 middle name, Chung은 family name이 되는 것이다. 미국의 고 케네디 대통령을 John F. Kennedy라고 부르지, middle name을 완전하게 발음하여 John Fitzgerald Kennedy라고 부르지는 않는다. 즉 middle name은 그냥 initial만 읽으면 된다.

(1-c) Chen is a popular family name in Hong Kong.

A What is a popular family name in Hong Kong?
B Chen is. What about Korea?
A In Korea, Kim is a popular surname.

Note

요즘은 문화교류가 미국뿐 아니라 아시아의 부자 나라들, 즉 Japan, Singapore, Hong Kong, Taiwan 등과도 자주 일어나고 있다. 특히 Hong Kong과 자주 무역을 하시는 분은 기억해 둘 만한 표현이다. 우리나라에는 '김', '이', '박'씨 성을 갖고 계신 분들이 많다. 예를 들어 "한국엔 '김'씨 성을 갖고 계신 분들이 많습니다"를 영어로 옮겨보면 Kim is a popular family name in Korea.라고 할 수 있다.

popular : 유명한, 많은 **cf** popular songs : 대중음악 / surname : '성'씨

(1-d) Mr. Lee, how come your wife's last name is Mrs. Kim?

A Mr. Lee if you don't mind, may I ask you a question?
B Sure, go ahead.
A Your family name is Lee, but how come your wife's last name is different?
B Korean women retain their maiden name even when they get married. It's a Korean law.

Note

영어권을 여행하거나 영어권 원어민을 만나서 대화할 때 그들이 자주 묻는 질문 중의 하나이다. 왜냐하면 대부분의 영어권 국가에서는 결혼을 하면 부인은 남편의 성(family name)을 따라 가기 때문이다. how come은 원어민들이 '어째서', '왜'라는 의미로 회화에서 자주 쓰는 표현이다. 뭔가가 몹시 궁금할 때 사용하는 표현이다. 한국의 법을 모르는 많은 영어권 사람들은 한국 분이 자기의 wife라고 소개를 하면서 "성"씨가 자기와 다른 부인의 이름을 알려주면 몹시 의아해 한다. 왜냐하면 혹시 "동거하는 부부인가?"라고 생각할 수 있기 때문이다.

(2-a) Family name 1

1)

A Can I have your name, please?

B My name's Delion. That's D for Doris, E for Edward, L for Love, I for Italy, and N for Nancy.

A And your initials, sir ?

B My initials are T. J.

2)

A Your name, please?

B My name is Chung. That's C for Charlie, H for Harry, U for Universe, N for Noel, and G for Great.

A And can I have your initials, please?

B Sure, my initials are B.L.

Note

원어민들(Native speakers), 특히 미국인(Americans)의 성씨(family name or last name)를 제대로 알아 듣기는 쉽지 않다. 그 이유(the reason)는 미국이 전세계 여러 나라의 후손 (descendants of various nations)들로 구성된 복합문화국가(multi-cultural society)이기 때문이다. 그러므로 전화상으로 이름을 받아 적는 것은 특히 어렵다. 참고로 우리나라의 '이'씨를 영어로 Lee라고만 하지는 않는다. 종종 Yie라고도 하고 자기가 편한대로 쓰면 된다.

(2-b) Family name 2

A Good morning, Boulevard Hotel. May I help you?

B Yes, please. I'd like to reserve a room.

A When and for how long, sir?

B This Friday and for two nights.

A O.K. May I have your family name, please?

B My name's Perot.

A How do you spell that, sir?

B That's P for Peter, E for Edward, R for Robert, O for Oliver and T for Tom.

A Thank you. And your initials, sir?
B D.O.
A I see. Thank you for calling.
B You're welcome.
A Have a nice day!
B You too!

Note

우리나라에서는(in Korea) 이름으로 사람을 구별하는 것이 보다 더 쉽지만, 복합민족(multi-cultural society)인 미국에선 성(family name)으로 사람을 구별하는 것이 더 용이(much easier and more effective)하다.

(3) Inquiring

1)
A Hello. My name is Kim from room 506. Can you tell me the time when the shop opens this morning?
B Certainly, sir. It opens at 10.
A Thank you so much.

2)
A When is the Italian restaurant open for breakfast?
B Breakfast is available from 8 until 9:30, ma'am.
A Is there any restaurant that opens before 7:30? I have an important meeting this morning.
B Oh, I see. Why don't you try the American restaurant? It's open 24 hours a day.

3)
A Hello, front desk?
B Yes, can I help you?
A Where can I buy daily newspaper?
B You can get the paper on the first floor or if you want

we can send a paper to your room.
A Let me get one at the lobby.

Note

"506호실의 '김'이란 사람"은 Kim from room 506이라고 할 수 있고, 또한 This is Kim from room 506.라고 할 수도 있음. / '가게를 열다'라고 할 땐 open을 쓴다. 덧붙여 '영업 중'이란 표현은 We are open.이라고 한다. We are opened.라고 하지 않음을 기억하기 바람. **Cf** We close at 10.(우린 10시에 닫습니다.) / Thank you so much : 이 표현을 조금 더 정중하게는 I appreciate it!이라고 할 수도 있음. appreciate 뒤엔 '사람'을 쓸 수 없다는 것을 주의하기 바람. 즉 I appreciate him. 이라고는 못함. / breakfast 앞엔 a 를 쓰지 않는다. 즉 for a breakfast라고 할 수 없다. lunch, dinner 앞에도 a를 못붙이기는 마찬가지 / be available : ~이 가능한 **Cf** Are you available for tomorrow's meeting? ⇒ "당신 내일 모임에 참가할 수 있어요?" / '~이 어떠냐'고 권유할 땐 try라는 동사를 쓴다. **Cf** Why don't you try Korean food?(한국 음식 드셔 보세요.) / Hello, Front desk? : 이 표현을 그냥 Hello, front? 라고 하면 어색하다. / Where can I buy (get) a daily newspaper? : 이 표현을 우리 식으로 I would like to read a newspaper.라고 하면 부자연스럽다. 이런 경우엔 돌려서 '신문 어디서 구입할 수 있어요?'라고 하는 것이 자연스럽다.

④ Domestic News

Roh at War with Dailies over Capital Relocation

The dispute involving projected relocation of the nation's administrative capital shows signs of further escalating into a fierce political fight between ruling and opposition camps with the nation's major vernacular dailies throwing their weight behind the latter. The presidential office of Chong Wa Dae on Sunday stepped up rhetoric to dismiss calls for scrapping its capital relocation project. Chief presidential secretary for national policy Kim Byong-joon on Sunday launched a fresh salvo at the opponents by saying, "The national project is being blindly opposed with more haste than caution." He rebuffed the assertion that Chong Wa Dae has pushed through the capital relocation project in a rough-and-ready manner. Kim also underlined that the government's plan to rebuild an administrative capital should be seen as part of its vision to move beyond a small regional power toward becoming a hub in Northeast Asia. "Such a dream should not be trampled and overridden any more. How can the nation possibly sharpen its competitiveness if Seoul's population increases by more than 3.5 million in 10 years?" "Opposition to the government's plan seems to stem from a deep-seated distrust in the head of state and insubordination to the 2002 presidential election," Kim said. Regarding growing calls for a referendum for the fate of the project, the presidential secretary dismissed it as a matter to be discussed at the National Assembly beforehand. His remarks came two days after the presidential office denounced the nation's two major conservative dailies-Chosun Ilbo and DongA Ilbo-for taking the lead in fostering opposition to the relocation plan.

President Roh Moo-hyun earlier joined the fray to accuse the conservative dailies for their opposition to the government's capital relocation project, saying "The campaign against the capital relocation is a campaign of no-confidence aimed at ousting the incumbent president." Immediately after the government virtually chose the Yongi-Kongju area in the country's central region as the site for its new administrative capital last week, ruling and opposition parties have been at loggerheads over the plan. (from The Korea Times)

Note

throwing their weight behind the latter : 야당편을 들면서 / stepped up rhetoric : 발언공세의 수위를 높이다 / rough-and-ready manner : 졸속으로 / sharpen its competitiveness : 경쟁력을 키우다 / stem from a deep-seated distrust : 뿌리깊은 불신에서 비롯되다 / take the lead in fostering opposition : 반대 조장에 앞장서다 / a campaign of no-confidence : 불신임 운동 / ousting the incumbent president : 현직대통령의 퇴진 / loggerheads : 치고 받기 싸움

⑤ Ann Landers

Reckless driving

Dear Ann Landers:

Last week, my husband and I were on our way to a restaurant to meet some of my relatives for lunch. The restaurant is about two hours away from our house. "Dwight" was doing at least 65 mph in a 35 zone. I calmly asked him to please slow down. Instead, he sped up to pass some bicyclists on the side of the road. We then came to a curve where several motorists have been killed in the past few years. He kept his foot on the gas pedal. I was terrified that his reckless driving would get us both killed. Finally, I said, "If you cannot slow down, stop the car, and let me out." Dwight immediately turned the car around, went back to our house, and told me to get out of the car. I begged him not to make me miss the luncheon. Dwight said nothing. He simply got back in the car and drove to the restaurant by himself. Dwight not only had lunch with my relatives, he also went along with them to visit my grandmother, who has not been feeling well. I was so furious when Dwight returned that I told him to leave the house and never come back. He is basically a good person, but this is not the first time he has behaved in an immature manner, and I've had it. Am I just too angry to see straight? Please tell me what to do.

—Angry in North Carolina

Dear North Carolina:

You two are in desperate need of marriage counseling, and Dwight could use some sessions on anger management. Yes, I know counseling costs money, but your marriage and Dwight's mental health need propping up-big time. Please get the help you need. This is no do—it-yourself project.

6 Reading Comprehension

The editors of The Encounters magazine would like to offer you the first issue of their new publication at no cost to you. Simply return the enclosed reply card and an issue of The Encounters will be sent to you. When you receive your copy, you will be offered the opportunity to subscribe to The Encounters at the rate of $36 a year (12 monthly issues)–an annual savings of $12 over the cover price of $4 per issue. If you subscribe at this time, you are entitled to renew annually at a savings of 25 percent off the newsstand price. We hope you will take advantage of this offer soon.

(1) How can you receive the issue of The Encounters described in the advertisement?

ⓐ By renewing your subscription.
ⓑ By mailing back the accompanying form.
ⓒ By taking the enclosed form to your newsstand.
ⓓ By subscribing to the magazine for two years.

(2) What is the future advantage of accepting this offer now?

ⓐ The first year is free.
ⓑ The editors will respond to all requests.
ⓒ Opportunities of employment will be available.
ⓓ Renewal prices are lowered.

Note

at no cost : 무료로 / simply : 간단히 / issue : 호 / subscribe to : 정기구독하다 / cover price : 표지에 적힌 가격 / savings : 절약 / be entitled to : 할 자격이 있다 / renew : 갱신하다

⑦ Humour in English

(1) The Proposal

A millionaire collected live alligators which he kept in the pool at his mansion. The guy also had a beautiful daughter who was single. One day he threw a big party during which he announced, "My dear guests, I put forth a proposition to every man here: I will give one million dollars or my daughter to the man who can swim across this pool full of alligators and emerge unharmed." Suddenly, there was a large splash, and everybody gawked as a man took the plunge and began swimming across the pool like Tarzan going to save Jane. The crowd cheered the guy on as he kept churning through the water. Finally, he made it to the other side unharmed. The millionaire was impressed, saying, "My boy, that was incredible. Fantastic! I didn't think it could be done. Well, I must keep my end of the bargain--which do you want, my daughter or the one million dollars?" The guy said, "Listen, fella, financially, I'm doing all right, so I don't want your money. And I'm married so I can't have your daughter. But what I do want is THE SON-OF-A-BITCH WHO PUSHED ME INTO THE GODDAMN POOL!!"

Note

millionaire : 백만장자 / alligator : 악어 / single : 미혼의, 독신의 / throw a party : 파티를 개최하다 / put a proposition to A : A에게 제안을 하다 / emerge unharmed : 무사히 나오다 **cf** emerge : (수면 위로) 나오다 / splash : 물의 철썩거림 / gawk : 멍청하게 쳐다보다 / take the plunge : 뛰어들다, 잠수하다 / churn through : 몸을 비틀며 뚫고 나가다 / make it to A : A에 닿다 / My boy : My son, My friend; (아니 이런) 부르는 투의 감탄사에서 상대가 어리므로 boy라고 한 것임. / incredible : 믿지 못할, 놀라운 / financially : 재정적으로 / son-of-a-bitch: son of a bitch; 개XX(=bastard) 약어로는 S.O.B. / goddamn : 망할, 빌어먹을(경멸의 뜻으로 쓰이는 강조사)

(2) An American Football Fan

An American football fan, looking with his binoculars, spotted an empty seat on the 50-yard line. He made his way down to the empty seat. "Is this seat taken?" he asked the man sitting next to it. The man replied, "This was my wife's seat. She passed away. She was a big fan." The other man said, "I'm sorry to hear that. May I ask why you didn't give the ticket to a friend or a relative?" "They're all at the funeral." the man replied.

Note

make one's way : (애써) 나아가다, 가다 / pass away : 죽다

Exercise

(1) Unbalanced Employment Market

As the year-end employment season is approaching, college graduates-to-be or graduates are busy seeking jobs, but their rate of employment at large enterprises remains at a low level. On the other hand, small and medium-sized companies, especially those engaging in so-called "3D"(difficult, dangerous, and dirty) businesses, are having serious difficulties in hiring workers. In a nutshell, a strange phenomenon of concurrent labor and job shortages exists in the local market. According to a recent survey of an employment-related information research company, the average competition ratio among college graduates to get a job in large enterprises was 67.3:1, almost similar to last year's 67.7:1. Until the first half of the year, many market experts anticipated that the employment scale by large enterprises would increase significantly, riding on a strong upturn of the domestic economy. However, as the future economies of the world's major countries have become opaque due to deepening fears of the possible "double-dip" recession of the U.S. economy and an anticipated war between the U.S. and Iraq, most domestic enterprises have been making downward adjustments of their employment plans these days. If this trend is left unchecked, the domestic job market in 2003 is feared to face its worst situation since the foreign exchange crisis gripped the country in late 1997.

On the contrary, some small and medium-sized companies are facing the suspension of their plant operations due to a failure to secure enough workers. Based on a survey of 8,400 companies with five to 300 employees, which was conducted by the Korea Institute for Industrial Economics & Trade, the shortage of manpower came to 204,900 persons. In particular, the lack of professionals and technicians with undergraduate or higher-level educations stood at 7,300 and 17,000, respectively. As a means of solving this problem, smaller companies have been largely dependent on foreign workers. It is not easy, however, to employ competitive ones. To settle the unbalanced employment market problem, it is desirable for large enterprises to expand their recruitment from the standpoint of investing in future manpower and contributing to social responsibility. College graduates seeking jobs, meanwhile, are required to reconsider their basic conception of employment so smaller companies can support the national economy by becoming better places for workers to demonstrate their abilities. (From The Korea Times)

Note

college graduates-to-be : 대학졸업 예정자들 / In a nutshell : 아주 간결하게 / concurrent labor and job shortages : 노동력과 일자리의 동시 부족 / Korea Institute for Industrial Economics & Trade : 산업연구원 / competitive ones : 경쟁력 있는 기술인력

(2) Continuing Hostage Situation in Iraq

After beheading Nick Berg of the US and Kim Sun-il of South Korea, an Islamic militant group calling itself Islamic Reponse has announced that it is currently holding another hostage. Al-Jazeera, the Islamic satellite broadcasting station, showed the image of a blindfolded man holding a US marine ID card. According to the ID card, the man's name is Wassef Al Hassoun and he was a soldier on active duty. The US military has confirmed that Hassoun has been missing since June 21, but they are not sure if the man on the tape is really him. Islamic terror groups have used ID cards in the past to falsely claim they are holding US military hostages. The group said that their hostage is of Pakistani origin, but the military says that Hassoun is of Lebanese descent.

In a seperate incident, a group that is suspected of supporting Al-Qaeda leader Abu Musab Al-Zarqawi appeared on a video broadcast by Al-Jazeera and said that they are holding three Turkish prisoners. They threatened to behead them unless all Turkish companies in Iraq withdraw within 72 hours. Turkey has rejected the demand. The increasing violence in Iraq has made many nervous about the handover of power from the Coalition to the interim Iraqi government. The handover was previously scheduled for June 30, but abruptly took place two days earlier than planned. The Allies will remain in Iraq to support the government against future terrorist attacks. An election for a new government is scheduled for next year. (From The Teen Times)

Note

militant : 투쟁적인 / hostage : 인질/ blindfolded : 눈가리개 쓴 / confirm : 확인하다 / falsely claim : 거짓으로 주장하다 / origin : 혈통 / descent : 출신 / broadcast : 방송하다 / behead : 참수하다 / withdraw : 물러나다 / demand : 요구하다 / increasing : 증가하는 / handover : 이양 / Coalition : 연합군 / interim : 임시의

제4장 Iraq

① Warm-up

(1) When will you leave for Belgium?
(2) His major is economics, but he studies architecture as a hobby.
(3) Stick around, George. I'll be with you in just a minute.
(4) Ed Burnstein was by far the most talented warrior in those days.
(5) You should be able to get a big discount on your airline ticket if you buy it through a wholesaler.
(6) We consider this difficult assignment a challenge to our marketing skills.
(7) He asked me so many questions during the movie that I hardly know what happened myself.
(8) They enjoy working as bank tellers.
(9) Over the past year, there have appeared several exciting new stars in the entertainment industry.
(10) Some products are manufactured to wear out after one or two years.

Note

1) leave for ~ : ~로 떠나다 cf leave Belgium : 「벨기에를 떠나다」, leave for Belgium : 「벨기에를 향해 떠나다」
2) major : 전공 / economics : 경제학 / architecture : 건축학 / hobby : 취미 / as : 「~로서」라는 뜻의 전치사 cf as for : 「~에 관하여」
3) stick : 꼼짝않고 그대로 있다 / stick around : 멀리 가지 않고 근처에서 기다리다 / be with you : 당신과 함께 하겠다, 당신에게로 돌아오겠다 / in just a minute : 곧바로, 즉시
4) by far는 최상급 혹은 비교급을 강조하는 수식어이다. talented : 재능있는, 유능한 / warrior : 전사(戰士), 군인 / in those days : 그 당시에 / by far : 훨씬, 몹시
5) 「~에 대한 할인」이라고 할 때는 전치사 on을 사용한다. discount : 할인 / airline ticket : 항공권 / wholesaler : 도매업자
6) consider : 고려하다, 간주하다 / assignment : 과제 / challenge : 모험, 도전
7) 부사 hardly의 위치는 일반동사 앞이나 be동사 뒤이다. question : 질문 / movie : 영화
8) enjoy는 동명사를 목적어로 취하는 동사이다. teller : (은행의) 금전출납계원
9) appear는 「나타나다, 출두하다」라는 자동사이므로 수동태가 불가능하며, 새로운 스타가 나타난 것은 현재까지 유효한 사실이므로 현재 완료형이 적합하다.
several : 몇몇의 / entertainment : 연예, 오락 / industry : 산업
10) product : 생산품 / manufacture : 제조하다 / wear out : 닳아 없어지다, 낡다

② Current Terms

(1) Aggregate Land Tax

Starting 2006, individuals will face an extra tax burden if they own real estate above a certain level, the Ministry of Government Administration and Home Affairs said yesterday. The move is part of the government's efforts to curb rising real estate prices and reduce the income gap between rich and poor, the ministry said. Currently, people pay only two regional taxes on their real estate holdings, namely aggregate land tax and property taxes. (from The Korea Herald)

Note

tax burden : 세부담 / real estate : 부동산 / Ministry of Government Administration and Home Affairs : 행정자치부 / curb : 억제하다, 자갈을 물리다 / aggregate land tax : 종합토지세 / property tax : 재산세

(2) The Outside Director System

Of the 163 outside directors it interviewed, the civic group found links between 51 of them and the management of the companies of which they are on the board. Seven were former or sitting executives, 33 were former or incumbent officials at financial authorities, and 11 were former or present officials at government branches or research institutes which are closely associated with the companies. The outside director system was first introduced in Korea in 1998. (from The Korea Herald)

Note

Outside directors : 사외이사 / civic group : 민간 단체 / executives : 경영진(간부) / incumbent : 현직의, 재직의 / associate : 관련시키다, 연합시키다

3 Practical English

(1) Have you been to Wall Mart?

A Have you been to Wall Mart?
B Yes, I have.
A How is it? Is it cheaper than Shopper's Ville?
B About the same I think.

Note

해석을 할 때 'have been to' 라는 표현을 단순히 "~에 가 본 적 있어?(단순경험)"라고만 해석하지 말고 다양하고 넓게 보기 바람. 예를 들어 Have you been to Paris?를 단순히 "파리에 다녀 온 적 있어?"라고만 하지 말고 "파리 관광 가 봤어?"라고 해석하면 대화의 분위기가 더 살 수 있다.

cf 생활영어에서는 많은 단어를 사용하지 않는다. 그래도 생활영어가 어려운 이유는 단순한 표현인데도 불구하고 해석이 다양하게 되기 때문이다. 예를 들어 상기의 표현 중에서 How is it?이 상황에 따라선 "(물건) 어때?" "(날씨) 어때?," "(음식 맛이) 어때?" 등의 다양한 뜻을 나타낼 수 있다.

(2) I have to buy a week's worth of groceries.

A Linda, any plans for this weekend?
B Not really, I have to go shopping.
A What will you buy?
B A week's worth of groceries.

Note

grocery는 "식료 잡화류"라는 뜻이지만 대개 식품이 큰 부분을 차지한다. 그래서 grocery store라고 하면 "식료품 가게"를 의미한다. 회화에서 Where do you usually go grocery shopping?이라고 하면 "주로 장은 어디서 보세요?"라는 뜻이다. 덧붙여 "run a grocery"라고 하면 "식료품점을 운영하다"이다. Go shopping이라는 표현을 우리말로 하면 "장보러 가다"가 가장 자연스럽다. 백화점 등에서 종업원이 "뭐 찾으시는 거 있으세요?"라고 물어볼 때 "그냥 구경만 하는 거예요."라고 영어로 표현하고 싶으면 I'm just looking around., I'm just window-shopping., I'm just browsing.이라고 하면 된다. **cf** 우리도 증가 추세에 있지만 미국에선 대부분이 맞벌이 부부(double income couple)이다. 그러다 보니 부인들이 슈퍼에 갈 시간이 많지 않다. 그래서 주말에 부부가 함께 일주일치의 식료품을 구입하는 경우가 많다.

(3) I go to the store on Sundays.

A What do you usually do on Sundays?
B I go shopping on Sundays.
A Me, too. Let's go together.
B Okay, call me when you go.

Note

'요일' 앞에는 전치사 on이 필요하다. 그런데 더 중요한건 '요일'이 복수형이 되는 경우이다. 예를 들어 "Monday+s"는 "매주 월요일"이라고 해석한다. 다른 표현으로는 every Monday가 있음. "Me, too."의 경우, 이 말은 "당신 말이 맞고 저도 그래요."이다. 다시 말해 앞서 말한 사람이 "긍정적인 표현"을 할 때 쓴다. 예를 들어 I like coffee.라고 할 때 Me, too.라고 하면 "나도 당신처럼 커피를 좋아해요."가 된다. 하지만 앞서 말하신 분이 "부정적 표현"을 하면 Me, too. 보다는 Me, neither.를 써야 한다. 예를 들면 I don't like coffee.라고 할 때 Me, neither.라고 하면 "저도 당신처럼 커피 싫어해요."가 된다.

(4) Where is the nearest convenience store?

A Excuse me, where is the nearest convenience store?
B Sorry, I'm a stranger here. But I think I saw one on the next street.
A Thank you so much. Where are you from?
B Japan, I'm a tourist here.

Note

'편의점'이라는 단어가 사용되기 시작한지는 얼마 되지 않는다. 옛날에는 대부분의 사람들이 낮에만 일을 하는 경제구조였지만 사회 규모가 커지면서 야간에도 근무를 하는 사람들이 늘어나고 있다. 그러다 보니 그들(야간 근무자)을 위한 시설이 필요하게 되었고 자연스레 편의점이 생성된 것이다. 편의점이란 "편리하다"라는 뜻의 convenience와 가게라는 뜻의 store가 합쳐져 만들어졌다. 예를 들어 길에서 어떤 사람이 "이곳의 지리"를 물어볼 경우 "저는 이곳 출신이 아니어서 잘 모르겠습니다."라고 할 때는 위의 표현인 I am a stranger here.를 쓰면 된다.

cf) 미국에서 보통 일반 수퍼는 밤이 되면 모두 문을 닫는다. (치안상) 이런 경우 우리는 24시간 open하는 편의점을 찾는다.

(5) When you go shopping, pick some butter up!

A Jane, I'm going shopping. Do you want me to buy anything?
B Will you pick some butter up?
A Sure, anything else?
B That's all. Thanks.

Note

영어공부를 할 때는 영어 단어나 표현에서 한 가지 뜻만 보면 안된다. 예를 들어 pick up을 "~을 집어 들다"라고만 알고 있으면 안된다. pick up에는 "사람을 모시러 가다," "물건을 사오다" 등 다양한 의미가 숨어 있기 때문이다. 그래서 Can you pick me up at 7?이라고 하면 "7시에 날 데리러 올래?"라는 의미가 된다.

(6) It was a total drag.

A How'd your blind date go?
B It was a total drag. I thought she was interesting at first, but I was wrong.
A What do you mean?
B Well, after a while, she kept asking me these typical boring questions. I mean, I think she asked me three times what I like to do in my spare time.

Note

Drag는 명사 bore와 같은 뜻으로, "따분하기 짝이 없는 사람, 진력나는 것(일)"을 뜻한다. "It was a drag" 하면 "It was a bad time"의 의미로, 아주 따분하거나 진력날 때 자주 쓴다. 이와 비슷한 표현으로는 "It sucked," "It was a let down" 등이 있다.

(7) At a hotel

A Front desk, Good morning.
B Good morning. It's room 1203.
A Yes, may I help you?
B Yes, please. Can I have my hair done in the hotel?
A Yes, ma'am. There is a beauty parlor open from 10 to 6:00.
B On which floor?
A The basement.
B And is there a bar in the hotel?
A Yes, ma'am. It's open from 5 p.m. till midnight.

B Thank you.
A You're welcome.

Note

호텔에서 문의할 경우의 한 가지 예임.

(8) Could you please arrange accommodations for me?

I'll be visiting your office on Oct. 18.
Could you please arrange accommodations for me?
I would prefer either Hyatt of Sheraton.
My itinerary is as follows:
Oct. 18 Arr. Singapore Check in
19 Meeting with Mr. Gan
20 Check out Lv. Singapore
I'd appreciate your help.

*** Related Expression**

Could you please reserve a single room at Intercontinental?
My budget for accommodations is $100/night.
I prefer a hotel by the airport.
Is there any hotel you can recommend near your office?
Could you arrange transportation from the airport to the hotel?

④ International News

Iraq

The flimsiest pretext–or none at all–seems good enough for the killers. Last month teams of suicide bombers in Karbala and Baghdad slaughtered 200 or more Shiites peaceably exercising their religious beliefs during the Ashoura festival–a right denied to them under Saddam's dictatorship. The Iraqi Shiites' most venerated leader, Grand Ayatollah Ali Sistani, blamed the Americans for the lack of security that made the bombings possible. Now authorities are bracing for the threat of more bombings on the Shiite calendar's next major holy day, April 12. About 1 million worshipers are expected in Karbala, with as many as 750,000 in Najaf and a similar number in Baghdad. The biggest fear is that more killings could eventually set off a holy war between the Shiites and their former oppressors from the Sunni minority. (from Newsweek)

Note

flimsy : (피륙·종이 등이) 얇은, 여린, 연약한, (근거·이유·이론 등이) 박약한, 빤히 들여다 보이는, 보잘 것 없는, 천박한 / pretext : (사실과 다른) 구실, 핑계 / peaceably : 평화적으로 / exercise : (권력 등을) 행사하다, (위력 등을) 휘두르다, (맡은 일을) 다하다, (좋은 일 등을) 행하다 / venerate : 존경하다, 숭배하다, 경모(敬慕)하다 / brace for : (공격 등에) 대비하다

5 Abby

Dad keeps daughter under virtual house arrest

Dear Abby:

My 15-year-old daughter, "Becky," is a sophomore in high school. She's an honor roll student, well-mannered and a good girl. My problem is her father. He's too strict with her. Becky has always been open and honest with me. This year she's discovered boys, and I know that's the reason her dad is being so overprotective. He rarely allows our daughter to talk on the phone, and when she does, it must be in our presence. He won't let her go anywhere without us. She's not allowed to go to supervised parties or attend any group activity other than cheerleading practice. My poor daughter has no social life. Becky's lifelong friends no longer call her to invite her to go places with them, because they know her dad won't allow it. They've stopped coming over because they know that the limit of their activity is going to be sitting on the couch watching TV with my husband and me. I think Becky deserves some privacy and a social life that does not include us. After she told us a 17-year-old senior boy had a crush on her, my husband refused to allow her to go to the movies with him and his parents. My husband won't even let the boy ride to the store with us. How can I get him to ease up, Abby?

—Caught in the Middle Somewhere in Texas

Dear Caught in the Middle:

Start by telling your husband that you love him and know

he is trying to be a protective parent, but he has gone off the deep end. In the name of love, he is crippling his daughter and if it continues, she will eventually withdraw from both of you.

Note

in somebody's presence : ~의 앞에서, ~의 면전에서 / ease up : 너그러운, 인자한(=lenient) / go off the deep end : 지나치다, 자제를 잃다(=go too far)

⑥ Reading Comprehension

In an uncertain world, training and education are your most important investments. People with a wide range of skills are best-positioned to advance. At Aberdeen University we offer an executive MBA program designed with this reality in mind. You won't specialize in any single area, such as finance or marketing. You'll develop a deep understanding of all areas of business. In addition, you'll hone your computer skills and, if you're not already, you'll become fluent in either Japanese or Mandarin. This program is not for the faint-hearted. It is for men and women determined to reach the top in international business. The program consists of 18 months of full-time study. The cost is $35,000, inclusive of course books and daily lunch but exclusive of other materials and living expenses. For more information, please write to The Dean, Executive MBA Program, University of Aberdeen.

(1) According to the advertisement, what kind of people are most likely to be successful in the future?

ⓐ Those with computer skills
ⓑ Those with language skills
ⓒ Those with a variety of skills
ⓓ Those with highly specialized knowledge

(2) For whom is this program designed?

ⓐ Business professors
ⓑ People who speak Asian languages
ⓒ People with highly-developed computer skills
ⓓ People who want a career in international business

(3) For what does the announced fee pay?

ⓐ Tuition only.
ⓑ Tuition, room and board.
ⓒ Tuition, books and lunch.
ⓓ Tuition, books and materials.

Note

uncertain : 불확실한 / training : 훈련 / education : 교육 / important : 중요한 / investment : 투자 / a wide range of : 다양한 / skill : 기술 / be best-positioned to : ~하는 데 가장 유리하다 / advance : 출세하다 / university : 대학 / offer : 주다, 제공하다 / executive : 간부, 경영자 / MBA : 경영학석사(=Master of Business Administration) / design : 만들다, 고안하다 / with A(목적어) in mind : A를 염두에 두고 / reality : 현실 / specialize in : ~을 전공하다 / single : 하나의 / area : 분야 / such as : ~와 같은 / finance : 재무 / marketing : 마케팅 / develop : (소질, 능력을) 계발하다 / deep : 깊은, 폭넓은 / understanding : 이해 / in addition : 게다가 / hone : 연마하다 / become fluent in : (언어가) 유창해지다 / either A or B : A나 B, 둘 중 하나 / Mandarin : 맨더린; 중국어의 한 가지로 대만과 중국에서 표준어로 채택하고 있음. / faint-hearted : 소극적인 / determined to : ~하기로 결심한 / reach the top : 정상에 이르다 / international business : 국제 비즈니스 / consist of : ~로 구성되다 / full-time : 정규의 / cost : 비용; 여기서는 '수업료' 를 의미 / inclusive of : ~을 포함하여 / course book : 교재 / daily : 매일의 / exclusive of : ~은 제외하고 / material : 학습자료 / living expenses : 생활비 / information : 안내, 정보 / write to : ~에게 편지를 쓰다 / dean : (대학의) 학장

⑦ Humour in English

(1) An Ideal Match

Bill and Hillary are out driving in the country near Hillary's hometown. They are low on fuel, so Bill pulls into a gas station for a fill-up. The attendant comes out and begins to pump gas into the first couple's tank. As he is doing this, he looks into the passenger window. “Hey, Hillary. We used to date in high school, do you remember me?” he asks. They chat for a few minutes. Bill pays and they leave. As they drive Bill is feeling very proud of himself and looks over at Hillary. “You used to date that guy? Just think what it would be like if you hadn't married me.” he says smugly. Hillary looks at Bill, shrugs and replies. “Well, I guess you'd be pumping gas and he'd be the President.”

Note

low on fuel : 연료가 바닥나다(=out of gas) / pull into : ~로 차를 대다 / fill-up : 기름을 가득 채움 / pump gas into : ~에 기름을 채워넣다 / first couple : 대통령 부부 / chat : (가볍게) 이야기를 나누다, 담소하다 / look over at : ~을 어깨너머로 쳐다보다 / what it would be like : 어떠했을지 / smugly : 으쓱해 하며, 뽐내는 투로 / shrug : (모르거나 대수롭지 않다는 투로) 어깨를 으쓱하다

(2) The 99th Birthday

A reporter, interviewing a man who had reached his 99th birthday, said, “I certainly hope I can come back next year and celebrate your 100th birthday.” “Look, young feller,” the old-timer replied, “I can't see why not. You look healthy enough to me.”

Note

feller : fellow의 속된 표현 / old-timer : 노인

Exercise

(1) Japanese Prime Minister to Stick with His Plan to Visit War Shrine

The Japanese Prime Minister, Junichiro Koizumi has said that he will definitely visit the Yasukuni shrine despite objections from Japan's Asian neighbors. His visit is dedicated to the nation's war dead. Yasukuni was a shrine used before and during World War II to encourage soldiers. Many Japanese war criminals are honored among the 2.5 million war dead there. The visit has infuriated China and South Korea, who still vividly remember war crimes committed by Japanese soldiers. August 15 is the anniversary of Japan's World War II surrender and also South Korea's Independence Day. The two Koreas have asked Koizumi not to visit the shrine on their Independence Day. If Koizumi goes ahead as planned, ties with China and the two Koreas will be hurt. In a poll published by the Asahi newspaper in Japan, 65 percent of respondents said they wanted Koizumi to be "careful" about the shrine issue. Only 26 percent of respondents thought Koizumi should ignore criticism and visit the shrine. (from The Teen Times)

Note

definitely : 확실하게(반드시) / Yasukuni shrine : 야수쿠니 신사 / despite objections : 반대에도 불구하고 / neighbor : 이웃나라 / dedicate : 경의를 표하다(바치다) / shrine : 신사 / encourage : 용기를 북돋우다 / criminal : 범죄자 / are honored : 존경받다/ infuriate : 격노하게 하다 / vividly : 생생하게 / crimes committed by : ~에 의해 저질러진 범죄들 / anniversary : 기념일 / surrender : 항복하다, 항복 / Independence Day : 광복절 / goes ahead as planned : 계획한 바에 따라 진행하다 / be hurt : 해를 입다(상하다) / poll : 여론조사 / respondent : 응답자 / issue : 문제 / ignore : 무시하다 / criticism : 비난

(2) The U.S. troops in Korea will cut the number by one-third.

A plan to cut the number of its troops in South Korea by one-third by the end of 2005 will force the South to shoulder more responsibility for defending itself against any North Korean military aggression. The U.S. plan calls for withdrawing 12,500 of the 37,000 U.S. troops stationed in South Korea, according to a statement released by the U.S. military in Seoul. The statement coincided with the beginning of talks between the two allies on another sensitive issue: moving U.S. troops further south away from the tense border with North Korea. Those troops were long considered a "tripwire" that would ensure U.S. intervention in the event of an attack from the North. Many in the South also see it as a healthy restraint on the United States, believing Washington won't take military action that could provoke the North when U.S. troops are in harm's way on the border. The American plans augur the biggest shift in the U.S. troop deployment on South Korean soil since the early 1990s, when the two allies coordinated the removal of 7,000 U.S. soldiers. The new scheme, part of a global realignment of American forces, comes at a time of heightened tension over North Korea's efforts to develop nuclear weapons. The U.S. delegation in Seoul, led by Assistant Secretary of Defense Richard Lawless, told the South Koreans the troop reduction would not affect U.S. defense capabilities in the theater because the United State plans to bring in more modern weapons systems, according to Kim Sook, head of the South Korean Foreign Ministry's North American bureau. The U.S. troop cut would include some 3,600 soldiers already earmarked for redeployment this summer from South Korea to Iraq. (from ybmFM Daily News)

Note

coincide : 일치하다, 부합하다 / tripwire : 인계철선 / intervention : 간섭, 개입, 중재 / restraint : 억제, 구속 / provoke : 자극하다, 유발하다 / scheme : 계획, 기획안 / realignment : 재정렬 / delegation : 대표단 / earmark : 따로 두다

제5장

Suspected SARS Case in Beijing

1 Warm-up

(1) You must have cogent reasons for opposing this proposal.
(2) Accounting is a very exacting profession; there is no room for error.
(3) The passenger's remarks were so ambiguous that I could not catch them.
(4) No, thank you. I don't care for anything else
(5) This product is guaranteed against all defects in materials or workmanship for a period of one year.
(6) It was assumed that the losses were covered by insurance.
(7) The closed bridge forced motorists to take an alternate route.
(8) Low-cost computer technology has increased the amount of counterfeit money in circulation.
(9) They were confident they could meet and even exceed their monthly production targets.
(10) Analysts think the company will try to boost sales by cutting their prices.

Note

1) co(=togeher)+gent(=drive) : 여럿을 함께 몰아가는 → 설득력 있는(convincing)
2) exacting : 아주 정확함을 요구하는 → 엄격한(strict), 힘이 드는(arduous, tiring)
3) ambi(=both)+(i)g(=drive)+uous : (입장이)양쪽으로 몰아가는 → 애매모호한(equivocal)
4) care for : 좋아하다, 원하다
5) guarantee : 보장하다 / against : ~에 대항하여 / defect : 결점, 결함 / material : 재료 / workmanship : 솜씨, 기술
6) assume : 가정하다, 추정하다
7) an alternate route : 다른 길
8) counterfeit money : 위조지폐
9) exceed : 능가하다
10) boost : 늘리다, 후원하다

② Current Terms

(1) Pension

Pension lodges are cheaper than hotels-priced between 60,000 won and 150,000 won per night-and their accommodations are classier than minbak. The so-called "love motels" usually catering to couples looking for rooms with red lighting and free condoms, have spread to all the tourist destinations as a frugal option, but are not popular with families, or couples who prefer a natural relaxing atmosphere. (from The Korea Herald)

Note

pension lodges : 펜션 / accommodations : 숙박 설비 / classy : 고급인, 멋진 / cater : 조달하다, 준비하다(to) / frugal : 저렴한, 절약하는, 검소한

(2) Hostile Mergers and Acquisitions(M&A)

The government will veto improvement plans from both Cho Hung and Korea Exchange Bank as well if the two banks also fail to aquire written consent from the unions. The two banks were allowed to remain independent on the condition that they improve their balance sheets and reduce non-performing loans. "We will not accept any revised management improvement plan that is submitted without the written consent of the bank unions," said the official, adding that banks that fail to receive approval from the government will have to suffer the consequences. "The management will be questioned for poor management, while also being forced to undergo hostile mergers, acquisitions, or be tied to a financial holding company." (from The Korea Herald)

③ Practical English

(1) I'll go for black(coffee).

M How about a break? You want anything to drink?
W Yeah, I could go for a coffee.
M Sugar or cream?
W I'll go for black.

Note

'Go for something'하면 「something으로 나아가다, ~쪽을 찬성하다, ~을 택하다」 의 의미이다. 같은 말로 "Make my coffee black," "Strong and black please"(진하게 블랙으로 해주세요), "No sugar or cream, please."(설탕과 크림을 넣지 마세요) 등이 있다.

(2) Where is the menu?

A Excuse me, where is the menu?
B The menu is on the wall.
A Oh, thanks. Let me have a tuna sandwich.
B What about drinks?

Note

우리나라 식당도 그렇지만 미국도 고급 식당이 아닌 경우엔 메뉴판이 일반적으로 벽에 붙여져 있다.
cf 식당에서 종업원을 부를 때 쓰는 표현 : 종업원이 남자이면 Waiter, 또는 Excuse me, Mister. 하면 되고 여자이면 Excuse me, Miss. 하면 된다. 단순히 종업원의 주의를 끌기 위해선 Excuse me! 라고만 하면 된다.

(3) Let's discuss it over lunch.

A What time is it?
B It's 11:30.
A Let's finish discussing it over lunch then.
B Do you know a nice place?

Note

미국인들은 유난히 식사를 하면서 business하기를 좋아하는 국민들이다. 'over lunch'라는 표현을 잘 보면 lunch(점심식사)를 두고 그 위로 "대화를 한다(discuss)"는 의미이다. 그럼 "우리 커피나 한 잔하면서 대화합시다."는 어떻게 될까? 이럴 땐 "Let's talk over coffee."라고 하면 된다.
cf 괜찮은 식당을 영어로는 a nice place라고 한다. 우리나라 말에서도 "냉면 잘하는 집 알고 있니?"라고 묻는 경우가 있다. 다시 말해 식당을 일반 구어체로 '집'이라고 한다. 이와 마찬가지로 영어에서도 굳이 restaurant이라고 하지 않고 place라고 한다.

(4) Shall we eat out tonight?

A Any plans tonight?
B Not really.
A Shall we eat out tonight?
B Okay, I know a nice seafood restaurant near here.

Note

미국인들은 '외식'을 자주 한다. 그러다 보니 값이 저렴하고 맛좋은 음식점들이 많이 생겨나고 있다. '외식'한다는 건 말 그대로 "밖에서 식사"를 한다는 것이므로 풀어보면 eat out이 됨을 알 수 있다.
cf 미국인들에게 '외식'이 잦은 이유는 다름 아닌 "맞벌이 부부(double income couple)"가 많기 때문이다. 다시 말해 대부분의 부인들이 일을 하러 나가기 때문이다. 그러다 보니 자연 외식하는 빈도가 잦아지고 심지어 미국 여자들에게 '요리'는 취미수준이 되고 있는 것이 사실이다.

(5) Christmas cards

1) Hope your Christmas is filled with all the joy in the world.
2) Have a very Merry Christmas!!! Don't you forget about me!!!
3) May the Light of Christmas fill your life!
4) Fun times are here again! Wishing you a Merry Christmas!
5) May the Joy of Christmas be yours!
6) We are sending our merriest greeting to your folks and you, Wishing you joy for Christmas and the whole year through.
7) Merry Christmas and let this kindly greeting say we are thinking of your Christmas Day.
8) Inside, outside, upstairs, down, hope you have the happiest Christmas Day in town.
9) With Christmas wishes kind and true. That all life's blessings come to you.
10) A Merry Christmas from our house to your house goes today an extra share of hearty wishes for the joy of everybody there.
11) Wishing you friends at your fireside happiness in your home, and joy in your heart.
12) In this magical season here's some holiday cheer to fill your heart through Christmas and all of your next

year.

13) We much regret that you're away from home and us this Christmas Day. But trust, that though we are not near you, you yet may have a lot to cheer you.
14) Always on my mind, yes, YOU ARE!!!

Note

Christmas card에 위의 내용을 한 번 써 보기 바람.

④ International News

Suspected SARS Case in Beijing

China has reported a suspected case of the potentially deadly SARS virus in Beijing for the first time since an outbreak of the contagious disease subsided in July. A 20-year-old female nurse fell ill with SARS symptoms on April 5 and was admitted to hospital two days later, China's Health Ministry said in a report from the state-run Xinhua news agency. The woman had a cold, fever and a cough. Five others have been isolated for observation, the report said. "Five people who had close contact with her have fever and other symptoms," Xinhua quoted the health ministry as saying. Also, 171 people who have had some form of contact with her are under observation, the report said.

SARS first emerged in southern China late 2002 and spread throughout the world, infecting around 8,000 people and killing over 770. Since last July only four cases have been reported in China, all in the southern Guangdong province. All four patients recovered. Two other scientists researching the mysterious disease in Taiwan and Singapore also contracted the disease. They also recovered and no other infections were reported. The six cases have been the only confirmed infections since the World Health Organization declared the epidemic over last year. Beijing was one of the cities hardest hit by the SARS outbreak that killed 349 people on the Chinese mainland. (from CNN)

5 Ann Landers

Showing off

Dear Ann Landers:

My husband and I moved into our new house 18 months ago. We had it decorated and furnished in a way that we consider quite lovely. Whenever we have guests, my husband insists that we show them around the entire house, including all the bathrooms, the laundry room and the broom closets. I don't feel this is necessary. There are certain rooms in the house I would rather not show anyone because they wouldn't pass scrutiny, but my husband says that it's ridiculous. If someone is invited for dinner, does that mean the entire house should be available for inspection? Your answer is going to make a difference.

—Depending on You in Alaska

Dear Alaska :

If you're looking for an ally, you have one in me. This might come as a shock to your husband, but most people are not particularly interested in bathrooms and broom closets. The detailed tour your mate insists on is really an ego trip for him, but the visitors find it borrr-rrr-rrring.

Note

broom closet : 빗자루 넣어 두는 광 / scrutiny : 면밀한 관찰 / make a difference : 효과가 있다 / ally : 우방, 자기 편 / mate : 배우자의 한 쪽

⑥ Reading Comprehension

This is Neil Young with a traffic update. Traffic is moving well into the city with the exception of the Truman Tunnel, where there is a 30 minute wait. Motorists are advised to take the Lincoln Tunnel, which only has a 10 minute wait. There has been a water main break on 57th Street between Second and Third Avenue. Avoid this area if at all possible. We'll return in 20 minutes with an update. This is Neil Young.

(1) How long is the wait at the Truman Tunnel?

ⓐ 10 minutes
ⓑ 15 minutes
ⓒ 20 minutes
ⓓ 30 minutes

(2) **Why should listeners avoid 57th Street between Second and Third Avenue?**

ⓐ There is heavy traffic.
ⓑ There is a stalled car.
ⓒ There has been a water main break.
ⓓ There is a long wait.

Note

update : 새로운 소식 / motorist : 운전자 / water main : 지하 수도관 / break : 터짐, 고장

⑦ Humour in English

(1) Guards Reading Prisoner's Mail

A prisoner in jail receives a letter from his wife: "Dear Husband, I have decided to plant some lettuce in the back garden. When is the best time to plant them?" The prisoner, knowing that the prison guards read all mail, replied in a letter: "Dear Wife, whatever you do, do not touch the back garden. That is where I hid all the money." A week or so later, he received another letter from his wife: "Dear Husband, You wouldn't believe what happened, some men came with shovels to the house, and dug up all the back garden." The prisoner wrote another letter back: "Dear wife, now is the best time to plant the lettuce."

Note

regarding : ~에 관한 / in jail : 감옥에 갇힌, 복역 중인 / plant : 심다, 파종하다 / lettuce : 상추 / knowing that ~ : ~임을 아는, ~인 줄을 알고서 / prison guard : 교도관, 간수 / whatever you do : 뭘 해도 좋지만, 무엇을 하든지 간에 / hide : 숨기다 / ~ or so : ~ 정도 / shovel : 삽 / dig up : 땅을 파헤치다, 파뒤집다 / write another letter back : 다시 답장을 보내다 / now is the best time to-inf. : 지금이 ~할 절호의 기회다

(2) An Old Handyman

Professor Kimball, a doctor of aeronautics, brought home a backyard swing for his children and started to assemble it. After reading the directions, attempting to fit bolt A into slot B, etc., he finally gave up and called Swenson, an old handyman working in the neighboring yard. Swenson came over, threw the directions away, and in a short while had the swing completely assembled. "It's beyond me," said the Ph.D father, in admiration, "how you got it together without even reading the instructions." "Tell you the truth," replied the oldtimer, "I can't read and when you can't read, you've got to think."

Note

aeronautics : 항공술, 항공학 / directions : 지시, 설명서 / handyman : 잡역부, 무슨 일이나 잘 하는 사람 / It's beyond me : 나로서는 이해할 수 없는 일이다 / get together : 조립하다 / oldtimer : (구어) 구식사람

Exercise

(1) Japanese Economy in Panic

Japanese companies have been following a "lifetime employment system." Employees devote themselves to the company they're working at, and the company takes care of the employees until they die. There is no "retirement age" in these companies since the companies let the employees work as long as they can. Last week, Fujitsu, which is one of the biggest Japanese companies, announced it would abolish its "lifetime employment system" and layoff 16,000 employees. It shocked the Japanese as well as people in other countries. It clearly shows how bad the Japanese economy really is. Fujitsu also decided to reform their overall companies in order to survive the economic crisis. Japan has been in recession for the past ten years, and now its economy is almost in a panic. The problems started in the early 90's due to a bubble economy, but in those days Japan missed their chances for reform.

In the last ten years, Japan's unemployment rate has doubled. Housewives are looking for jobs to bring home the bread and butter instead of their jobless husbands. Bankrupt businessmen are selling Ramen to make a living. The GNP is tied up and hasn't shown any big increase since this economic crisis began. Experts say unless Japan reforms its economic structure nationwide, it will face the worst economic situation in its history. (from The Teen Times)

Note

lifetime employment system : 종신고용제 / devote themselves to : ~에 전념하다 / retirement age : 정년퇴직연령 / as long as : ~하는 한 / Fujitsu : 후지쯔 / announce : 발표하다 / abolish : 폐지하다 / layoff : 해고하다 / employee : 직원 / shock : 충격을 주다 / as well as : ~는 물론 / reform : 개혁하다 / overall : 전반적인 / in order to : ~하기 위하여 / economic crisis : 경제위기 / recession : 경제침체 / panic : 공황상태 / in the early 90's : 1990년대 초에 / bubble economy : 거품경제 / miss : 놓치다 / unemployment rate : 실업률 / double : 두배가 되다 / Housewife : 주부 / bring home the bread and butter : 가족을 부양하다 / jobless : 무직의 / bankrupt businessmen : 도산한 사업가들 / make a living : 생계를 잇다 / is tied up : 묶여 있다 / nationwide : 전국적으로 / face : 직면하다

(2) 82% of Americans Support Pullout of US Troops Stationed in Korea.

Amid continuing reports of rising anti-American sentiment in Korea among the younger population and some liberal lawmakers, negative sentiment toward Korea is also taking its toll in the United States. Results of a poll released show that 82 percent of Americans support the current Bush administration's plan to cut one-third of Uncle Sam's forces in South Korea by the end of next year. In the survey conducted by the right-wing

U.S. FOX television news company not known for its objectivity, 59,630 of the 72,327 Americans who took part said the pullout was a "good idea" and that the American troops were needed "elsewhere." Only 9 percent of the Americans surveyed in the United States, said it was a bad idea that endangered South Korea. (from ybmFM Daily News)

Note

amid : ~의 한복판에(서), ~에 둘러싸여 / one-third : 3분의 1 / Uncle Sam : (美구어, 美속어) 미국 정부, (전형적인) 미국 사람 / objectivity : 객관성 ; 객관적 실재(實在); 객관적 경향 / pullout : (군대 따위의) 철퇴, 철수; (자금의) 회수 / endanger : ~을 위험에 빠뜨리다, 위태롭게 하다

제6장

Kahn Interested in Change of Club

① Warm-up

(1) It is imperative that we schedule a meeting with the potential clients as soon as possible in order to ensure that they understand what our company has to offer.

(2) In order to save time, photocopy as many copies of the agreement as you can, so that if we run out during the meeting there will be some extra available.

(3) The recommendations can be divided into three distinct sections; each deals with different aspects of the serious problem of inner city crowding.

(4) This new muscle toning machine will enable the customer to lose weight and at the same time to relax in front of his TV.

(5) Please contact a sales representative if you have any problems or queries about the product that you have just purchased.

(6) During her opening remarks, the history professor attempted to explain the basic theories which she would attempt to elucidate in her lecture.

(7) This new CD player is durable and easy to use and

is guaranteed to keep on operating under all possible conditions without suffering damage.

(8) The procedures for emergency evacuation of this aircraft have been fully documented in the pamphlet located in the seat pocket in front of you.

(9) It is believed by most delegates at this international trade conference that the discussion will help to foster positive international relations through economic cooperation.

(10) In compliance with the safety regulations as set out in the company manual, all employees must participate in a mandatory fire drill once a month.

Note

1) potential client : 잠재고객 cf prospective buyer : 물건을 살 가망이 있는 고객
2) save : 절약하다 ⇒ 전치사로 쓰일 경우 except의 의미가 있음.
3) be divided into : 분류되다
4) enable+목적어+to부정사 구문임.
5) contact : '연락 주세요'라는 표현으로 자주 쓰임. ⇒ 타동사이므로 전치사가 필요 없음. / query : 질문
6) opening remarks : 개막 연설, 개회사 ⇒ 반드시 ~ing형을 사용함. / elucidate : 상세히 설명하다, 상술하다
7) and의 앞과 뒤는 균형이 맞아야 한다. and 뒤에는 형용사가 왔으니 그 앞에도 형용사가 와야 함.
8) procedure : 절차
9) foster : 조장하다, 활성화하다(promote)
10) in compliance with : ~을 준수하여, ~에 순응하여 cf in accordance with : ~와 일치하여

2 Current Terms

(1) Bird Flu

Ducks at a farm near the chicken farm where more than 20,000 chickens died of fatal bird flu last week were also infected with the livestock disease, said the Ministry of Agriculture and Forestry yesterday. The ministry said that it ordered all 3,300 ducks at the farm in Eumseong-gun, Chungcheong Province, about 130 kilometers from Seoul, to be killed buried. "It is highly possible that the ducks caught the same strain as the highly pathogenic Avian influenza, which was found in Hong Kong in 1997," said an official from the ministry. (from The Korea Herald)

Note

bird flu : 조류독감 / infect : 감염시키다 / livestock disease : 가축병 / Ministry of Agriculture and Forestry : 농림부 / strain : 변형 / pathogenic : 병원의, 발병시키는 / Avian influenza : 가금 인플루엔자

(2) BRICs

At present, the equity markets of Brazil, Russia, India and China("BRICs") account for just five percent of the combined market values of the United States, Britain, Japan and Germany. Although strong growth is expected in the BRIC markets, the U.S. is expected to remain the largest market by 2050, accounting for about 45 percent of the total stock market universe. China, however, will have risen to become the second largest market, at 25 percent, and India will rank third, at more than 10 percent. (from The Korea Herald)

Note

Equity market : 주식사장 / BRICs : 브릭스(브라질, 러시아, 인도, 중국의 머리글자를 딴 약어) / combined : 결합된, 합동의 / account for : 차지하다 / rank : 등급을 매기다, ~위에 서다, 평가하다

③ Practical English

(1) Taking a bus or taxi

Michael How can I get to the subway station from here?
Julie Well, you can take Bus No. 81.
Michael Where is the bus stop for Bus 81?
Julie It's just across the street from the main gate of the university.
Michael That sounds easy.
Julie Of course, if you're in a hurry, it's best to take a taxi.
Michael How much would a taxi cost?
Julie From here, a taxi would cost about 1,500 won.

Note

get to : 도착하다 ⇒ I got to the airport late. So, I missed the flight to Chicago.(나는 공항에 늦게 도착했다. 그래서 시카고로 가는 비행기편을 놓쳤다.) / across : 맞은편에 ⇒ Star Cinema is across from Seoul Department Store.(스타 극장은 서울 백화점 맞은편에 있습니다.) **cf** cross : 건너다 ⇒ Cross the street only when the traffic signal turns green.(교통 신호가 녹색으로 바뀔 때 길을 건너세요.) / cost : 비용이 들다

(2) In the taxi

A Excuse me, where is the taxi stand?
B It is at the back of this building.

A Thank you.

(In the taxi)

A Hi, ma'am. Where to?
B Hilton Hotel, please.
A Which one? There are two Hiltons here.
B Oh, I'm sorry. The Hilton hotel beside the bay.
A Oh, you mean Hilton Pavilion. Right?
B That's right.
A Are you here on vacation?
B No, actually I have a business presentation here.
A Where are you from?
B Switzerland.

(3) Taking the subway

Michael I'm going to meet a friend in Sinchon.
Julie To get to Sinchon, you first have to get on line 1 from here.
Michael Which direction should I go on line 1?
Julie When you stand on the platform, look for the sign that says to Uijeongbu.
Michael After that, what do I need to do?
Julie You need to transfer at City Hall station.
Michael So I get off line 1 at City Hall?
Julie Yes. Then simply follow the signs that lead to line 2. That will take you to Sinchon.

Note

get on : 타다 **cf** get off : 내리다, get to : 도착하다 ⇒ I got on the wrong bus. So, I wasted a lot of time(버스를 잘못 타서 시간만 낭비했다). Please get off at Shinchon(신촌에서 내리세요). / direction : 방향, 지시(복수형) ⇒ I was trying to get to Chicago but I ended up going in the opposite direction(시카고에 가려고 했지만 반대 방향으로 가고 말았다).

(4) Reply : Kimpo Airport

I haven't gone through the Kimpo Airport and I was wondering if you would be able to tell me which is the best line to take to COEX.

The best way to get to COEX is the limousine bus from the airport. The limousine bus stops at Palace Hotel, Novotel Hotel, and COEX. It takes 40 minutes. Subway is less expensive, but there's no direct line from Kimpo to COEX. If you don't mind changing, you could take the bus to Tangsan Station and take subway to COEX.

Let me know if you have other questions.

④ International News

Kahn Interested in Change of Club

German goalkeeper Oliver Kahn is considering leaving Bayern Munich and would be interested in a move to a top European side. The 34-year-old national captain says he needs a new challenge after 10 years in Munich, in which he has won 15 titles. In an interview, published on the German Football Federation homepage, Kahn said he would need to move in time for the new season.

Kahn, who is with the German national squad at Winden Im Elztal near Freiburg preparing for the forthcoming Euro 2004 finals in Portugal, said he doubted whether a high transfer fee would be an obstacle to a move. Coach Felix Magath, who is to take over the trainer's job at Bayern

Munich, said he knew nothing about Kahn's intentions. "I am assuming that Oliver Kahn will still be in goal at Bayern Munich next season," said Magath. (from CNN)

5 Abby

Loud kids, sarcastic parents are recipe for miserable meal

Dear Abby:

Last night, my husband and I had dinner at the only "good" restaurant in our small town. Seated at the table behind us was a couple with three small children. During our entire meal, those children screamed and carried on while their parents did nothing. The disruption was so incessant that another couple walked out without finishing their dinner. The manager offered to seat us elsewhere, but the children's high-pitched voices could be heard throughout the place. I repeatedly looked over at the parents, and the man shot me a sarcastic remark implying that if I was annoyed, it was "my problem". If you were the manager of the restaurant, what would you have done?

Dear Annoyed:

Had I been the manager, I would have approached the parents and said it was time for one of them to take the youngsters outside for a "time out" until they were ready to behave themselves in the restaurant. I would rather risk losing one couple's business than that of a room full of patrons.

⑥ Reading Comprehension

The pollen count hit a record high today. It was last this high 10 years ago. The lack of precipitation has caused the pollen to remain in the air longer. This means millions of area residents will have difficulty breathing and will experience symptoms similar to a cold or bronchitis. No new rain is expected for the next two weeks; those affected are advised to stay in air conditioned environments and wear a protective mask when outside. Tomorrow the count will be even higher.

(1) What is the problem?

ⓐ A high pollen count
ⓑ Excess rainfall
ⓒ The flu virus
ⓓ A broken air conditioner

(2) When will the problem abate?

ⓐ By today
ⓑ By tomorrow
ⓒ In two weeks
ⓓ In ten years

(3) What advice does the announcement give?

ⓐ Breathe deeply
ⓑ Take frequent showers
ⓒ Stay outdoors
ⓓ Wear a mask outside

Note

pollen count : 일정한 장소의 공기 속에 들어있는 꽃가루의 수 / precipitation : 강수, 강우, 강우량 / resident : 거주자 / symptoms : 증세 / bronchitis : 기관지염 / affected area : 영향을 받은

지역 / abate : 감소되다

7 Humour in English

(1) A Cure for Nightmare

A man had been tormented for years by nightmares. Whenever he went to sleep, he dreamed that grotesque animals and reptiles were rushing in and out from under his bed. Finally he told a friend that he had been cured. "I told my brother about it," he said, "and he stopped it." "Is your brother a psychiatrist?" "No, he's a carpenter," the man replied. "He sawed the legs off my bed."

Note

torment : 괴롭히다 / grotesque : 기괴한, 괴상한 / reptile : (뱀 따위의) 파충류 / rush : 달려들다, 돌진하다 / psychiatrist : 정신과 의사(학자) / saw : 톱질하다

(2) A Nice Management Method

Two women were comparing notes on the difficulties of running small business. "I started a new practice last year," the first said. "I insist that each of my employees take at least a week off every three months." "Why in the world would you do that?" the other asked. She responded, "It's the best way I know of to learn which ones I can do without."

Note

compare notes : 정보(의견)를 교환하다 / do without : ~없이 해 나가다

Exercise

(1) Police Maintain Strict Control of Protests against the WEF.

Police have been put on high alert to guard against possible violent demonstrations by student activists and civic associations against an international economic meeting currently under way in the capital. The meeting coincides with the second anniversary of the deaths of two Korean middle school students. The two girls were struck and killed by a U.S. military truck June 13, 2002. The World Economic Forum, an international think tank that groups leading policymakers and economists, is holding a two-day meeting in Seoul. Police announced that they would maintain strict control of any antiglobalization protests against the WEF at the Shilla Hotel and said they had deployed 1,300 policemen near the hotel in central Seoul. (from ybmFM Daily News)

Note

think tank : 두뇌 집단, 싱크 탱크; (속어) 두뇌, 머리

(2) Are Order and Liberty at Odds?

Americans feel vulnerable, and they are: We need look no further than TWA Flight 800 and the bomb set off in Centennial Park in Atlanta. The cause of the TWA tragedy may yet emerge as a catastrophic mechanical failure, but the possibility that it is the evil hand of terrorism is real, and it rightly provokes a frisson of fear. Our concentrated populations, our electric grid and power supplies, our skyscrapers, our jumbo jetsand subways, our computer networks and crowded arenas, offer endless targets. The day after the crash, a tape was played in Manhattan Federal Court: what Abdul Hakim Murad told the Philippine police when he was interrogated for his part in a terrorist plot. He described making a bomb out of liquid nitroglycerin poured into a container of contact-lens cleaner with a Casio watch as a timer to set it off. "I studied the 747," he said.

"I know where to put it." Another suspect, Ramzi Ahmed Yousef, has been accused of using a similar combination to construct an explosive that blew up a Philippine Airlines flight to Japan in 1994, a murderous test run for a plot to blow up 11 American planes simultaneously. (Source : U.S. News & World Report)

제7장 Annan : No Death for Saddam

① Warm-up

(1) The aim of Greencom is to be an outspoken advocate for the protection of our natural environment and the preservation of many animal species which face extinction.

(2) For your convenience, extra blankets have been placed in all the hotel rooms to make sure that your stay is as warm and comfortable as possible during the winter months.

(3) The government will make all efforts to compensate the victims of the recent flash floods for damage done to their houses, farms and livestock.

(4) Most cartons and boxes can be recycled profitably because they can be turned into new products and sold once again.

(5) It was impossible to appreciate her natural complexion because she always like to wear a thick coat of make-up whenever she was around other people.

(6) The first thing to do if you find that a product you have purchased is defective, is to take it directly back to the store to get a replacement.

(7) That the committee members could not agree with

each other about solving those problems has caused more serious problems.

(8) The program is designed to improve competitive strength; moreover, it will also increase the potential for higher earnings.

(9) Mr. Markowitz travels around the entire country searching for small towns that would be appropriate locations for his hotel chain.

(10) The analyst predicted that the company would not go bankrupt and might even show a profit.

Note

1) advocate는 그 뒤에 전치사 for, of 들을 동반한다.
2) for your convenience : 편의상
3) compensate A for B 구문이다. flash flood : 갑작스런 홍수
4) recycle : 재활용하다
5) complexion : 용모, 안색
6) defective : 결함이 있는
7) 'That the ~ those problems'까지가 명사절로서 주어이며 caused가 동사, problems가 목적어인 문장임. 명사절은 단수 취급함. 문장에 목적어가 있으므로 능동형 문장을 만들어야 함을 알 수 있음.
8) design : 고안하다, 만들어내다 / competitive : 경쟁의 / potential : 잠재력, 가능성 / arnings : 수입 / moreover : 게다가, 더욱이
9) appropriate : 적당한
10) analyst : 분석가, 전문가 / predict : 예측하다 / go bankrupt : 도산하다, 파산하다

② Current Terms

(1) Task Force

The government has taken the first step to streamlining the nation's financial supervisory system yesterday, as a task force under the Planning and Budget Ministry put forward a set of proposals for the seemingly tough job. The Financial Supervisory Service and its decision-making body, the Financial Supervisory Commission, have been widely credited for helping the nation ride out a foreign exchange crisis, the resulting recession earlier than expected, by focusing on structural reforms. (from The Korea Herald)

(2) International Energy Agency(IEA)

As energy costs rise, consumers fear economic recovery could suffer. The International Energy Agency(IEA), adviser on energy to 26 industrialized countries, said on Tuesday that prices were too high and that OPEC should act to cool the market. "Current levels are too expensive," said Norio Ehara, the IEA's head of non-member countries division Asia Pacific and Latin America. "When OPEC meets in February we want them to calm down the market. We need some balance." (from The Korea Herald)

Note

The International Energy Agency(IEA) : 국제에너지기구 / industrialized countries : 선진국들 / non-member : 비회원의 / calm down : (노여움, 흥분 등을) 가라앉히다

③ Practical English

(1) Business English 1

A I'm planning to attend a seminar about electronics in Taiwan from Sep.10 to Sep. 25. Could I meet you during those two weeks?

B You're coming to Taiwan? Very good! When can I see you?

A How about Sep. 12? I think I'm free on that day.

B Very good. Why don't you call me again when you arrive in Taiwan? Which hotel will you check in to?

A I made a reservation at the Mandarin Hotel.

B That's great, my company is located very close to the hotel.

A Fantastic. I'll get in touch with you when I arrive in Taiwan.

B Okay, I'll talk to then.

Note

1) 날짜 표기 : '2000년 9월 10일'은 영어로 September 10th, 2000이라고 하면 자연스럽다. 물론 September를 줄여서 Sep. 이라 할 수도 있고 '10일'을 꼭 10th라고 하지 않아도 큰 지장은 없음.
2) a seminar about electronics : '전자관련 세미나'라고 하는데 여기서 중요한 것은 electronics란 단어이다. 학문 분야는 단어가 s로 끝나는 것이 많이 있음. ⇒ politics(정치학), linguistics(언어학), economics(경제학), physics(물리학) 등
3) 일반 학교문법에선 Are you coming to Taiwan?처럼 전형적인 의문문을 쓰지만 일상회화에선 You're coming to Taiwan?과 같이 평서문의 뒤를 살짝 올려서 말하면 된다. 다른 예로 "결혼하셨나요?"라는 표현을 Are you married?라고 하는 것이 정석이지만 일반 회화에선 You are married?처럼 할 수도 있다.
4) 예를 들어 "가는 것이 어떨까요?"라고 하면 Shall we go? 또는 Why don't we go? 정도로 표현할 수 있다. 날짜나 시간에 대한 상대의 의견을 물을 땐 how about ~ ? 이 자연스럽다. 그래서 "지금 하시는 것이 어때요?"라고 할 땐 How about now? "내일 하시는 것이 어때요?"라고 할 땐 How about tomorrow?라고 하면 된다. 물론 "이 물건 어때요?" 라고 할 때도 How about this one? 이라고 할 수 있다.
5) "어느 호텔에 묵을 예정입니까?"라는 표현을 할 경우 'check in'이란 표현을 쓸 수 있다. check out은 check in의 반대 개념. When is your check out time?은 "몇 시에 (호텔) 퇴실하세요?"

라는 의미이다. 일반적으로 낮 12시가 check out time이다.

6) Mandarin Hotel은 동남아시아에서 가장 큰 특급 체인 호텔이다. 호텔의 등급은 일반적으로 star를 사용한다. 그래서 five star hotel이라면 '특급호텔'이라고 보면 되고 일반적인 호텔은 three star hotel이다.

attend : ~에 참석하다 / from A to B : A에서 B까지 / meet : ~를 만나다(사업상의 모임) / be free on ~ : 시간을 내다, ~는 시간이 있다 / please call me : 전화 주세요 / check in : ~에 묵다 / be located very close to ~ : 그리 멀지 않은 곳(가까이에 위치한 곳)에 있다 / then : 그때

(2) Business English 2

A Hello, can I speak to Mr. Tan Chow, please?

B Speaking. Is this Mr. Smith?

A Yes. I arrived in Taiwan two days ago. Can I meet you?

B Yes, of course, I have been waiting for your call. How about tomorrow morning around 10:30?

A Well, let me check my seminar schedule. I'm sorry but I have to attend a seminar tomorrow morning. How about in the afternoon?

Note

1) Can I speak to ~ ? [Can I speak with ~?] : (전화상으로) ~ 계십니까? [~와 통화할 수 있습니까?]

2) 전화상으로 "접니다."라고 할 때는 간단히 Speaking! 또는 This is he! 내지는 This is she! 라고 하면 자연스럽다. Speaking! May I help you? 라고 하면 상당히 격식을 차리면서도 '친근감을 느끼게 하는 표현'이 된다. 그리고 전화상으로 "혹시 ~ 이십니까?"라고 물어볼 때 Are you ~? 라고 하면 자연스럽지 못하다. 이런 경우엔 Is this ~? 라고 하는 것이 훨씬 자연스럽다.

3) 대화상 "~에 도착했다."라고 할 땐 동사 arrive를 쓴다. 예문처럼 '타이완에 도착했다'라고 할 땐 I arrived in Taiwan. 이라고 하면 된다. 중요한 건 '나라 이름' 앞에는 전치사 in을 붙인다는 것이다. 그리고 "뵐 수 있을까요?"라는 표현은 간단히 Can I meet you? 라고 하면 자연스럽다.

4) I've been waiting for your call : 전화 기다리고 있었습니다 **cf** I was waiting for your call.이란 표현도 쓸 수 있으나 격식을 덜 차린 표현임.

5) "~하시는 편이 어떠세요?"라는 말은 간단히 How about ~ ? 이라고 할 수 있다. 그래서 "내일 아침 10시30분 정도 어떠세요?"라고 하면 How about tomorrow morning around 10:30?가 된다. '~시경'이라고 할 땐 around를 쓴다. 계속해서 "오후는 어떠세요?"라고 할 땐 How about in the afternoon? 이라고 하면 된다

(3) Business English 3

B You mean tomorrow afternoon? That's okay for me.
A Where can I meet you?
B The hotel's lobby, I told you my company is just a stone's throw away, remember?
A Yes, I do. Alright. I'll wait for you there tomorrow afternoon around 3:30. Is that okay for you?
B Of course. Would you like me to bring any samples or catalogs?
A How about meeting in the lobby and then going to the company to see the products? You said the company is very close to the Mandarin.
B That's a better idea. I'll see you tomorrow afternoon.

Note

1) 비즈니스 대화상 가능하면 정확성을 기하기 위해 상대가 한 말을 다시 한번 짚어 볼 필요가 있다. 이런 경우에 쓸 수 있는 표현이 You mean ~이다. 예를 들어 "오후 두 시 말씀이죠?"라고 하고 싶으면 You mean 2 p.m.?이라고 하면 자연스럽다.
2) 우리말의 '뵙다' 또는 '만나다'는 단순히 meet을 사용하면 된다. "저녁 드셨어요?"와 "저녁 먹었어?"의 경우 둘 다 Did you have dinner?라고 하면 된다.
3) 아주 가까운 거리를 '넘어지면 코 닿을 곳'이라고 하는데 이런 상황에서 native speaker 들은 "손으로 돌 던지면 닿을 곳"이라고 표현한다. 그래서 It's just a stone's throw away.라는 표현을 쓴다. 덧붙여 hotel의 lobby는 보통 1층 휴게실을 의미한다.
4) 우리말로 시간을 나타낼 때 '~시 경(쯤)'이란 말을 자주 한다. 이런 경우에 about이나 around를 쓸 수 있다.
5) 영어로 '~해 드릴까요?'를 "제가 ~해 드리길 원하십니까?"라고 하면 상당히 존칭해서 말하는 느낌을 준다. 예를 들어 Can I help you?를 Would you want me to help you?라고 하면 무척 존대하는 표현처럼 들린다.
6) '~라고 하셨잖아요?'라고 할 때 영어로는 단순히 You said ~라고 하면 된다. 다른 예로 "내일이라고 말씀하셨잖아요?"는 You said tomorrow.라고 하면 된다.

That's okay for me [That's okay with me] : 좋습니다 / is just a stone's throw away : 넘어지면 코 닿을 곳 / Is that okay for you? : 괜찮으시다면 / Would you like me to ~? [Would you want me to ~?] : 제가 ~하기를 원하십니까? / go to the company to see the products : 제품을 보러 회사로 가다 / very close to ~ : ~에서 가깝다

(4) Business English 4

B Excuse me, are you Mr. Smith from America?
A Yes, I am. I guess you are Mr. Tan Chow?
B Yes, I am. How do you do?
A Nice to meet you.
B How was your trip? You must have jet lag.
A Yes, I do. Otherwise everything is fine. And I like the Taiwanese hospitality.
B Oh, thank you. Shall we go to the company?
A Alright.

Note

1) 사람을 잘못 보고 사과를 할 땐 'I am sorry I thought you are someone I know.'(죄송합니다. 제가 아는 분인 줄 착각했어요.) 라고 하면 된다.
2) 자신을 다른 사람으로 착각하고 묻는 상대에게 "저는 그 사람이 아닙니다."라고 답하려면 어떻게 해야 될까? (Are you Mr. Williams?) 이럴 땐 Sorry I am not.이라고 하면 된다. 그리고 처음 사람을 만나 정중히 인사를 할 땐 How do you do? 라고 하지만 친근감있게 인사하려면 How's it going? 도 괜찮다.
3) "이렇게 만나게 되어 반갑습니다."의 표현은 학교에서 배웠던 것처럼 Nice to meet you. 라고 하면 된다. 덧붙여 I've heard a lot of you.(말씀 많이 들었습니다.) 라고 하면 듣는 사람의 기분도 좋을 것이다.
4) 해외출장(business trip)이 잦은 분들의 경우, 우리나라에선 잠을 잘 시간인데 출장 간 곳은 time difference로 인해 한낮이라면 그 느낌이 어떨까? 해외출장(business trip) 시에는 장시간의 비행으로 인해 피로감을 느끼게 되는데 이러한 현상을 jet lag라고 한다.
5) 대만이나 동남아 사람들은 그 특유의 성격 때문인지는 몰라도 항상 미소짓는 얼굴을 하고 있다. 그래서 그들에 대해서 얘기할 때 종종 쓰이는 단어가 hospitable 또는 hospitality이다. 예를 들어 "필리핀 사람들은 상냥하고 친절해요."라고 할 땐 "Filipinos are hospitable."이라고 하면 된다.

Excuse me : 실례합니다만 / ~ from America : 미국에서 오신 / I guess you are ~ : 혹시 / How do you do? : 처음 뵙겠습니다 / How was ~? : ~ 어떠셨어요? / jet lag : (시차 때문에 생긴) 여행 피로감 / hospitable : 친절하다

④ International News

(1) Annan : No Death for Saddam

U.N. Secretary-General Kofi Annan said on Monday he does not support the death penalty for Saddam Hussein and emphasized any court trying the former Iraqi leader had to meet international norms and standards. Annan, who offered U.N. help in the judicial process, said he was encouraged by Bush administration comments that Saddam would be treated humanity "even though this is a treatment he in the past did not accord those who fell into his hands." But he said the world body had not supported the death penalty in any court it set up previously. "So as secretary-general I am not going to now turn around and support a death penalty."

The president of Iraq's Governing Council, Abdelaziz al-Hakim, said in Paris that Saddam could face execution. He also said he recognized the need for an international role in the proceedings but gave no details. Annan said he hoped the removal of Saddam's "rather long shadow" would speed Iraqi reconciliation but was about cautious, when the United Nations, whose Baghdad headquarters were bombed on Aug. 19, would return to Iraq. Sir Jeremy Greenstock, the senior British envoy in Iraq, said Annan was not expected to name a special representative to replace Sergio Viera de Mello, who was killed by the bomb, until spring or summer. Greenstock, who saw Annan during a brief stop in New York, said the secretary-general was unlikely to set up a U.N. presence in Iraq until after the U.S.-led occupation ended in July. (from Reuters)

Note

headquarters : 본부 / support : 지지하다 / try : 재판하다 / norm : 기준, 표준 / judicial : 재판의, 사법의 / humanity : 인도, 인류

(2) Save Our Potatoes

Potato Growers of Idaho is pursuing a new plan to reduce a potato surplus after dropping a drive to get the federal government to buy extra spuds. The growers' group wants to form a cooperative called Potato Management Co., which would try to cut the surplus by at least 10% by buying up potatoes and getting them off the market. The surplus is depressing prices. (Source: USA TODAY)

Note

pursue : 추구하다, 쫓다 / surplus : 잉여농산물, 과잉 / drop : 중단하다 / drive : 운동(campaign) / get+O+to부정사 : O가 ~하게 하다(사역의 의미) ⇒ get the federal government to buy extra spuds(중앙정부가 과잉 생산된 감자를 매입토록 하다) / spud : potato / extra spuds : 과잉 생산된 감자들 / cooperative : 협동조합 / buy up : 매점하다 / depress : 시세를 하락시키다, 우울하게 하다

5 Annie

Live-in mother

Dear Annie:

My wife and I have been married for three years, and we have a 6-month-old son. The problem? My wife's mother is living with us. Last year, we invited my MIL (and her two large dogs) to move in so that we could help her get back on her feet. Mom had been on welfare, and we opened our home until she could find a job. She pays us a little rent each month. When my wife became pregnant, I informed my mother-in-law that she had nine months to move out. It has been nearly 15 months, and Mom hasn't budged. Last week while shopping, my wife noticed a store with a sign for part-time help. She pushed her mother to go in and get a job application. The next day, Mom was supposed to return the application to the manager, but she refused to go back to the mall. Our neighbors often inform us when people are looking to hire temporary help, but Mom never follows through. Mom has so much stuff stored in our house that we no longer have access to our basement or garage. And her dogs have done a lot of damage to our carpets and doors. My wife and I want to be able to raise our child in peace. Are we the bad guys for asking her to move? Can I get a moving van, load up her stuff and move it to a storage area?

—Canada

Dear Canada:

Mom obviously is reluctant to find her own place when yours is so inexpensive and offers security. Your wife should be the one to discuss this with her mother. She must make it clear that Mom has overstayed her welcome. It sounds as if Mom has some emotional issues that are hampering her ability to support herself. She could use some counseling (check the YWCA, United Way or a local women's center), and couple it with an ultimatum that if she doesn't make a serious effort to find a job, you will be forced to make good your threat to load up the moving van.

Note

live-in : 입주하고 있는, 동거하는

⑥ Reading Comprehension

Attention passengers. Our morning shuttle to Chicago has been canceled due to a blizzard. I regret to say that the weather service estimates the storm will last at least all day, thus flights will be delayed indefinitely. We apologize for the inconvenience and ask you to report to the customer desk for further information on refunds and exchanges.

(1) Why was the flight canceled?

ⓐ Rain
ⓑ Snow
ⓒ Lightning
ⓓ Tornadoes

(2) How can customers respond to this inconvenience?

ⓐ Take a morning flight on a different airline
ⓑ Take a bus
ⓒ Get a flight in the afternoon
ⓓ Get the money back

Note

blizzard : 폭풍설, 심한 눈보라 / estimate : 예상하다 / last : 계속되다 / indefinitely : 무한정으로 / inconvenience : 불편 / customer desk : 고객 카운터 / refunds : 환불 / exchanges : 항공편을 바꿔 타는 것 / lightning : 번개 / tornado : 선풍, 회오리바람

⑦ Humor in English

(1) The Truth Can Hurt.

It was a bright spring morning and four high school boys decided to skip school. They showed up at school after lunch and told the teacher that their bus had a flat tire along the way and that was why they were late. To their relief, the teacher smiled and said: "You boys missed a test this morning. Please take seats apart from one another and get out your paper and pencil." When the boys were seated the teacher said, "Each of you please answer just one question. Which tire was flat?"

Note

skip school : 학교를 빠지고 농땡이 치다 / show up : 나타나다, 등장하다 / have a flat tire : 차 바퀴가 펑크나다 / to one's relief : 한시름 놓게

(2) A Conversation of Drunks

Two drunks were walking along the street. "What a beautiful night. Look at the moon," said one. "You're wrong. That's not the moon ; that's the sun," said the other drunk. They started arguing for a while, when they came upon another drunk. "Mister, please help settle our argument. Tell us what thing shining up in the sky. Is it the moon or the sun?" The third drunk looked at the sky and said, "Sorry, I don't live around here."

Note

drunk : (구어) 주정뱅이 / come upon : ~와 만나다

Exercise

(1) Man's Last Enemy

Good food and good health are important, but they are not the only things necessary to make man happy. People can be well-fed and healthy and yet spoil life for themselves and others by being thoughtless, selfish, and bitter. Ill feelings between people cause unhappiness, and bad feelings between nations may lead to wars. Wars are created in the minds of men, and we do not want wars any more than we want diseases. Hatred and misunderstanding between countries are primitive emotions which we can no longer allow, for our knowledge and technical skill are so advanced that any war could put the whole world in danger. The modern world is a huge and complicated place. Each year trade, transport, and communication grow more complex and more rapid. Every part of the world becomes more closely connected with every other part. Not long ago a big war could take place in one part of the earth without any general effect. That is no longer possible. You and I and all the other ordinary people can make a great contribution to the creation of peace and prosperity in the world by trying to understand other nations. We must get rid of, from within ourselves, the envy, fear, and hatred that make us bitter, blind, and destructive. Man's final enemy is that which is suspicious, greedy and cruel within himself. Man must bring this under control, or all the other triumphs of man will come to nothing. (Source: James Hemming, "Man's Last Enemy")

(2) A Letter to His Brother

Dear Johnston:

Your request for eighty dollars, I do not think it best to comply with now. At the various times when I have helped you a little, you have said to me, "We can get along very well now," but in a very short time I find you in the same difficulty again. Now this can only happen by some defect is, I think I know. You are not lazy, and still you are an idler. I doubt whether since I saw you, you have done a good whole day's work, in any one day. You do not very much dislike to work, and still you do not work much, merely because it does not seem to you that you could get much for it. This habit of uselessly wasting time is the whole difficulty; it is vastly important to you, and still more so to your children, that you should break this habit. It is more important to them, because they have longer to live, and can keep out of an idle habit before they are in it, easier than they can get out after they are in. You are now in need of some ready money; and what I propose is, that you shall go to work. "tooth and nail," for sombody who will give you money for it. To secure you a fair reward for your labor, I now promise you that for every dollar you will get for your own labor in money, I will then give you one other dollar. (Source: Abraham Lincoln, A Letter to His Brother)

제8장

Quake Razes Jewel of Iranian Heritage

1 Warm-up

(1) It is imperative that he remain in contact with NASA ground control at all times during this historic mission to land on the planet Mars.

(2) Preference will be given to employees who have shown commitment to the company over the last few years, and not to those who have taken advantage of their privileged positions.

(3) The stock exchange began trading this morning at a surprisingly past pace, because of new investor confidence and higher share values in the last week.

(4) Every time we discuss the issue of her brother's death last year, she breaks down in tears and needs to be consoled.

(5) You have missed most of your classes this semester, and consequently you will have to make up for lost time and take some extra classes on weekends.

(6) The remainder of the month will be spent going over the treaty, and finalizing the terms of the cease-fire between the two countries.

(7) The two countries have always had a tenuous relationship with each other because of many

disagreements about land ownership and border demarcations.

(8) Most people think that France has a dismal chance of winning the next World Cup because they have not paid enough attention to training and participation in international competition.

(9) One day when I jumped on to a bus I found that I had left home without any money in my pocket.

(10) I wonder how she can manage to get along on so low a salary.

Note

1) 〈It is important[imperative] that 주어 + 동사…〉 구문에서 동사는 should가 생략된 동사 원형을 사용 ⇒ 주어가 3인칭 단수라 할지라도 동사 원형이 오는 특성이 있음.
2) preference : 선호, (구인광고시) 우대
3) pace, cost, rate, expense 등은 전치사 at과 어울린다. **cf** at the cost[rate/pace/expense] of를 덩어리로 암기해 두기 바람.
4) break down in tears : 정신없이 울다 ⇒ break down : 부서져 떨어진다, 기계가 고장나다 **cf** break out : (전쟁이나 화재가) 일어나다 / break in : 난입하다 / break off : 취소하다, 헤어지다
5) make up for : 보충하다(compensate for)
6) remainder : 나머지 **cf** reminder : 기억나게 하는 것
7) tenuous : 얇은, 빈약한, (관계가) 돈독하지 않은
8) a dismal chance : 기회가 별로 없다는 의미 ⇒ dismal : 음침한, 황량한
9) 버스를 타기 전에 집을 떠나온 것이므로 과거완료형이 된 것임.
10) salary[wage]에는 high[low]를 사용함.

manage to : 이럭저럭 해 내다 / get along : 살아가다

② Current Terms

(1) The Political Funds Law

If former President Kim gave Kang money left over from his campaign, it would constitute a violation of the Political Funds Law. But the statute of limitations to prosecute him under that law has already expired. But the former president can still be charged with misappropriating money from state coffers if it turns out that the funds came from the intelligence agency or from corporate contributions made after his victory in the 1992 election. (from The Korea Herald)

Note

constitute : 구성 요소가 되다 / Political Funds Law : 정치 자금에 관한 법률(정치자금법) / prosecute : 기소하다, 구형하다 / misappropriate : 유용하다, 사사로운 용도로 쓰다 / coffer : 금고, 재원 / intelligence agency : 정보 기관

(2) Achilles' Heel

Arranging family reunions had been one of the most sought-after agenda items Seoul in negotiations with Pyongyang. But the two sides had only once held such an event in 1985, and the North had since shunned the issue, apparently nervous about the exposure of its controlled people to the South's capitalism. "The reunion issue has been like an Achilles' heel for North Korea. What is significant is that the North has dared to tread in this formerly taboo area," said Prof. Kang Seong-yoon of Dongguk University. (from The Korea Herald)

③ Practical English

(1) Can you give me a hand?

M That's quite a load you're carrying there.
W Uhg. Can you give me a hand?
M Sorry, I hurt my back last week. Doctor told me to take it easy. I'll hold the door open for you though.
W Gee, thanks a lot.

Note

Can you give me a hand? : hand가 들어가는 광범위하게 쓰이는 표현 중 하나이다. 대신 쓸 수 있는 표현으로 Can you help me out? 혹은 I could use some help over here.(도움이 좀 필요한데요.) 혹은 I'd really appreciate your help.(도와 주신다면 정말 감사할 거예요.) 등이 있음. ⇒ 'could use'는 구어체로 need란 뜻으로 기억해 두기 바람.

(2) We're all booked up.

M I'd like to reserve two rooms for four people next month.
W What dates will you be here?
M July 17 to the 26th.
W I'm sorry, sir. We're all booked up at that time. Would you like me to refer you to our sister hotel on the other side of the island?

Note

book : 예약하다(reserve)

cf 식당이나 호텔에서 자주 사용되는 표현 ⇒ We are full.(꽉 찼습니다.), We have no rooms/tables/seats available.(방/테이블/좌석이 빈 게 없습니다.), Everything is taken.(모두 사용되고 있습니다.)

(3) Back and forth

M How's the tennis game going?
W It's been back and forth all day. First Sampras is ahead, then McEnroe.
M Sounds exciting.
W It is. It's a really close match. No one can predict the outcome.

Note

back and forth : '뒤였다가 앞이었다가' 하는 것처럼 어떤 상황이 계속 뒤바뀌는 것을 묘사하고 싶을 때 쓰는 표현이다. 비슷한 구들을 살펴 보면 up and down, good and bad(좋기도 하고 나쁘기도 하고), constant change(계속 바뀌다) 등이 있음. ⇒ Life is full of ups and downs(인생은 성공과 실패의 연속이지).

④ International News

Quake Razes Jewel of Iranian Heritage

Virtually leveled in a devastating earthquake, the historic heart of Bam was one of the wonders of Iran's cultural heritage, boasting a 2,000-year-old citadel that was the largest mud-brick structure in the world. Built entirely of mud bricks, clay, straw and the trunks of palm trees, the city's old quarter dates back to pre-Islamic times, although most of the monuments were from Iran's modern heyday under the Safavid rulers of the 16th and 17th centuries.

Then, the city occupied six square kilometers, was surrounded by a rampart with 38 towers, and had a population of between 9,000 and 13,000. Located in a vast plain between the Barez and Kabudi mountain ranges, Bam prospered because of pilgrims visiting its Zoroastrian fire temple and as a commercial and trading center on the famous Silk Road between the Far East and Europe. The five-story citadel, constructed entirely from unbaked bricks, had undergone frequent repairs over the years but traced its origins back to the Parthian era around the time of Christ. The city's grand mosque dates from the 10th century. An oasis in the arid Dasht-e Kavir region known as the Emerald of the Desert, Bam boasts extensive underground water reserves, which have allowed the planting of rich palm groves and citrus gardens. (from AFP)

Note

raze : 파괴하다 / ruin : 폐허 / citadel : 성채 / wonder : 불가사의 / heritage : 유산 / level : 무너뜨리다 / monument : 기념비

⑤ Annie

Applicant angst

Dear Annie:

I have worked for 23 years doing building maintenance. Three years ago, I decided it was time for a change. I still have a job, so I can take my time and be selective about sending out my resume. Recently, I was called in for an interview. Since I had downloaded the application off the Internet, I redid it so it would look nice. I wanted to show my attention to detail. The interviewer was impressed that I had taken the time to edit the application and indicated that the interview went smashingly well. I e-mailed the interviewer, thanking her. That was two weeks ago. I haven't heard a word since, and the position opens up in three days. I think if an employer asks me to spend my time preparing a resume, downloading and filling out their application, dressing up and driving an hour to an interview, the least they could do is send me a note saying they hired someone else. To say I'm disappointed is a huge understatement. What's worse, I've had four interviews that went the same way. Why can't a company give me five minutes and a stamp to say I didn't get the job? Even an e-mail or a phone call would have been OK. This is so discouraging, I'm ready to give up.

—Disappointed in Seattle

Dear Seattle:

Too many companies do not feel the need to let an applicant know he didn't get the job, but you are right, they absolutely should send a note indicating that the position has been filled. It often helps to follow up the initial interview with a phone call four to five days later and ask if a decision has been made. It shows you are interested and keeps you in their thoughts. Instead of stewing over it, call the interviewer and ask her what happened. You have nothing to lose, and you might hear some useful information.

Note

angst : 불안, 공포, 걱정, 고뇌

⑥ Reading Comprehension

Nevada began its transition to a modern economy during the Great Depression of the 1930s. After the legalization of gambling in 1931 and the reduction to six weeks of the residence requirement for divorce, Nevada became a marriage, divorce, and resort center. The principal resort areas are Las Vegas, Reno, Laughlin, and Lake Tahoe. Las Vegas attracts many tourists from southern California and foreign countries and also hosts business and professional conventions. Reno draws many pleasure seekers from the San Francisco Bay area and from the Pacific Northwest. Laughlin emerged as a tourist center in the 1980s, and Lake Tahoe continues to serve as a fashionable playground. Construction of the Hoover Dam on the Colorado River substantially aided the economy of southern Nevada, and its cheap hydroelectric power opened the way for manufacturing. The importation of both hydroelectric power from the Bonneville Dam on the Columbia River and piped-in natural gas brought industrial development to the northwestern region. In the 1950s the establishment of the Nevada Test Site by the federal government expanded employment opportunities and stimulated the development of technical industries within the state. Overshadowing the new industrialization, and fundamentally responsible for the current prosperity, is the diversification and expansion of the tourist trade.

(1) The first paragraph primarily describes

ⓐ Nevada's economy during the Great Depression
ⓑ Las Vegas, one of the most important centers in Nevada
ⓒ the way the change in marriage law in Nevada influenced the

economy

ⓓ the booming tourist industry in Nevada since the Great Depression

(2) What is the best title for the whole passage?

ⓐ Nevada in the 20th century
ⓑ History of the tourist industry in Nevada
ⓒ The entertainment boom in Nevada in the 1950s
ⓓ The creation of a modern economy in Nevada

Note

transition : 변화, 전환 / gambling : 도박 / legalization : 적법화, 합법화 / reduction : 축소, 저하, 적응 / substantially : 실질상 / overshadow : 무색하게 하다, 가리다 / industrialization : 산업화 / diversification : 다양화, 변형, 분산

7 Humor in English

(1) Might vs. Bright

After ordering a milk shake, a boy had to leave his restaurant seat to make a telephone call. Since he did not want his drink to disappear, the boy put a paper napkin under the glass and wrote on it, "World's Strongest Man." Then he went to make his call. When the boy returned, his glass was empty. And under it was a new napkin with new writing. "Thanks for the treat, signed, World's Fastest Runner."

Note

order : 주문하다, 명령하다 / make a (telephone) call : 전화를 걸다 / treat : (음식 등의) 대접, 한턱

(2) A Wild-eyed Doctor

A man injured his leg skiing one weekend. His doctor told him to soak it in hot water. He tried soaking it in hot water but the leg became more swollen and more painful. His maid saw him limping and said, "I always thought it was better to use cold water, not hot, for swelling." He tried switching to cold water, and the swelling rapidly subsided. Then he called his Dr. again to complain. "You told me to soak my leg in hot water and it got worse. My maid told me to use cold water and it got better." "Really?" answered the doctor, "I don't understand it–my maid said hot water."

Note

injure : 상처 입다, 다치다 / soak : 담그다, 적시다 / swollen : swell(부풀다, 팽창하다)의 과거분사 / painful : 고통스러운 / maid : 가정부 / limp : 절뚝거리다 / subside : 가라앉다, 빠지다 / complain : 불평하다

Exercise

(1) Reinforced Patrolling to Prevent Suicides on Bridges over the Han River

The Korea Times reports police have reinforced patrolling activities after sunset on bridges over the Han River in Seoul, following the suicides from the bridges of a number of businessmen and social leaders involved in corruption scandals. A man in his 60s committed suicide by jumping off Hankang Bridge, one of 24 bridges over the river, the first day of police patrols aimed at preventing suicide attempts. (from ybmFM Daily News)

Note

reinforce : 강화(증강,보강)하다; 지원군을 보내다, 증원하다 / corruption : 부패, 매수, 타락

(2) Moore's Bush-bashing Movie "Fahrenheit 9/11"

The director the controversial movie "Fahrenheit 9/11" that is very critical of the Bush administration says his goal is have a new president in the Oval Office. Michael Moore told ABC's "This Week" that his film is an "op-ed" piece. He says he's not trying to pretend that it's some sort of "fair and balanced journalism." Moore also accused the media of becoming cheerleaders for the war in Iraq, saying reporters have refused to ask "tough questions" of the Bush administration. (from ybmFM Daily News)

Note

Fahrenheit : 화씨의; 화씨 온도계 / the Oval Office : (美 구어) 대통령 집무실; 미국 정부 / op-ed : (美) 신문에서 사설란의 맞은 편; 보통 서명이 든 특집 기사가 실림

(3) Clinton's Interview for His Memoirs, "My life"

While he supports President Bush's decision to oust Saddam Hussein and his regime in Iraq, former President Bill Clinton says the timing was all wrong. In an interview in "Time" magazine, Clinton said he has "repeatedly defended President Bush against the left on Iraq," but he should have waited until the UN inspections were finished. Clinton's interview with "Time" was his first print interview as part of his high-profile publicity campaign in conjunction with Tuesday's release of his memoir, "My Life." (from ybmFM Daily News)

Note

oust : 내쫓다, 쫓아내다, 퇴거시키다, 배제하다 / inspection : (공식) 시찰, 감찰; 정밀 검사 / print : 출판물, 신문 / high-profile : 명확한 태도(정책), 주의를 끌려고 하는 태도 / publicity : 선전, 광고, 홍보 ; 널리 알려짐, 명성 / memoir : (pl.) (필자 자신의) 회고록, 회상록, 자서전

제9장

Duty over Freedom

① Warm-up

(1) A formal dinner will be held to honor our ex-president Mr. Lee, who dedicated himself to being the best CEO this company has ever had.

(2) The possibility of avoiding the consequences of first degree murder is precluded by law, so people who are proved guilty in a court of law will have to pay for their crimes.

(3) Identification is required in order to purchase alcoholic drinks at licensed bars and restaurants in this country according to the law.

(4) Due largely to cutbacks in our company this year, we will be unable to offer our employees any pay raises this year.

(5) Marathon participants must be in good physical condition or else they run the risk of injury.

(6) The president's optimism about the future gave all the employees a renewed sense of confidence.

(7) Ms. Chung has worked in this company for ten years.

(8) To explain any aspect of society the sociologist must determine the laws influencing human behavior in social contexts.

(9) One difficulty in isolating the components of economic movements is that those components are not completely independent of one another.

(10) Snowbound for most of the year, the bay area is a wilderness of forests, rivers, and lakes.

Note

1) formal dinner : 정찬 / dedicated : 헌신적인
2) preclude : 막다, 방해하다, 배제하다, 금지시키다
3) identification : 신분증
4) due largely to : 주로 ~ 때문에
5) or else : 「그렇지 않으면 ~」 이라는 의미를 나타내며 주로 명령문 또는 must나 have to를 포함하는 문장 뒤에 이용됨. run[take] the risk of : ~의 위험을 무릅쓰다
6) give ~ a renewed sense of confidence : ~의 자신감을 회복시키다 / optimism : 낙관주의 **cf** pessimism : 비관주의
7) 'for ten years' 라는 부사구가 있으므로 계속을 나타내는 현재완료형이 쓰였음. [지금도 일하고 있다]는 것을 강조하고 싶다면 has been working의 현재완료진행형도 사용할 수 있음.
8) 부정사의 부사적 용법임.
9) difficulty in ~ 의 구문임.
10) for most of the year : 「한 해 중 대부분 기간 동안」 ⇒ '한 해 중 대부분의 기간'은 기간을 나타내는 전치사 for와 '한 해의 대부분'을 나타내는 most of the year가 합쳐진 것임.

② Current Terms

(1) Bad Bank

Yesterday's government measure calls for the state-run Korea Asset Management Corp. and financial institutions to fund the new agency, called Bad Bank. KAMCO will likely pump up to 500 billion won into the program, said Kim Suk-dong, a Finance Ministry director general. The agency will apply to people who are defaulting on less than 50 million won from at least two institutions for three to six months, providing them with fresh loans for a period of up to eight years. (from The Korea Herald)

Note

Korea Asset Management Corp. : 자산관리공사 / Bad Bank : 배드뱅크 / pump : 공급하다 / default : 디폴트(채무 불이행), 채무를 이행하지 않다

(2) Bed Town

Although the numbers of students assigned to each class are still relatively higher here than schools in the United States and Japan, it is a welcome sign so far, said an official of SMOE. "More people moving to new towns built around Seoul, and the trends among young couples toward having fewer children are behind less crowded classrooms," added the official. "The overcrowded classes are negatively effecting the learning environment," said an official at Pundang, a "bed town" south of Seoul. "It makes it hard for teachers to pay full attention to all the students in his or her class, and for the students to receive intensive learning," he added. (from The Korea Herald)

Note

SMOE : 서울특별시 교육청(Seoul Metropolitan Office of Education)

③ Practical English

(1) Introduction 1

Let me introduce myself.
May I introduce myself?
Allow me to introduce myself.
Would you allow me to introduce myself?
Please allow me to introduce myself.

Here's my card.
Let me give you my business card.
This is my business card.
This is my card and if there is anything I can do for you, please call me any time.
Here's my card and if you ever need anything, please feel free to get in touch with me.
Can I have your calling card?

• **Related Conversation**

A Let me introduce myself. I'm Paul Peterson of Davis Electronics. I'm glad to meet you.

B Nice to meet you, Mr. Peterson. I'm Sylvia Stone, the vice president of this company.

A Here's my card and if you need anything, please don't hesitate to let me know.

(2) Introduction 2

I would like to introduce you to Mr. Tan Niu, the president of Neo Taiwan Electronics.

May I present Mr. Lee and Mr. Park? They are the co-directors of Seoul Tec.

Let me introduce Mr. Saisaki, the vice president of Tokyo Industry.

Ladies and gentlemen, may I introduce Mr. Edward Kieve, the director of the Israeli Mechanic R&D team?

May I have your name, please?
Sorry, but what did you say your name was?
Pardon me, but how do you spell your name?
I'd be grateful, if I could get your name.

• Related Conversation

A I'd like to introduce Mr. Bellafonte. He is in charge of the import and export department of Neo Francois in Paris.

B Sorry, but what did you say his name was?

A Mr. Bellafonte.

Note

introduce you to ~ : 당신을 ~에게 소개한다 / president : 사장 **cf** C.E.O. : 회장(chief executive officer의 약자) / co-director : 공동이사 **cf** 여기에 쓰인 접두어 개념인 co- 는 'together'라는 의미임. / the vice president of ~ : ~회사의 부사장 / Ladies and gentlemen : (좌중을 향해) 여러분 / the director of ~ R&D team : 연구 개발팀 이사 / sorry : (상대방에게) 죄송하다 / one who is in charge of the import and export : 수출입을 총괄하는 분

(3) Introduction 3

Mr. Lee Hi, Mr. Jackson. I am glad to run into you here! How are you?

Mr. Jackson Good to see you again. I'm doing well, and you?

Mr. Lee Fine, thank you. May I please introduce a friend and colleague, Tony Kim of Best & Ever Computers. Tony, this is Steve Jackson with Future & Media Corporation.

Mr. Jackson Hello, it's nice to meet you, Mr. Kim.

Mr. Kim Nice to meet you, Mr. Jackson.

Mr. Lee Would you like to join us for lunch, Mr. Jackson?

Mr. Jackson Thank you for the offer, but I'm meeting a client here. Oh, by the way, Mr. Lee, will you give me a call later at the office? I have a question for you.

Mr. Lee Sure, I'd be happy to. Nice to see you again, Mr. Jackson.

Mr. Jackson Good to see you again, Mr. Lee. Well, it was very nice meeting you, Mr. Kim and have a nice lunch.

Mr. Kim Thank you, and you too.

Mr. Lee We are trying to land contract with Future & Media. And he is a director being charge of marketing department. The final sales contract will be agreed, soon and I think we have a good shot at making this sale, indeed.

Mr. Kim That's great! Good luck to you, Scott! Ah, by the way, my wife wants to know if you are free for dinner. We'd like to have you over for dinner, if that's okay with you.

Mr. Lee That's very kind of her. I'd love to.

Mr. Kim Great! Alright, let's order.

Note

Would you like to join us for lunch? : 점심 식사를 같이 하시지 않겠어요? / Give me a call : 전화 좀 주세요 / I'd be happy to : 알겠어요, 기꺼이 그렇게 하겠습니다 / land contract with ~ : ~와 계약을 맺다, 성사시키다 / have a good shot at ~ : ~에 좋은 성과를 올리다

• Useful Expression 1

I am glad to run into you here! (=I am glad I bumped into you.)

What brought you here?

This is amazing!

I never expected to see you here.

What a pleasant surprise!

Who do I have here?
How glad to see you here.
What made you come here?

• Useful Expression 2

Give your family my best regards.
Give my regards to him.
Give my best wishes to him.
Say hi to her.
Remember me to your mother.
Thank your parents for me.
Give my love to Jane.
Please, say hello to Mr. Kim.

(4) Greeting 1

Nice to meet you, Mr. Murakami. It's a great pleasure to visit your company.

I'm glad to have an opportunity to do business with you.

It's my pleasure to get acquainted with your members.

Mr. Peterson, I'm glad to pay this visit to your company.

Mr. Philips, I haven't seen you for a long time and I'm glad to see you again.

Hello, Ms. Turner. I'm so happy to meet you here again. How have you been?

Haven't we met before? My name is Arnold Nixon, I'm a car dealer.

Excuse me, don't you remember me? We met at the Pusan International Trade Fair last year.

• Related Conversation

A Welcome to Canada, Mr. Kim. I hope you enjoy your

stay here.

B Nice to meet you, Ms. Lowe. It's a great pleasure to visit your country.

A Hello, Mr. Kwan. I haven't seen you for a long time. Nice to see you again.

B Hello, Ms. Carson. How have you been?

Note

It's a great pleasure to ~ : ~하게 되어 영광이다 ⇒ It's a great pleasure to meet you, Mr. James (James 씨, 만나 뵙게 되어 영광입니다.) / I am glad to have an opportunity to ~ : ~할 기회를 얻다 ⇒ I am glad to have an opportunity to visit your factory.(운영하시는 공장을 방문할 기회를 주셔서 기쁩니다.) / get acquainted with : ~와 거래한다, ~사와 친분이 생긴다 **cf** acquaintance party : 학교 선후배간의 만남이나 직장에서 신입사원과 일반사원과의 만남의 시간 / be glad to see you again : 다시 만나게 되어 반갑다 / 일반적으로 business상에서 '여자를 존칭해서 부를 경우'엔 Ms. 라는 칭호를 쓴다. 이 표현은 '결혼을 한 여자나 미혼인 여자 모두에게' 쓸 수 있는 표현임. / How have you been? : 그동안 어떻게 지내셨나요? / Haven't we met before? : 전에 뵌 적이 없었나요?, 우리 전에 만났었죠? ⇒ 물론 이런 표현은 sales를 하는 business person들이 주로 사용하는 상투적인 표현임.

(5) Greeting 2

It's my pleasure to meet you, Mr. Dubner. I've heard a lot about you from my associates in Osaka.

Mr. Krantz, I've been looking forward to meeting you for a long time. Mr. Francisco has often spoken of you.

How do you do? Mr. Ive told me to look you up when I got to London.

I think I have to go now.

Ms. MacDemand, I'm afraid I must be going now.

I'm sorry but I must say goodbye as I have another appointment now.

Mr. Tanaka, thank you for visiting.

Thank you for meeting me, Mr. Lasseter. I really appreciate your kindness.

Thank you very much. I had a good time.

* **Related Conversation**

A How do you do? I'm Peter Dubner. Glad to meet you.

B Nice to meet you, Mr. Dubner. Mr. Catmull has often spoken of you.

A Excuse me, but I think I must go now.

B Can't you stay a little longer?

Note

(business) associate : 제휴사 / I've heard a lot about you : 말씀 많이 들었습니다 ⇒이것은 business 상에서 많이 쓰는 표현이므로 반드시 익혀 두기 바람. / I've been looking forward to meeting you : 뵙기를 고대하다 **Cf** 'look forward to ~ing'를 꼭 기억하기 바람. / A has spoken of you : A씨가 귀하에 대한 말씀을 많이 했다 / Mr. Ive told me to look you up : 이브 씨가 귀하를 찾아 뵈라고 말씀하셨어요 ⇒ look ~(사람) up : ~를 만나보다, ~를 찾아 뵈다 / I have to go now : 이제 그만 가봐야 하겠습니다(= It's time to go now.) / I have another appointment : 다른 약속이 있다 / Thank you for visiting : 방문해 주셔서 감사합니다 **Cf** Thank you for watching : 우리 프로그램을 봐 주셔서 감사합니다 / I really appreciate your kindness : (헤어질 때) 귀하의 친절에 감사드립니다 ⇒ 이 경우에 I appreciate you 라고는 하지 않는다. 이유는 'appreciate'은 '상대에게 감사하다'라는 의미가 아니고 '상대의 행동에 감사하다'라는 뜻으로 쓰이기 때문임. / I had a good time : 유익한 시간을 갖다

4 Domestic News

Duty over Freedom

The Supreme Court chose duty over freedom when it upheld a decision by the lower court, which had sentenced a conscientious objector to one and a half years in prison. Among the 12 justices on the bench, only one issued a minority opinion, which said, "The freedom of conscience deserves greater respect than the duty for national defense when they are in conflict." While granting the right of thought, conscience and religion, the Constitution demands that all citizens perform the duty of national defense under the conditions prescribed by law. But it has no reference to which of the two should be given supremacy when they are in conflict.

In upholding the lower court's ruling on Thursday, the Supreme Court went against the 1998 U.N. resolution calling on states which had yet to permit conscientious objection to take measures to ensure that it was upheld in specific cases. That was disappointing, not only to conscientious objectors, but also to many civic groups, which demanded conscientious objection be adopted in the nation's legal system. It was not the first time for the highest court to rule against conscientious objection. "Guilty" decisions were made against those refusing to serve in the military for religious reasons back in 1969 and 1992.

This time, however, conscientious objectors had high expectations that the earlier decisions would be reversed, because in May a district court in Seoul acquitted three young men who had refused compulsory military service on the grounds of their religious convictions. True, it is theoretically possible for the Constitutional Court, which is deliberating on a similar case, to overturn the Supreme Court's ruling. But legal experts say it is practically impossible, as many in the Constitutional Court are certain to share the highest court's majority opinion. In addition, it will take many years for the Supreme Court to deliberate on a similar case again, if it ever does.

But that does not necessarily mean that it is now impossible to make room for conscientious objection. On the contrary, the Supreme Court's decision will certainly prompt civic groups to put greater pressure on the administration and the political community to revise the military service law to legalize alternative service. Indeed, six of the 12 justices, including the one who issued the minority opinion, wrote an additional opinion that it is necessary to make alternative service available. It will not be too difficult to exclude conscientious objectors from active duty, given the fact that quite a few young men are already exempt from military service for various reasons, although they are judged to be physically or mentally fit. They include some engineering majors who are given civilian jobs as a form of alternative service.

Each year, about 600 young men, many of them Jehovah's Witnesses, reportedly choose to go to prison instead of bearing arms. To incarcerate them is to deny them a "legitimate exercise of the right to freedom of thought, conscience and religion," as pointed out by the United Nations. The administration and the political community are advised to pay attention to their plight and hasten to revise the military service law to permit them to carry out some form of alternative service. (from The Korea Herald)

Note

incarcerate : 감금하다, 투옥하다 / plight : 곤경, 궁지, (어려운) 상태

⑤ Annie

Romantic choices

Dear Annie:

My 21-year-old daughter, "Misty," is socially immature. She always has been attracted to the "bad" boys who lack ambition, motivation, jobs, cars and families. We wonder why she is drawn to this type, since Misty was brought up with scads of love and attention. She has no reason to feel that she doesn't deserve a boy with a positive future.

Misty's latest romance is with a young man of 25 who has no family in the area and works as a waiter at a coffee shop. He has no car and seems to be staying with a friend. In other words, he is one couch short of homeless.

Misty has begun describing this fellow as her fiance, although we've heard nothing about an engagement. The worst part is that her sister and I have a gut feeling about the guy that scares us. We've never felt this way about any of Misty's other boyfriends, but this one seems dishonest, although we have no evidence to back up our fears. We have talked about our feelings with Misty, but she insists the creep treats her like a queen. He now is pushing for her to let him move into her place.

I have asked Misty to think carefully before she gets engaged or married, and to give this relationship a little more time before she lets him move in. Do you have any other suggestions? We are worried sick.

—Misty-Eyed Mom

Dear Mom:

We trust your gut instincts that the current beau is a

creep, but that isn't going to be enough for Misty to drop him. Perhaps she was raised to be a confident young woman, but she nonetheless lacks a healthy sense of self-worth.

Misty needs to know her mother not only loves her, but has faith in her. Your worries may be justified, but your criticism of Misty's romantic choices is undermining her decisions, and she is tuning you out. Is there someone Misty respects enough to listen to about this? Her father perhaps? A girlfriend, employer or the family clergyperson? In the meantime, get to know the creep. It might help.

6 Reading Comprehension

Misconceptions about alcoholism are common. Many people, for example, think that alcoholics are careless, pleasure-seeking people. Actually, alcoholics often feel guilty about their drinking and are very self-conscious around other people. Another common myth is that alcoholics are always drunk. In truth, there are three types of alcoholics. Episodic drinkers, for example, drink only now and then. Habitual excess drinkers are also only occasionally drunk, but their episodes are much more frequent than those of the episodic drinker. The addict is a person who must drink continually simply to function. It is the addict who needs medical assistance to withdraw from the support of alcohol.

(1) Which of the following is the best title of the above passage?

ⓐ Different Kinds of Alcoholics
ⓑ Alcoholism: Fact and Fiction
ⓒ Alcoholism: Causes and Effects
ⓓ The Psychology of Alcoholics

Note

alcoholism : 알코올 중독 / alcoholic : 알코올 중독 환자 / self-conscious : 사람 앞을 꺼리는, 수줍어하는 / episodic : 일시적인 / episode : 증상, 발현

⑦ Humour in English

(1) A Sleeping Pill

Tom had the problem of getting up late in the morning and was always late for work. His boss was mad at him and threatened to fire him if he didn't do something about it.

So Tom went to his doctor, who gave him a pill and told him to take it before he went to bed. Tom slept well and in fact beat the alarm in the morning. He had a leisurely breakfast and drove cheerfully to work. "Boss," he said, "The pill actually worked!" "That's all fine," said the boss, "but where were you yesterday?"

Note

be late for work : 직장에 지각하다 / be mad at : ~에 화내다 / threaten : 협박하다 / fire : 해고하다 / take a pill : 알약을 복용하다 / in fact : 사실상 / beat : 이기다, 능가하다 / leisurely : 한가한, 느긋한 / actually : 실제로, 정말로 / work : 효과가 있다

(2) Dead Men Never Talk

"And ladies and gentlemen," shouted the charlatan in the market place, "I have sold over a million bottles of this great cure-all, and I have never received a single complaint. I ask you, what does that prove?" "It proves that dead men never talk," came a voice from the crowd.

Note

charlatan : 허풍쟁이, 협잡꾼 / market place : 장터, 시장 / cure-all : 만병통치약 / complaint : 불평 / prove : ~임을 알다

Exercise

(1) Taiwanese Going Bananas

Recently, the military force of Taiwan was put on a very important job. They were ordered by the government to eat as many bananas as possible. The members of the government did the same thing. They stood outside and munched bananas for a long time. There is a simple reason for this. They were trying to help the banana farmers of their country. Most of the bananas are exported to countries like Japan. So bananas bring in a lot of money for the farmers and the country. But this time, Japan did not take as many bananas as they usually do. Taiwan got flooded with bananas, and their price kept going down. Finally, the government asked citizens to do their duty by buying and eating as many bananas as possible. (from The Teen Times)

Note

Taiwanese Going Bananas : 바나나 사 먹으러 가는 대만인들 / Recently : 최근에 / the military force of Taiwan : 대반군대 / put on a very Important job : 중요한 임무가 주이지다 / eat as many bananas as possible : 가능한 한 많은 바나나를 먹다 / munch : 우적우적 씹어먹다 / export : 수출하다 / bring in : ~의 이익을 생기게 하다 / get flooded with : ~로 넘쳐나다 / citizens : 시민 / duty : 임무(의무)

(2) Record Soju Shipments during First Half

Soju shipments rose to a record high during the first six months of this year as the low-priced traditional Korean spirit gained popularity amid the depressed economy, the National Statistical Office said yesterday. Sales of beer and whiskey declined from a year earlier, prompting the government to postpone a tax increase on alcoholic beverages scheduled to begin next year. Soju shipments in the first half rose 7.2 percent to 590,000 kiloliters, while beer sales shrank 10,000 kiloliters to 833,000 kiloliters and whiskey sales nosedived 16.9 percent to 4,967 kiloliters. (from The Korea Herald)

제10장

Lifting Age Limits on Teachers Likely to Compound Youth Unemployment

① Warm-up

(1) You will be able to access the computer facilities at this office after hours if you have the correct identification card.
(2) The recent report on development in third world countries has brought up some important questions concerning the value of food aid to these countries.
(3) The automobile division of our company is very successful because of good teamwork and strict management.
(4) The building has remained unoccupied ever since it was scheduled for demolition earlier this year.
(5) We believe that the ongoing economic reform must continue well into the 21st century.
(6) Salary increases have been calculated this year according to the official guidelines.
(7) He advised me to buy my air ticket immediately, or it would be too late.
(8) The manager has, on the advice of a consultant, dispatched one hundred to the site of the gas leak.
(9) With their new programs and displays the educational staff of the museum invite us to discover the

technological history of this region.

(10) Safety in the workplace continues to be a major industrial issue, and today most firms emphasize safety equipment and avoidance of hazards.

Note

1) access : 접근하다, 이용하다(have access to) ⇒ have access to에서 access는 명사로 그 뒤에 전치사 to를 동반함.
2) question은 그 뒤에 about이나 concerning이 나와 그 뒤의 명사와 연결됨. **cf** raise a question : 질문을 제기하다
3) '자동차부'라고 할 때 부서는 division이라고 함.
4) unoccupied : 사람이 살지 않는, 거주하지 않는
5) ongoing : 진행하고 있는 / reform : 개혁
6) 주어가 사물인 '월급 인상분'이므로 수동적으로 '계산되어져야' 함. 한편 이 문장의 주어가 increases로 복수이므로 have been 이 된 것임. official guideline : 공식적인 지침
7) 'advise+목적어+to부정사' 로 쓰임.
8) 현재완료 구문임. dispatch : 파견하다
9) staff는 집합적으로(복수) 쓰였음.
10) workplace가 추상명사가 아닌 보통명사이므로 a workplace, the workplace, workplaces 중에서 선택이 가능하다. 보통 일상생활에서 일반적으로 쓰이는 장소는 정관사 the를 붙임.

② Current Terms

(1) Injury Time

Defending champion Bayern Munich was ousted from the German Cup, losing to second-division Alemannia Aachen 2-1 Wednesday night in the quarterfinals. Eric Meijer headed in the go-ahead goal in the 81st minute. Stefan Blank had beaten Liver Kahn in the 33rd minute to put Alemannia Aachen ahead, but Michael Ballack had tied it in the first-half injury time. (from The Korea Herald)

Note

oust : 내쫓다, 쫓아내다 / go-ahead : 전진하는 / tie : 동점을 이루다 / injury time : 인저리 타임

(2) No-work-no-pay Principle

Meanwhile, in a meeting of labor officials from major corporations, the KEF yesterday resolved to oppose the general strike planned for June 12 by the Korean Confederation of Trade Unions(KCTU). Denouncing it as an illegal strike, the KEF urged major corporations to fight it anyway they could, including the use of irregular workers, sticking to the no-work-no-pay principle, filing civil and criminal suits against union leaders and closing down factories. The KEF issued guidelines setting out these and other steps to assist management in dealing with illegal strikes. (from The Korea Herald)

Note

KEF : 한국경영자총협회(Korea Employers Federation) ⇒ 일명 '경총' / Korean Confederation of Trade Unions : 전국민주노동조합총연맹 ⇒ 일명 '민주노총'

3 Practical English

(1) Hotel 1

(Could you recommend a hotel?)
Could you recommend a good hotel?
I am looking for a reasonable hotel near downtown,

could you recommend one?

Have you already reserved a hotel room?

Have you already made a reservation at the hotel?

Let me show you a reasonable hotel at the price you're looking for.

(At the front desk)

1. Have you any rooms vacant tonight?
2. Is there a room available for tonight?
3. I'd like to check-in for three nights.
4. I'd like to have a single room with a nice view.
5. Do you have any quiet rooms here?
6. Do you have a room with an ocean view?
7. I'd like to book a room.

*** Related Conversation**

A : Good morning, sir. May I help you?

B : Yes, I'd like to book a room for three nights.

A : I see. Do you have any preference?

B : I'd like a room with an ocean view.

Note

recommend : 소개하다 **cf** French 식당에 갔을 때 익숙하지 않은 음식의 이름들이 나열되어 있다면 waiter에게 What can you recommend? ("어떤 음식을 추천하시나요?") 라고 물어 볼 수 있음. / '숙박료가 적당하다'라는 말이 '단지 숙박료가 싸다'를 의미하지는 않는다. 그렇기 때문에 cheap hotel이란 표현보다는 reasonable hotel이란 표현이 더 낫다. / reserve : 예약하다 **cf** a reserved table : 예약석 / '원하시는 가격'이란 말은 다시 말하면 '적당한' 가격을 의미한다. 그래서 reasonable hotel이라고 하면 자연스럽다. / vacant room : 빈 방(=available room) / check-in for three nights : 3일간 숙박 **cf** Three days라고 하지 않고 three nights라고 하는 것을 꼭 익혀두기 바람. / a room with a nice view : 전망이 좋은 방 **cf** quiet room : 조용한 방 / a room with an ocean view : 바다 전경이 있는 방(바다가 보이는 방)

(2) Hotel 2

Have you booked already?

My name is Oishito Sasaki. I've a reservation here for tonight.

Can I see the list for the room charges?

Does this rate include breakfast?

This room rate includes tax and all service charges.

I want to stay here for two more nights.

Excuse me, I'd like to leave one day earlier.

Can I change my room? The elevator is really noisy.

Sir, here is your key and please follow the bell man.

Could I have the key?

Note

reserve : 예약하다(=book) **cf** a reserved table : 예약석 / hotel 방을 미리 예약하면 대부분의 경우 hotel 비용을 절약할 수 있음. / list for the room charges : 객실료 리스트 / 대개의 경우 B & B hotel이란 광고를 보게 된다. 말 그대로 Bed and Breakfast의 약자로 '방값과 아침식사가 제공된다'는 것임. 물론 특급 호텔보다는 중저가 호텔에서 주로 사용하는 마케팅 전략임. / service charge : 봉사료(=tip) / two more nights : 이틀 더 숙박하다 / 종종 자신이 예약한 날보다 먼저 check-out 해야 할 경우가 있다. 이런 경우에 leave ~ earlier라고 하면 자연스럽다. **cf** I would like to leave two days earlier : 이틀 먼저 check out하고 싶다 / 방의 소음과 관련된 표현의 또 다른 예 : Room 1009 is really noisy, will you please tell them to be quiet? (1009호가 너무 시끄러워요. 좀 조용히 하라고 해 주세요.)

*** Related Conversation**

A How may I help you?

B How much is the room rate?

A The rate is $65 a night. Please follow the bell man.

B Does the rate include breakfast?

A No, I'm sorry. Breakfast is extra.

B I see, thank you.

*** Further Study**

What time is breakfast served?

Where is the dining hall?

Please bring my breakfast to my room.
What time does the dining room close?
The toilet doesn't flush properly.
Hello, I can't take a shower. There is no hot water.
I locked myself out.
What is the rate?
One hundred fifty dollars a night. This includes a continental breakfast.

Note

대부분의 호텔에는 restaurant이 함께 있으나 24시간 영업을 하지는 않는다. **cf** How late do you open? : 몇 시까지 영업해요? / restaurant : 식당(=dining hall) / What time does the dining room close? = How late do you open? / flush : 변기의 물을 내리다 ⇒ Flush after use! : (일부 화장실의 경우) 용변보신 후 물을 내려 주세요! / take a shower : 샤워를 하다 / There is no hot water : 뜨거운 물이 안 나온다 / I locked myself out : 이 표현은 '문' 또는 '자동차' 안에 key를 두고 문 밖이나 차 밖에서 문이 잠긴 경우에 사용할 수 있는 유용한 표현임. lock oneself out이란 말을 꼭 익혀두기 바람. / (room) rate : 객실료

(3) Hotel 3(Check-in)

Clerk Good evening, sir. Welcome to the Gloria. Do you have a reservation?

Mr. Lee Yes, I have a reservation. My name is Lee, Scott H. Lee. I have a reservation for a room with a king size bed for 12 nights.

Clerk Okay, just one moment, please. Ah, Mr. Lee. We have your reservation for a non-smoking suite. Is that right?

Mr. Lee Exactly! I was wondering if I could get a room with a view of the city?

Clerk Of course. We have a room on the 15th floor with a great view.

Mr. Lee Great!

Clerk Will it be cash or charge?

Mr. Lee Let me use my credit card.

Clerk Yes, will you fill out this registration form?

Mr. Lee Okay. Do I have to check out by noon?

Clerk Yes, but if you need more time to check out, please let us know one day earlier.

Mr. Lee Thanks.

Clerk Here is your key. I'll have the bellboy show you the room and carry your baggage.

Mr. Lee Well, would you ring me up at 5:30 every morning?

Clerk Sure thing. And if you need anything, please call us at any time.

Note

we have your reservation : 예약이 되어 있다 / cash or charge : 현금이에요? 신용카드예요? / Let me use my credit card : 신용카드로 지불할게요 / registration form : 숙박계 / check out : (호텔 등에서) 계산을 하고 나오다

*** Free Talking Tips**

Ring me up at 5:30.
Can I deposit my valuables?
I'd like a wake-up call at seven.
I'd like to order room service.
Could you send someone up?
Can I have laundry service?
I'm locked out of my room.
I'd like to extend my stay.
Are there any messages for me?
May I change my room?
Do you take traveler's check?
Can you please call a cab for me?

(4) Hotel 4

Hello, I'd like to make an outside call.
Can you send someone to help me with my luggage?
Can you call me a taxi?
I'd like to put some valuables in the hotel safe.

*** Related Conversation**

A Front desk.
B This is 301. Can you send someone to help me with my luggage?
A Of course. Is there anything else?
B Yes, please, have a taxi waiting for me.
A Okay, sir. You can get a taxi in 15 minutes.
B Thank you.

(5) Hotel 5

A Do you have any vacant rooms?
B Yes, we have 2 suites left.
A What is the rate?
B One hundred fifty dollars a night. This includes a continental breakfast.
A Does it include tax and all service charges?
B Yes, it does.
A Do you have room service?
B You bet, sir!
A Could I have a suite with a balcony?
B I'm sorry. Those are all booked.
A Well, can I have a room with an ocean view?
B Sorry, sir. They are all occupied.
A Okay, I'll take whatever is available.
B All right, here is your key. Please follow the bellman.

A Oh, yeah, could you arrange for someone to pick up my luggage at 9:30 tomorrow morning?

B Certainly.

A And could you give me a morning call at 7?

B No problem.

A Thank you.

④ Domestic News

Lifting Age Limits on Teachers Likely to Compound Youth Unemployment

These days, it is not uncommon to find people in their early 40s who have been laid off because of harsh restructuring by their companies in order to tide over aggravating business conditions. It is also nearly impossible for people over 30 years of age to enter private companies. Despite such a restrictive trend in the private sector in employing workers, the government is increasing the number of its employees, betraying its earlier promise to streamline its structure. The expansion of manpower in the public sector adds to the financial burden on taxpayers. As public workers are ensured to keep their jobs until their legal retirement ages, young people, who are suffering most from the unstable labor market, are endeavoring to land jobs in the government sector.

The government is further relaxing its regulations on employing public workers, contrary to tighter personnel management by the private sector. Another example is the

Education Ministry's plans to lift the age limit of those who are qualified to take state exams for teaching jobs at primary and secondary schools across the country. At present, aspiring teachers over the age of 40 are forbidden to take the test. But there are exceptions for vacant seats or posts that require professional knowledge and skills. The Education Ministry has decided to abolish the age limit in recruiting teachers from 2006, following the National Human Rights Commission of Korea's ruling against it. The commission stated the restriction infringed on the principle of guaranteeing equal rights. Even though removing the age limit looks plausible, it is expected to invite a whirlwind of protests, not only from the private sector but also from the government. First of all, other state agencies and public companies will be pressurized to follow suit because teachers hold the same status as government workers. Second, the step will further worsen job opportunities for youths whose unemployment rate is nearly 8 percent, over twice the nation's average. Third, the recruitment of older teachers is feared to impede the development of the educational system for primary and secondary schools as they are largely unable to meet the demands of Internet-savvy students. In this regard, the Education Ministry ought to reconsider the plan to remove the age limitation in tests for employing teachers. (from The Korea Times)

Note

harsh restructuring : 가혹한 구조조정 / promise to streamline its structure : 구조조정하겠다는 약속 / legal retirement ages : 법적인 정년 / endeavor to land jobs : 일자리를 잡으려고 노력하다 / lift the age limit : 연령제한을 철폐하다 / infringed on the principle : 원칙을 침해하다 / plausible : 그럴듯한 / invite a whirlwind of protests : 반대의 회오리를 몰고 오다 / status as government workers : 공무원과 같은 지위 / impede the development : 발전을 저해하다 / Internet-savvy students : 인터넷에 능통한 학생들

⑤ Abby

Dear Abby:

I hope my letter will benefit others. I am going to be 50 next year, and recently started a job in a 22-story office building. I have never been self-motivated when it comes to exercise. However, I recently hit on the idea of using the stairwell in my office building to get regular exercise, and it is working out very well. I arrive at work half an hour early and change into shorts and a T-shirt in the washroom. Then I go to the stairwell, and walk up all 22 stories, take the freight elevator down to the bottom and do it again. Sometimes I do it a third time if I have the time and energy to spare. Just walking up gets my heart really pumping, so I thought your readers might appreciate this idea. It's cost-free, convenient and not time-consuming unlike going to the club after work.

Because I don't perspire much, I just wipe myself down with a wet paper towel, dry myself with another one, change my underwear, get dressed and go in to work. I am so awake and alive by the time I start the day I recommend this to anyone. The challenge each day is whether I can do it faster than the day before, and there is a real sense of accomplishment when I reach the top. I feel this would not be the case if I just ran around the block a couple of times.

—Fit and Happy in Toronto

Dear F and H:

I commend you for your commitment to personal fitness. However, your regimen could be dangerous to anyone with an undiagnosed heart condition. Those who decide to try it should first consult their doctor about having a stress test. May I also suggest that most people who exercise strenuously tend to perspire profusely (perhaps more than you think) and a sponge bath with a damp paper towel may not be enough to deal with the problem. Out of consideration for your fellow employees, perhaps you should consider running the stairs after work instead of before to avoid the possibility of offending anyone. (Whew!)

Note

benefit : 도움을 받다, 혜택을 입다(receive some useful aid) / work out : 잘 되다(have a good result) / freight : 화물(goods to be shipped, cargo) / convenient : 편리한(suited to one's comfort or ease) / perspire : 땀을 흘리다(to become wet on pars of your body) / recommend : 건의하다, 추천하다(to cause to receive favorable attention) / challenge : 도전, 위험(a demanding or stimulating situation) / sense of accomplishment : 성취감 / commend : 칭찬하다, 건의하다(praise, to cause to receive favorable attention) / commitment : 언약, 약속(a message that makes a pledge) / regimen : 운동 요법(a prescribed course of exercise) / undiagnosed : 진단 미 확정의 / strenuously : 열심히, 격렬하게(vigorously) / tend to : 경향이 있다(to have a tendency) / profusely : 많이 넘치도록(given, flowing or growing freely and in large quantities) / avoid : 피하다(to miss or keep away from) / offend : 감정을 상하다(to cause displeasure) / whew : (놀라움, 당황을 나타냄) 어휴!(phew)

⑥ Reading Comprehension

Imagine how it must feel to drive at 100 mph. As you accelerate beyond your usual 55 mph, you can feel the tension build, your grip on the steering wheel tighten. After a time, when you return to your usual 55 mph, you notice a strange phenomenon. The 55-mph speed seems much slower–almost like a leisurely 40 mph. Make use of this psychological principle to develop increased reading speed.

When you're reading normally at 250 wpm, practice reading for a while at 350 wpm. Then you'll feel more comfortable at 300 wpm. This ensures maximum progress.

(1) What is the main purpose of this passage?

ⓐ To describe the mental effects of accelerating while driving a car.
ⓑ To persuade readers to drive at a normal speed.
ⓒ To explain the relationship between driving and reading.
ⓓ To advise readers on how to increase their reading speed.

Note

mph : 시속(miles per hour) / accelerate : 가속하다 / grip : 잡음, 잡다 / steering wheel : 운전대 / phenomenon : 현상 / leisurely : 느린, 여유있는 / wpm : 분당 단어수(words per minute) / ensure : 보장하다

⑦ Humour in English

(1) Convenient Math

A father asked the young man who'd been seeing his daughter about his finances. "What will be your yearly income?" the father asked. "Fifty thousand," the young man said. "Not too shabby. When you add my daughter's forty thousand, that'll be decent enough." "Oh, I already counted hers in the fifty!"

Note

finance : 재력, 소득 / yearly income : 연간 수입, 연봉 / shabby : 초라한 / decent : 버젓한, 상당한

(2) Ruthless Boss

A man went to his boss and said, "I must have a raise. My mother is very ill. I have to scrape bottom to keep my kids in school. I can't afford to have my car fixed. My house is falling apart. When I get home from work, I have a dozen chores to do." The boss replied, "You're fired. You have too many outside activities."

Note

scrape : 몹시 절약하다, 빠듯할 정도로 줄이다 / afford : ~의 여유가 있다, ~을 살 돈이 있다 / fall apart : 산산조각이 나다, 붕괴되다 / chore : 잡일, 허드렛일

Exercise

(1) Pushes to Reinvestigate the Bombing of KAL in 1987

Largely forgotten for the past decade, former alleged North Korean agent Kim Hyun-hee has recently come back into the limelight as the majority Uri Party pushes to reinvestigate the mysterious bombing of a Korean Air flight in 1987, according the state-run Korea Herald. Despite official findings that Kim staged the bombing on an order from the North's current leader Kim Jong-il to hinder the 1988 Seoul Olympics, there has been persistent skepticism among bereaved families and civic activists. Some have even claimed the attack might have been planned by South Korea's then conservative government ahead of the December 1987 presidential election to help elect an anti-communist candidate. (from ybmFM Daily News)

Note

limelight : 세상의 이목을 끄는 / stage : 꾀하다, 기도하다, 기획하다, 계획하다 / hinder : 지연시키다, 방해하다, 훼방놓다 / skepticism : 의혹, 회의; 회의론[설]; 무신론 / bereave : (죽음, 병 등이 육친 등을) 앗아가다

(2) Korean TV Dramas to Hit the Middle East

"Autumn Fable" and "Winter Sonata," the two local TV dramas which have been leading the Korean Wave in Asia, will be broadcast throughout the Middle East, including Egypt and Iraq, beginning Saturday. The Egyptian Radio & TV Union (ERTU), the biggest broadcasting company in the region, will air the two dramas until the end of this year. This will be the first time that Korean TV dramas have been shown in the Middle East. The Government Information Agency has been pushing forward the broadcasting plan in an effort to coordinate it with Korea's dispatch of additional troops to Iraq, hoping to make Middle Easterners more familiar with Korea.

"Seeing how popular the two dramas were in other Asian countries, we expect that Middle East people will feel closer to Korea after the broadcasts," said Kim Jung-pyo, the agency's deputy director. Under the agreement between KBS and ERTU, the Egyptian broadcaster received the dramas free of charge and the Government Information Agency produced the Arabic subtitles. The two dramas were selected for a number of reasons. "First of all, they do not have any political color to them," said Kim, emphasizing that any kind of political tone could worsen Middle East sentiment toward Koreans at a time when some Iraqis are opposed to the dispatch of Korean troops. Also, the basic structure of a pure love story was said to match Middle East people's tastes, according to Arab experts the agency consulted, Kim said. "Since an inroad is being made, we hope that the Middle East region will now be included in the Korean Wave phenomenon. This will be a good opportunity for Korean TV dramas to make a firm entry into the area," Kim said. (from The Korea Herald)

제11장

Filipino Troops Leave Iraq to Save Hostage

① Warm-up

(1) For further information, fill out this form and send it to ARCO International, Box 105, NY, New York.
(2) They hope to open a branch in New York City next year.
(3) This highway map shows only the main highways and large cities.
(4) Sooner or later, everyone gets their chance at success.
(5) Some of the world's worst problems could be solved if only its leaders would communicate with each other.
(6) The company has a fantastic picnic in the park every year.
(7) Carrying traveler's checks rather than cash is safer when going abroad.
(8) The training session in March was longer and more difficult than the one in January.
(9) Mr. Lee was much confident that he would be promoted.
(10) As we drove into the city at rush hour we encountered heavy commuter traffic on the freeways.

Note

1) fill out : (문서나 양식을) 기입하다 **cf** fill up : ~을 채우다, 충만시키다 / form : 문서의 양식
2) branch : 지점, 지부
3) highway map : 고속도로 지도 / main : 주요한 / large : 큰
4) sooner or later : 조만간 / chance : 기회 / success : 성공
5) if only : ~하기만 하면 **cf** if ever : ~하는 경우가 있다손 치더라도 / solve : 풀다, 해결하다 / communicate : 의사 소통하다
6) fantastic : 환상적인
7) A rather than B : B보다는 오히려 A / aborad : 해외에서, 밖에서 / when과 going 사이에는 〈주어+be동사〉가 생략되어 있음.
8) 비교급 구문이며 'the one'은 the training session을 말함.
9) confident : '~라는 것을 확신하여'라는 의미의 형용사임. ⇒ confident는 much나 very와 함께 사용하면 가능 **cf** well : 부사나 전치사 앞에 놓여서 '상당한'의 의미로 사용되는데, 형용사 앞에는 오지 않음.
10) commuter : 통근자 / traffic : 통근차에 의한 교통체증 / '교통'은 heavy(많다) 혹은 light(적다)로 양을 나타냄.

② Current Terms

(1) Boss Politics

In a broader perspective, however, the current disturbance can be seen as a critical transition in the evolutionary process of Korean democracy as well. Democratic institutions in this country have just been weaned from decades of "boss politics" dominated by a few charismatic faction heads with stalwart regional support bases. The nation is groping for a new leadership which meets the needs of changing times, and this has yet to emerge. (from The Korea Herald)

Note

perspective : 시각, 견지 / disturbance : 소동, 소란, 불안, 방해 / evolutionary : 진화적인 / wean : 떼어 내다, 버리게 하다 / boss politics : 보스 정치 / faction : 도당, 당파, 파벌 / stalwart : 매우 충실한 / grope : 손으로 더듬어 찾다, 암중 모색하다

(2) Berlin International Film Festival

Korean director Kim Ki-duk was named best director at the 54th annual Berlin International Film Festival on Feb. 14 for his film "Samaria," or "Samaritan Girl," a movie on a teenage girl's sexual exploitation and her detective father's revenge and forgiveness. This is the first time a Korean director has won the award at the festival. Kim, one of the most controversial filmmakers in Korea, had been nominated for "Bad Guy" in 2002. (from The Korea Herald)

Note

annual : 해마다의, 연례의 / exploitation : 착취, 개발 / detective : 탐정 / revenge : 복수 / forgiveness : 용서 / controversial : 논의의 소지가 있는, 쟁점이 되는

3 Practical English

(1) Make an appointment 1

When shall I visit you?

Would you please let me know a convenient time for you?

When is it possible for you to meet me?

When is the most convenient time to meet you?
Ms. Yamaguchi, I'd like to meet you to discuss this matter.
Could you call me sometime this afternoon at your convenience?
Could you make some time to discuss the Beijing project?
When you're free, please get in touch with me.
Can I drop by your office early tomorrow morning?

Note

visit : 방문 cf visitor : 방문객 / a convenient time : 편안하신 시간 cf convenience store : 편의점 / When is it possible for you to meet me? : When can you meet me? 라고 하는 것보다 훨씬 격식을 차린 표현이다. 우리말도 그렇지만 영어에도 '존대법'이 있다는 사실을 꼭 기억해 두기 바람. / discuss : ~를 토론하다 ⇒ discuss는 타동사이고 타동사는 바로 뒤에 목적어(명사, 대명사, to부정사, 동명사, that절 등)를 써야 한다. 따라서 discuss 뒤에 전치사(about)를 쓰면 안됨. / Could you call me? : Can you call me? 라고 하는 것보다 격식을 차린 표현이다. / the Beijing project : 베이징 프로젝트 ⇒ 이 표현을 the project of Beijing이라고 할 수도 있지만 글은 '짧게 쓰는 것'이 좋은 표현임을 꼭 기억해 두기 바람. / free : 시간이 날 때, 한가할 때

*** Related Conversation**

A Mr. Ramos, would you please let me know a convenient time for you?
B How about this Friday afternoon?
A Ms. Yamaguchi, could you make some time to discuss this matter with me?
B Sure, please come to my office anytime tomorrow.

(2) Making an appointment 2

We'd like to make an appointment for this evening with Mr. Rogers.
Shall we discuss our overseas marketing strategy?
Ms. Hill, I have something important to discuss with you.
Mr. Lane, do you think it would be possible for us to

meet you tonight?

Mr. Elford called this morning and said he wanted to talk to you.

Would you please tell Mr. Tan that Ms. Wilkinson wanted to discuss the new project with him?

Can I ask why you want to see me?

What did you want to see me about?

Could you please tell Steve why he wants to see me?

Note

make an appointment : 누구와 시간 약속을 정하다 **cf** Did you make an appointment with Mr. Rogers? : Roger 씨와 시간 약속 정했어요? / Would it be possible for me to meet you? : Can I see you? 보다 훨씬 더 공손하고 존경을 나타내는 표현임. / call : ~가 전화를 했다 **cf** Did anyone call? : 전화 온 데 없었어? / tell ~ that … : ~에게 전해주다 **cf** Can you tell Smith that I was here? : Smith 씨에게 내가 여기 왔었다고 전해 주실래요? / Can I ask why you want to see me? : 이 문장을 Can I ask why do you want to see me? 라고 하면 안된다. 그 이유는 ask 뒤에 '목적어 역할'을 하는 일반 평서문 문장이 와야 하기 때문이다.

*** Related Conversation**

A Ms. Pan, I'd like to make an appointment for this evening with Mr. Rogers.

B Sure, what time do you prefer?

A Tom, what did you want to see me about?

B I'd like to discuss the new project.

(3) Make an appointment 3

How about tomorrow? (Are you free tomorrow?)

Would December 20th be all right for you?

Shall I look forward to seeing you this Friday?

What time would suit you on November 3?

Would Wednesday or Thursday be all right?

Mr. Shoeman, what time do you think you can meet me?

Ms. Park, could you meet with me on Thursday evening?

If possible, I prefer Friday.
How about this coming Friday?
I am free tomorrow, how about you?

Note

How about tomorrow? (Are you free tomorrow?) : Are you available tomorrow? 라고도 한다. / would ~ be all right for…? 라는 표현을 익혀두기 바람. **cf** Would Ramyon be all right for you? : 라면 괜찮아? (라면 먹을래?), 그리고 이에 대한 긍정적인 대답은 That would be all right for me. 라고 하면 됨. / this Friday : 이번 주 금요일 **cf** coming Friday : 다음 주 금요일(=next Friday) / suit : ~이 적당하다 / Mr. Shoeman, what time do you think you can meet me? : 이 문장을 약간 변형해서 Can you meet me at 11? 이라고 하면 "11시에 날 만날 수 있겠어요?"라는 의미가 된다. / 'meet+사람' 또는 'meet with+사람' : ~와 만나다 / if possible : 가능하면 **cf** If possible, can you come to my office? : 가능하시다면 제 사무실로 오실래요? / be free : '괜찮다'는 것은 곧 '시간이 난다'라는 의미로 볼 수 있음. / How about you? : '당신은요?'라고 상대의 의향을 물을 때 쓰는 표현임.

*** Related Conversation**

A Cindy, would the first day of November be all right for you?
B I'm afraid I have a previous engagement on that day.
A Would Monday or Tuesday afternoon be all right?
B I prefer Tuesday afternoon.

(4) Make an appointment 4

John, what about 3:30?
You mean 3:30? Okay, it's also convenient for me.
Sorry, but I can't make time in the morning. What about after 2?
All right. 4:30 would be fine with me.
Sally, I'll visit you on Thursday around 3 in the afternoon. Is it all right for you?
Please drop by my office around 2:30 on Friday.
Is it okay for you if I visit you around 4 o'clock tomorrow?

What time shall we meet on Friday?

Note

you mean ~ : 상대방이 한 말에 대해 '확인'을 할 때 쓰는 표현임. **cf** You mean Korea? : 한국이라고 말씀하셨나요?, You mean NO PARKING here? : 이곳에 주차하면 안 된다고 하셨나요? / It's also convenient for me : 저도 그 시간이 괜찮아요 **cf** Is it convenient for you? : 그거 편해요? / can't make time : '미안하지만 시간을 낼 수 없다' 또는 '시간을 만들 수 없다' **cf** Can you make time tomorrow? : 내일 시간 낼 수 있어요? / fine with me : 그 시간이 좋다 **cf** Is this fine with you? : 이거면 되겠어요? / drop by : 들르다(stop by, come by) **cf** Drop by my office anytime! : 야, 아무때나 내 사무실에 들려!, Can I stop by your office this afternoon? : 오늘 오후에 잠깐 들려도 되나요? / 4 o'clock : 정확히 4시 **cf** around 4 : 4시쯤 / 요일 앞에는 전치사 on을 붙여야 함.

* **Related Conversation**

A When is the most convenient time to meet you?

B 3:30 is okay for me.

A What time can I see you?

B Please drop by around 5 o'clock in the afternoon.

(5) Make an appointment 5

Mr. Milton, I'm afraid I have a previous engagement on Monday.

Mr. Smith, can we change it to another day?

I think I can make it sometime next week.

Why don't you come to my office? We have plenty of parking space.

Ms. Maxwell, I'm afraid I'm fully booked tomorrow afternoon.

Shall we discuss the matter over lunch? I know a nice place near here.

Can I meet you tomorrow afternoon instead of tomorrow morning? I'm fully booked all morning.

Where shall we meet on Friday?

Note

previous engagement : 선약, 미리 한 약속 cf previous show : 이전 공연, previous class : 이전에 있었던 수업 / another day : 다른 날 / make it : ~를 할 수 있다 cf Can you make it? : 너 이거 할 수 있어? / come to my office : 내 사무실로 오라 / plenty of parking space : 충분한 주차공간 / be fully booked : 무척 바쁘다, 시간이 없다 cf Are you booked tomorrow? : 내일 바쁘신가요? / a nice place : 식당(=restaurant) / instead of : ~대신에 cf Let me have beer instead of whisky : 위스키 대신 맥주 주세요

*** Related Conversation**

A Mr. Bernard, can I meet you tomorrow to discuss this matter?
B I'm afraid I'm fully booked tomorrow. How about this Friday?
A When can you see me?
B I think I can make it sometime next week.

(6) Make an appointment 6

A Would you please let me know a convenient time for you?
B How about this Friday afternoon?
A When is it possible for you to meet me?
B Please come to my office to discuss the matter.
A Would you please tell Mr. Tan that Ms. Wilkinson wanted to discuss the new project with him?
B What time do you prefer?
A Can I ask why you want to see me?
B I'd like to discuss the Beijing project.
A Would December 20th be all right for you?
B I'm afraid I have a previous engagement on that day.
A Shall I look forward to seeing you this Friday?
B Shall we make it on Thursday? Because I'm fully booked on Friday.
A Is it okay for you if I visit around 4 o'clock tomorrow?

B I'm afraid I'm fully booked tomorrow afternoon. How about tomorrow morning around 11 o'clock?
A What time shall we meet on Friday?
B Anytime will be fine with me.
A Mr. Smith, can we change it to another day?
B It's fine with me except next Wednesday.

4 International News

Filipino Troops Leave Iraq to Save Hostage

Filipino peacekeepers were heading home Monday from Iraq after the Philippines pledged to withdraw its troops to fulfill a demand made by Iraqi insurgents threatening to behead a Filipino hostage. The kidnappers holding Filipino truck driver Angelo dela Cruz said earlier they would release him if all Philippine peacekeepers are withdrawn before the end of the month. Foreign Secretary Delia Albert said in a statement Sunday that the remaining 22 peacekeepers from the original 51-strong deployment would make an "exit call" on the new Polish commander at Camp Charlie in Iraq's Babil province on Monday.

They would be accompanied by Roy Cimatu, a special envoy of President Gloria Macapagal Arroyo helping Filipino diplomats in Iraq secure dela Cruz's release. "After the call, the remaining contingent will then proceed to Kuwait, and from there, return to Manila by commercial flight," Albert said. The Philippine Embassy in Kuwait is arranging their flight back to Manila, she said. Some peacekeepers who earlier left Iraq were due home Monday, officials said. A prominent left-wing group, Migrante, which has called for the Philippine troop pullout in recent protests, welcomed the development. (from AP)

Note

mob : 떼지어 몰려들다, 쇄도하다 / withdraw : 철수시키다, 후퇴시키다 / insurgent : 폭도, 반란자 / strong : ~의 인원을 가진 / deployment : 배치, 전개 / secure : 확보하다, 안전하게 하다 / contingent : 파견단, 분견대 / proceed : 나아가게 하다

⑤ Abby

Dear Abby:

I am a retired 80-year-old general surgeon. I am writing because I disagree with your response to "Grieving in L.A.," whose friend died of cancer and was never told that she was terminally ill. The writer felt guilty. The greatest factor in living, and in recovery from any illness or injury, is the patient's determination to live and recover. It is more important by far than the best of medical advice, supervision and treatment. To destroy hope is to seed defeat. The focus at home and in the professional environment should be directed at encouragement and a positive attitude. Any emphasis on "you are going to die" is, therefore, totally counterproductive.

—Eugene S. Kilgore Jr., M.D., Tiburon, Calif.

Dear Dr. Kilgore:

Intelligent minds can differ. Read on:

Dear Abby:

Before my first wife died of cancer in 1960, her doctor called me into his office. He said he would tell her all the facts and how much time she had left. I told him it was my responsibility. The doctor said it was her right that she might want to say something to the family or have something done. He was right! When I gave her the facts, she told me to get our minister, as she wanted to be baptized. Abby, my wife literally got out of her deathbed to be baptized at the hospital. Every person who is dying has the right to know. I have never regretted doing what I did. Please tell your readers who are wrestling with this question not to hold back the truth.

—L.L. in Fort Smith, Ark.

Dear L.L.:

You have made a compelling argument.

Note

general surgeon : 일반 외과의사 / cancer : 암(diseased growth in the body) / terminal : 말기 증세의(being or situated an end) / guilty : 죄책감(feeling responsibility for having done something wrong) / recovery : 회복(a return to a good condition) / injury : 손상(any physical damage) / patient : 환자(a person under medical care) / determination : 결의(an opinion, judgment reached after consideration) / supervision : 감독, 통제(leadership, direction) / seed : 종자, 심다(a small seed-like fruit by which a plant is propagated) / encouragement : 장려(the act of giving hope or support to someone) / emphasis : 강조, 중요성(special force given to certain words or ideas) / totally : 완전히(completely, wholly) / counterproductive : 역효과의(having the opposite effect to that intended) / responsibility : 책임(the proper sphere or extent of your activities) / minister : 목사(clergyman, a member of the priest or rabbi) / baptize : 세례를 주다(to perform the ceremony of baptism) / literally : 사실상(exactly, according to the words and not the intention) / get out of : 벗어나다, 나오다, 내리다 / deathbed : 임종의 자리(to be close to death) / wrestle with : (~ 문제로) 씨름하다 / hold back : 감추다, 주저하다 / compelling : 어쩔 수 없는(that compels one to do something) / argument : 논쟁, 언쟁(a dispute where there is strong disagreement)

⑥ Reading Comprehension

There is widespread fear among the public today that the family is falling apart. Much of that anxiety comes from a basic misunderstanding of the nature of the family in the past and a lack of appreciation for its flexibility in response to broad social and economic changes. The general view of the family is that it has been a stable and relatively unchanging institution through history and is only now undergoing changes; in fact, change has always been characteristic of it.

(1) Which of the following can be inferred from the passage?

ⓐ In modern times, broken families cause many problems.

ⓑ The stability of the family is desirable for the development of society.

ⓒ We don't need to be alarmed by changes in the family nowadays.

ⓓ Today's view of the family is not what it used to be.

Note

widespread : 널리 퍼진, 만연된 / anxiety : 근심, 걱정 / appreciation : 올바로 평가[이해]하기 / flexibility : 유연성, 융통성 / stable : 흔들리지 않는, 안정된 / institution : 협회, 기관 / undergo : ~을 경험하다, 겪다 / characteristic : 특징, 독특한

7 Humour in English

(1) The Meaning of Marriage

"Honey," said a husband to his wife, "I invited a friend home for supper." "What? Are you crazy? The house is a mess, I didn't go shopping, all the dishes are dirty, and I don't feel like cooking fancy meal!" "I know all that." "Then why did you invite a friend for supper?" "Because the poor fool's thinking about getting married."

Note

supper : 저녁식사, 만찬 / mess : 혼란, 뒤죽박죽 / fancy : 대단히 좋은, 멋진 / fool : 바보, 어리석은 사람, 놀림감

(2) A Young Woman Complaining of Pain

A young woman went to her doctor complaining of pain. "Where are you hurting?" asked the doctor. "I hurt all over," said the woman. "What do you mean, all over?" asked the doctor, "be a little more specific." The woman touched her right knee with her index finger and yelled, "Ow, that hurts." Then she touched her left cheek and again yelled, "Ouch! That hurts, too." Then she touched her right earlobe, "Ow, even THAT hurts," she cried. The doctor checked her thoughtfully for a moment and told her his diagnosis, "You have a broken finger."

Exercise

(1) China's Industry Output Up 15.5%

Growth in China's industrial output slowed in the year through July to 15.5 percent from 16.2 percent a month earlier, moderating for the fifth month in a row as the government kept up its drive to cool the economy. The slowdown was greater than expectations. The median forecast of seven economists surveyed by Reuters was for an increase of 15.9 percent. The State Statistical Bureau issued the data on Tuesday. The figure chimed with the message given in the central bank's second-quarter monetary policy report which forecast growth may slow in the third quarter, but that the economy would maintain steady and rapid expansion for the full year.

Industrial output growth has edged lower since peaking in the year to February at 23.2 percent. The downward trend followed credit curbs and government orders to curb overinvestment in sectors such as steel in order to put economic growth on a more sustainable footing. Industrial output from January to July was 17.3 percent higher than a year earlier, the State Statistical Bureau said in a statement. Production of steel rose only 18.5 percent in the year to July, but was 1.2 percentage points higher than in the year to June, it said. Steel production growth peaked this year at 37.7 percent in the 12 months to February. (from Reuters)

Note

output : 생산, 산출 / moderate : 완화하다 / slowdown : 감속 / monetary : 통화의, 화폐의 / curb : 억제하다 / overinvestment : 과잉투자 / sustainable : 지속적인

(2) Korea, Malaysia to Hold Summit Today

President Roh Moo-hyun and Malaysian Prime Minister Abdullah Ahmad Badawi will hold summit talks in Seoul today to discuss measures to enhance bilateral exchanges and strengthen their cooperation on the international stage. Abdullah arrived in South Korea yesterday for his three-day visit, which comes at Roh's invitation. Roh is expected to ask Abdullah to assist Seoul's efforts to seek understanding from developing countries and the Islamic region about its dispatch of an additional 3,000 troops to post-war Iraq, in that Malaysia chairs the nonaligned conference and the organization of Islamic countries. While in the South, the prime minister will meet economic leaders and attend a Korea-Malaysia business forum. (from The Korea Herald)

제12장

N-E Asia History Body Proposed

① Warm-up

(1) To curb the decline in profits, the company asked all managers to control costs in their areas.

(2) I believe that I could make a significant contribution to Exxone Corporation.

(3) Providing that you agree with our analysis of future economic trends, you have to invest your money in government bonds.

(4) The pension plans cover only domestic employees; consequently international employees must make other arrangements.

(5) All of the staff greatly appreciated management's understanding and decision.

(6) Despite the background of increasing business investment, weak domestic consumer demand was still squeezing many companies.

(7) Visitors are confronted by Rodin's two great masterpieces at the front entrance.

(8) By late Monday, the summit talks had reached an agreement.

(9) The euro dollar plunged below 85 US cents on Monday.

(10) Once merged, these two companies will beat all the competition and join forces to become the biggest fast food chain in Asia.

Note

1) decline에는 in이 따름. curb : 억제하다, 통제하다
2) contribution은 make와 함께 쓰임. significant : 상당한 / contribution : 공헌
3) Providing that~ : Provided that~과 같이 If~의 의미로 쓰이는 접속사임. providing : 만일 ~이라면 / analysis : 분석 / trend : 동향, 추세 / government bond : 국채
4) pension plans : 연금 제도 / domestic : 국내의 / make arrangements : 준비하다, 마련하다 / consequently : 그 결과
5) appreciate 다음에는 사물이 옴. cf thank 다음에는 사람이 옴. staff : 직원 / management : 경영층
6) investment : 투자 / demand : 수요 / squeeze : 쥐어짜다
7) confront : 마주치다
8) 정상 회담을 나타낼 때는 summit talks라고 씀. summit : 정상 / talks : 회담 / reach an agreement : 합의에 도달하다
9) 어떤 금액이나 가치가 ~보다 못하다고 표현할 때는 beneath(바로 밑에)나 under를 쓰지 않는다. Beneath나 under는 어떤 공간상에서 위치를 나타낼 때 쓰인다. 쉽게 생각해서 탁자를 생각하면 탁자 바로 밑에 껌이 딱 달라 붙어 있을 때 껌이 탁자 beneath에 있다고 말할 수 있다. 그리고 탁자 밑에 쓰레기 통이 있을 때는 쓰레기 통이 탁자의 under에 있다고 할 수 있는 것이다. 그러나 수치를 나타낼 때 A가 B보다 위에 있다 혹은 밑에 있다고 할 때는 below 혹은 above (위로)를 써서 나타낸다. plunge : 떨어지다 / below : 밑으로
10) 분사구문의 주어는 주절의 주어와 일치시켜야 한다. 의미상 두 회사는 합병되는 것이므로 수동의 의미가 적합하다. merge : 합병하다

② Current Terms

(1) Emerging Market

Bank of Korea Gov. Chon Chol-hwan said yesterday that requiring all domestic financial institutions to comply with a capital adequacy ratio recommended by the Bank for International Settlements(BIS) is problematic. "It is questionable to uniformly apply the BIS standard to all domestic financial firms," the central bank head said in a speech to a group of top corporate managers. "There is no need to have financial institutions in emerging markets conform to the ratio." Financial institutions which don't have contact with international markets, such as the National Agricultural Cooperatives Federation, should not be required to maintain their capital adequacy ratios above the recommended level. (from The Korea Herald)

(2) Pacific War

Japan's move to approve the textbook elicited angry reactions from officials, news media and civic groups in Korea. Seoul officials said the government plans to set the textbook issue as an agenda item for the third Korea-Japan ministerial talks slated for next month in Tokyo. In 1982, when Japan's history textbook issue was first raised, Japanese intellectuals successfully campaigned against a textbook glorifying the Pacific War and justifying its colonial occupation of the Korean Peninsula from 1910 to 1945. (from The Korea Herald)

③ Practical English

(1) Telephone English 1

This is John.
This is Winglish.
This is Tony Kim of Winglish.
Can I speak to Ms. Smith, please?
Would you please transfer me to the Overseas Department?
Would you connect me with the sales department?
I want to speak to Mr. Miller, please.
Overseas Department, please.

May I ask who is calling?
Who's calling, please?

*** Related Conversation**

Case 1)

A Hello, Winglish. Can I help you?
B Yes, please. Can I speak to Ms. Smith, please?
A May I ask who is calling?

Case 2)

A Good morning. May I help you?
B This is John. Would you transfer me to the Overseas Department?
A Hold on, please.

Note

전화상으로 "저는 존입니다."라고 할 때는 일반적으로 This is John. 이라고 한다. 만일 이런 상황에서 I am John. 이라고 하면 "나 존이다."라는 상당히 무례한 표현이 된다. 참고로 친구 사이에선 It's me, John. 이라고 한다. / '~와 통화하다'는 speak to ~라고 한다. 참고로 "스미스 양과 통화하고 싶으세요?"는 Would you like to speak to Miss Smith? 라고 하면 된다. / transfer : 옮기다, 건네다 / 전화상으로 '돌려주다'는 '연결하다'라는 의미의 connect를 쓰면 자연스럽다. / 전화상으로 정중하게 '전화거신 분이 누구인지' 묻고 싶을 때는 May I ask who is calling? 이라고 하면 된다. ⇒ 이 표현을 Who are you? 라고 하면 상당히 부자연스럽고 무례한 느낌을 준다. / '전화를 끊지 않고 기다리다'라고 할 때는 hold on이란 표현을 쓴다. 말 그대로 '대기하라'(hold on)는 의미임.

(2) Telephone English 2

Ms. Smith is not here right now.

She stepped out for a while.

I am sorry, Mr. Rodrigues is not at his desk.

Sorry, she is in conference now.

He is absent today. Would you like to speak with Mr. Moore instead?

Sorry, she is not here right now. She will be back at 2:30.

May I leave a message?

Would you please take a message for Mr. Summerville?

Would you tell him (her) to call me back when he (she) returns?

Could you tell her that her (his) flight to Rome is confirmed?

*** Related Conversation**

Case 1)

A Can I speak with Ms. Orlando, please?

B May I ask who is calling, please?

A This is John of Winglish.

B Sorry, she is in conference now. May I take a message?

Case 2)

A Good afternoon. Can I speak to Mr. Sanchez, please?
B Sorry, but he is absent today.
A Could you please take my message?
B Of course.
A This is Will Smith and please tell him to call me back tomorrow morning.

(3) Telephone English 3

Could you call me back at 4?
I'd like Mr. Smith to call me back when he returns.
Can I call you back as soon as I finish my meeting?
Could you please try again later?
John is on the other line, will you hold or will you call back in 10 minutes?

Can I have your number, please?
Could you leave your number?
Why don't you leave your number so I can tell him to call you?
How can I get in touch with you?
She/He is not here right now, do you want me to take your number?

*** Related Conversation**

A Can I speak to Mr. Johnson, please?
B He is on the other line, will you call back in 10 minutes?
A Could you tell him that David Moore called?
B Yes, sir.

Note

call back : 다시 전화하다 cf I'll call you back at 4 : 내가 4시에 다시 전화할게 / Would you like Mr. Smith to call you back? : 스미스 씨가 전화해 드리길 원하십니까? / '~한 직후'라고 할 때는 as soon as라는 표현이 자연스럽다. cf "그 report 끝내자마자 바로 전화 주실래요?" : Could you call me back as soon as you finish the report? / '다음에 다시 전화걸다'라는 표현은 try를 쓰면 자연스럽다. 물론 try에는 '전화걸다' 뿐만 아니라 '시도하다,' '~을 해보다'라는 의미도 들어 있다. ⇒ Can I try it? : 내가 한번 해 봐도 됩니까? / 전화상으로 '기다리다'라는 말을 할 때는 hold를 쓴다. / '다른 전화'라고 할 때는 the other line이라고 한다. cf Is Jane on the other line?(제인이 다른 전화를 받고 있어요?) / '남기다'라는 동사는 leave를 쓴다. cf "전화 잘못하셨습니다."라고 할 땐 Sorry, you have the wrong number. 라고 하면 된다. / "번호를 남겨 주시면"이란 표현은 "If you leave your number" 라고 하지 말고 "Why don't you leave your number?" 라는 표현을 쓰면 훨씬 더 자연스럽다. / '연락하다'는 get in touch with ~라는 표현을 쓰면 된다. cf Can I get in touch with you tomorrow?(내가 내일 연락 드려도 되나요?) / "지금 안계시다"라는 말은 not here right now라고 하면 된다. / "번호를 남겨 드릴까요?"라는 말은 "제가 당신의 전화번호를 받아 적을까요?"라는 의미이기 때문에 Do you want me to take your number? 라고 하면 된다.

(4) Telephone English 4

Can I speak with someone who speaks German?

Can you get me anyone who understands Korean?

I'd like to speak with anyone who knows about computer programming.

I want to talk to someone who knows medical terms for plastic surgery.

Sorry I can't hear you well. Will you speak a little louder?

Will you speak up?

This is a bad line, can you say that again, please?

*** Related Conversation**

Case 1)

A Can I speak with someone who speaks German?

B Hold on, please.

Case 2)

A I'd like to speak with anyone who knows about computer programming.

B Speaking. May I help you?

Case 3)

A Can I speak to anyone who knows Hebrew?

B Sorry, this is a bad line, can you say that again, please?

Note

'독일어를 할 줄 아는 사람'은 someone who speaks German이라고 하면 된다. 이에 대한 답인 "미안하지만 독일어를 하시는 분은 아무도 안 계십니다."는 Sorry but there's nobody who speaks German. 이라고 하면 된다. 독일어를 할 줄 아는 누군가가 있다면 Hold the line, please.(잠시만 기다리세요) 라고 하면 된다. / get : 연락이 닿다, (전화 등으로) 연결하다 / '~를 아시는 분'을 영어로는 anyone who knows about ~이라고 하면 된다. **cf** Can I speak with a computer expert? (컴퓨터 전문가와 통화할 수 있을까요?) 이때 "제가 압니다. 말씀하세요."라고 말할 때는 단순히 Speaking, may I help you? 라고 하면 된다. / '잘 안 들린다'라는 말은 I can't hear you well. 이라고 하면 자연스럽다. "내 말 들려요?"라고 할 때는 Can you hear me? 라고 하고, "목소리를 좀 더 낮춰 주실래요?"는 Will you speak a little softer? 라고 하면 된다. / '전화선이 좋지 않다'는 bad line이라고 하면 된다. **cf** The line is dead : 전화선이(전화가) 불통이야

④ Domestic News

N-E Asia History Body Proposed

In the wake of mounting concerns over China's alleged distortions of Korean history, a South Korean scholar on Tuesday proposed the establishment of a joint history committee consisting of experts from Seoul, Tokyo and Beijing. "South Korea should take the initiative in setting up the committee to maintain a regional identity in

Northeast Asia beyond nationalistic views on history," Bae Geung-chan, a professor at the Institute of Foreign Affairs and National Security, said in a report. The analysis, titled "Northeast Asian Age and Korea's Diplomatic Task," said South Korea stands at a better position to lead the project as it has never threatened neighboring countries by force nor has it pursued the domination of other countries. Because Japan and China are in a tight competition to win regional dominance in Northeast Asia, it will be hard for them to take the initiative in discussing a common perception of history, Prof. Bae explained.

As the committee produces its research findings, the three nations should ultimately reflect the result in their history textbooks without distortion, he stressed. The professor's suggestion draws special attention as the Seoul government has declared several times it will take countermeasures against Beijing's tinkering with historical facts. China's Foreign Ministry deleted Koguryo, one of the three kingdoms of ancient Korea, from an introduction to Korean history on its Web site a few months ago. However, the Beijing government still resists Seoul's request to correct the content on the Internet site. (from The Korea Times)

Note

in the wake of mounting concerns : 우려가 커지는 가운데 / beyond nationalistic views on history : 국수주의적인 역사관을 초월하여 / Institute of Foreign Affairs and National Security : 외교안보연구원 / domination of other countries : 타국의 지배 / common perception of history : 역사의 공동인식 / should ultimately reflect the result : 궁극적으로 그 결과를 반영해야 한다 / tinkering with historical facts : 역사적 사실을 어설프게 뜯어고치다

⑤ Abby

Dear Abby:

I have been dating my girlfriend for six months. We have a close relationship and are deeply in love. She is going away to college this fall. The school is two hours from our hometown. We had a talk about what we are going to do when school begins. She wants to break up with me because we won't see each other as often. I personally believe we can work it out. How can I convince her that we should remain a couple? In my heart, I feel we are meant for each other.

—Heartbroken in Hawthorne, Calif.

Dear Heartbroken:

If you want to keep the lines of communication open with your girlfriend, do not pressure her into an exclusive relationship when she goes off to college. She wants the entire "college experience," to meet new people and not feel tied down. It is a healthy attitude for both of you.

Couples in love give each other the freedom to be themselves. To do otherwise is controlling, and people run away from those who make them feel smothered. If you are meant for each other, you can get together when she comes home on weekends and holidays. She will be far more interested in seeing you if you have not made her feel guilty about other men with whom she may have seen a movie or gone for coffee. While she's gone, think of new ways to broaden your life. This should be a period of exciting growth for both of you.

Note

break up : 해산하다, 헤어지다, 분쇄하다 / work it out : 해답을 내다 / exclusive : 배타적인, 독점적인(excluding all others) / tie down : 구속하다, 제한하다 / smother : 질식시키다(to kill by depriving of air, suffocate) / broaden : 넓히다, 확장하다(to[cause to] become broad or broader)

6 Reading Comprehension

Canada's housing market is showing signs of gradual recovery. After struggling for nearly nine years against a protracted economic recession, housing is finally showing a substantial amount of growth. According to Canada Mortgage and Housing Corporation(CMHC), lower mortgage rates and prices will boost construction of new homes by 11 percent this year and 9 percent next year. In addition, sales of existing homes are expected to jump 14 percent over the course of the year. Despite these encouraging figures, the market is still much weaker than it was a decade ago. CMHC economist, Pat Trent, says slow population growth, high unemployment rates and declining real incomes are largely to blame for the situation.

(1) What is being reported in the article?

ⓐ An improvement in Canada's housing situation
ⓑ The rate of return on real estate investments
ⓒ A rise in the number of homeless people over the decade
ⓓ How the economic recession affected emigration rates from Canada to the United States

(2) What is expected to increase by nine percent in the next year?

ⓐ Mortgage rates
ⓑ Employment rates
ⓒ Sales of existing homes
ⓓ Construction of new homes

(3) How has the market changed from the previous decade?

ⓐ It has become weaker.
ⓑ It has become stronger.
ⓒ It has become stronger.
ⓓ It has experienced domestic growth but international decline.

(4) According to Pat Trent, what has caused the overall market trend?

ⓐ A reduction in trade barriers
ⓑ Speculation by Canadian economics
ⓒ Increased costs of building supplies
ⓓ High unemployment rates and slow population growth

Note

housing : 주택 / sign : 조짐 / recovery : 회복 / struggle against A : A에 대항해 싸우다, 투쟁하다 / protracted : 질질 끄는, 지연된(procrastinated) / economic recession : 불경기, 경기 침체 / substantial : 실질적인, 상당한 / mortgage rates : 주택 할부 대출 금리 / boost : 부양하다, 부추기다 / in addition : 더욱이, 게다가 / over the course of the year : 올해에 / encouraging : 고무적인 / declining : 감소하는 / real income : 실질 소득 / A be to blame for B : A는 B에 대한 책임이 있다, B는 A의 탓이다

⑦ Humour in English

(1) An Honest Little Boy

A lady lost her handbag in the bustle of Christmas shopping. It was found by an honest little boy and returned to her. Looking in her purse, she commented, "Hmmm··· That's funny. When I lost my bag there was a $20 bill in it. Now there are twenty $1 bills." The boy quickly replied, "That's right, lady. The last time I found a lady's purse. She didn't have any change for a reward."

Note

bustle : 혼잡 **cf** be in a bustle : 분잡하다, 크게 떠들고 있다 / change : 잔돈

(2) If I Were a Millionaire

"Take a pencil and paper," the teacher said, "and write an essay with the title 'If I Were a Millionaire.'" Everyone but Philip, who leaned back with arms folded, began to write furiously. "What's the matter," the teacher asked. "Why don't you begin?" "I'm waiting for my secretary," he replied.

Note

millionaire : 백만장자 **cf** billionaire / but : (전치사) ~을 제외한(=except) / lean back : (상체를) 뒤로 젖히다 / with arms folded : 팔짱을 끼고, 수수방관하여 / furiously : 맹렬히, 재빨리, 열심히

Exercise

(1) Nelson Mandela

Nelson Mandela was born in South Africa in 1918. His father being a tribal chief of an ethnic group, trained Nelson to be a tribal chief. But, Nelson chose to go to college to become a lawyer. In 1944, Nelson joined the African National Congress(ANC), the largest Black group against the South African Government. He led protests against the

Government, which led to his arrest in 1956. But he was found not guilty and was released. In 1960, the Government enacted the law which outlawed the ANC. Nelson led more protests against the Government, which led to his arrest in 1962. This time, however, was found guilty and was sent to prison for life.

Nelson as a symbol of the protest against the apartheid drew attentions from many people around the world. They consistently called for his release. More protests were held in South Africa, which led to the sociopolitical instability of the country. In 1989, the President of South Africa met with Nelson to work together for peace, which Nelson agreed. The Government allowed people to be members of the ANC, and Nelson was released from prison in 1990. Nelson Mandela work with the Government to create a new constitution. In 1994, both Blacks and Whites voted in the nation's first free election, and Nelson was elected president. He became the nation's first Black president. Nelson helped South Africa terminate apartheid and move toward democracy. (Source: Adapted from World History and You. Bernstein, Vivian〈1997〉.)

Note

tribal chief : 족장, 추장 / lead to : 결과를 낳다(=cause, have as a result) / enact : 법률을 제정, 통과시키다(=make or pass a law) / outlaw : 불법으로 선언하다, 무법자(=declare sth unlawful)

(2) Lost Olympic Spirit

The incompetent and irresponsible decisions of Olympic judges are fouling up the Games. In particular, unfair and erroneous judgments in favor of global sports powers have become a butt of criticism for degrading the Olympics into a political arena. Coincidentally or not, Korean athletes have ended up as victims of misjudgments in favor of U.S. competitors on more than a few occasions. The short-track 1,500-meter finals in Salt Lake City in 2002 and the baseball semifinals in Sydney in 2000 are such examples. One more such case is going on in Athens right now. In the men's gymnastics all-around event, Yang

Tae-young of South Korea lost the gold medal to Paul Hamm of the United States due to a scoring mistake by the judges. The International Federation of Gymnastics (FIG) admitted the mistake by suspending three judges but would not reverse the ruling, saying the Koreans' formal protest was too late. In athletic events, players vie for the tenth of a second, but would we need the clock in addressing an injustice?

But the Korean team officials' belated action cannot be excused. They should have been more familiar with the rules, making the right move at the right moment. Still this should be no reason for depriving an athlete of the honor earned by the efforts of a lifetime. Domestic athletic associations ought to strive harder for better sports diplomacy. But players should be rewarded or ignored according to their own ability or luck, not the incompetence of their delegations. Also to share the blame is the Korean news media in Athens. While major U.S. media outlets, including the New York Times and USA Today, pointed out the problem in the gymnastics event, most Korean sports journalists remained silent, bent on following other medal hopefuls, giving them heavy psychological burdens and ruining their condition. It was the U.S. media that first carried stories and columns calling for the gold medal to be given to Yang, or at least allowing him to share it.

Yielding to dominant U.S. public opinion, the U.S. Olympic Committee has reportedly expressed willingness to share the gold medal. Albeit begrudgingly, Paul Hamm also said he could give back the medal to Yang "if FIG ruled so." It would be best if the governing body of international gymnastics solve this matter reasonably. If not, the Court of Arbitration for Sports or the International Olympic Committee should step in to address the error. This is the only way to maintain the Olympic spirit, for which the Games have returned to their birthplace after 108 years. (from The Korea Times)

제13장 Crimes Surge amid Economic Slump

① Warm-up

(1) It is necessary to act cautiously when faced by a known felon, as the possible suspect may decide to flee before sufficient evidence has been gathered.

(2) It is interesting to note that our summer vacation coincides with my birthday and our third wedding anniversary next month.

(3) The police had no previous knowledge of the suspect's whereabouts until they received a tip-off from one of his business associates who led them directly to his hiding place.

(4) The UN is a unique organization as it includes representatives from all the major countries on earth and provides a forum to discuss international issues.

(5) Some seats are still available for tonight's performance, but you will have to make a reservation before five because they will probably be sold out by then.

(6) Use extreme caution when handling this antique vase as it is worth more than you or this museum could ever afford to repay.

(7) It was such an excellent report that Mr. Shultz

overlooked the fact that it had been turned in late.

(8) Because of the weather conditions, we'd like to postpone this Friday's meeting until sometime next week.

(9) Adequate liquidity is maintained to meet the cash flow needs of financial requirements.

(10) The young woman was so excited when she was called in for an interview that she told everyone she knew.

Note

1) felon : 악당 / flee : 도망가다
2) coincide with : ~와 (우연히) 일치하다
3) previous knowledge : 사전 지식 / whereabouts : 행방 / tip-off : 비밀정보
4) representatives : 대표자들 **cf** staff는 그 자체가 직원들의 총칭으로 -s를 붙이지 않음.
5) sold out : 매진되다 / make a reservation : 예약을 하다
6) Use extreme caution : 매우 주의하세요 **cf** with caution : 주의하여
7) turn in : 제출하다 / overlook : 간과하다, 눈감아주다.
8) postpone : 연기하다
9) adequate : 적절한 / liquidity : 유동성 / cash flow : 현금 자금 / financial : 재정상의 / requirement : 필요, 요구
10) call in : 요청하다 **cf** call off : 취소하다, call forth : 용기를 불러 일으키다

② Current Terms

(1) Kasin

Meanwhile, Kim's dishonorable retirement from Hyundai Construction will likely offer the terminally ailing contractor a fresh opportunity for independent survival, industry analysts said. In addition, Kim's departure would signify the end to the era of the so-called kasin, which refers to all-powerful company executives enjoying close relations with the founding family, they said. "The so-called problematic kasin trio, which includes former Hyundai Securities Chairman Lee Ik-chi and former Hyundai Construction Vice President Kim Jae-soo, have all been removed from the group's key management posts," said an industry analyst. (from The Korea Herald)

(2) Zayitun

The 3,000 troops, including combat-ready security forces, at Washington's request will help rebuild the oil-rich region of Kirkuk. They are required before deployment to take a six-week course on topics such as Arabic language and culture. The additional troops, whose unit is nicknamed Zayitun–the Arabic word for olive–will make South Korea the third-largest military contingent in Iraq after the United States and Britain. (from The Korea Herald)

Note

combat-ready : 전투 준비가 되어 있는 / rebuild : 재건하다 / deployment : 배치, 전개 / nickname : 애칭으로 부르다 / contingent : 분견대, 파견단

③ Practical English

(1) Travel English 1(Scheduling a trip)

Julie Hello. I would like information about flights to San Francisco.

Travel Agent When are you planning to travel?

Julie I am going to travel from December 28 to January 10.

Travel Agent Let me see if there are any seats available. How many people are traveling?

Julie Two people. Please tell me the cost of the tickets, too.

Travel Agent There are two seats available on Korean Air, departing Seoul on December 28 and returning on January 10. The cost for two is 2,000,000 won.

Julie That sounds okay! Can I make a reservation?

Travel Agent Of course. I`ll just need your name and phone number.

Note

I would like information about flights to San Francisco : 이 문장은 "샌프란시스코 행 비행기편에 관한 정보를 얻고 싶은데요"를 의미한다. 이 문장은 '주어(I)+조동사(would)+동사원형(like)+목적어(information)+전치사(about)+전치사의 목적어(flgiths)+부사구(to San Francisco)'로 구성되어 있음. / Let me see if there are any seats available : 이 문장은 "자리가 있는지 확인해 볼게요"를 의미한다. 이 문장은 주어 you가 생략된 명령문 형태로 '사역동사(let)+목적어(me)+동사원형 목적보어(see)+동사의 목적어 역할을 하는 명사절(if there are any seats available)'로 구성되어 있음. if는 '~인지 아닌지'를 의미하며 whether로 바꾸어 쓸 수 있다. if절은 '유도부사(there)+동사(are)+주어'로 구성되어 있음.

flight : 비행기, 항공편 / available : 사용할 수 있는, 도와 줄 수 있는 / depart : 출발하다 / make a reservation : 예약하다

(2) Travel English 2

A Good morning. May I help you?

B Good morning. I'd like to make a reservation to Bangkok, please.

A Yes, sir. When do you want to fly?
B Friday morning, please.
A Ok. Economy or business class, sir?
B Economy class, please.
A All right. Let me check if the flight's available.
B Thank you.

Note

May I help you? : 뭘 도와 드릴까요?(=How may I help you?) / make a reservation : 예약하다 **cf** reserved seats : 예약석 / business class : 비즈니스석, first class : 일등석, economy class : 일반석, 보통석(가격이 가장 저렴) / be available : ~이 가능한, ~할 여유가 있는 **cf** Are you available tomorrow? : 당신 내일 시간 좀 낼 수 있어요?

(3) Travel English 3

A I'm sorry, sir. It's full. How about the afternoon flight?
B What time?
A It's a 3:50 p.m. flight.
B That's fine. Let me take it.
A Sir, can I have your full name, please?
B My name is Charles Barclay.
A Thank you. Would you wait for a moment, sir?

Note

afternoon flight : 오후 비행(편) **cf** morning flight : 오전 비행(편), red eye special : 심야 (특별) 비행편 / 종종 항공사에선 비행시각을 말할 때 군대식으로 15:50 (It's fifteen fifty)라고도 한다. **cf** 오후 5시 : 17:00로 쓰고, 읽을 때는 seventeen hundred라고 함. / take : 물건을 취하다 **cf** Take it or leave it : 이 물건을 구입하시든지 아니면 그냥 가쇼 / full name은 first name과 last name을 합쳐서 부르는 이름이다. **cf** 미국 대통령 George W. Bush의 first name은 George, last name은 Bush, 그리고 W는 middle name initial이다. / for a moment : 잠시(=for a while, for a minute) / It's full : 만원이다, 빈자리가 없다 / a 3:50 p.m. flight : 오후 3시 50분 비행기 / let me take it : 그것으로 하겠습니다 / full name: 성과 이름 / wait for a moment : 잠시 기다리다

(4) Travel English 4(At the Airport)

Immigration Officer Good morning, sir. May I see your passport?

Mr. Lee Yes, here is my passport.

Officer What's the purpose of your visit?

Mr. Lee I've come here on business. I'm going to attend a trade show.

Officer How long are you going to stay in the country?

Mr. Lee I'll be staying here for about two weeks.

Officer Have you been in the United States before?

Mr. Lee Yes, I have. This is my third visit to this country.

Customs Officer Do you have anything to declare?

Mr. Lee No, I have nothing to declare.

Officer Do you have any fruits, plants, or food in your bag?

Mr. Lee No. Not at all.

Officer How much money do you carry?

Mr. Lee Well, I have $1,000 in traveler's check.

Officer What are these?

Mr. Lee Ah, they are my personal effects. That's all I have.

Officer Okay, thanks for your cooperation. Have a nice trip!

Mr. Lee Thank you.

Note

immigration officer : 이민국 직원 / customs officer : 세관원 / Do you have anything to declare? : 신고할 것이 있습니까? / traveler's check : 여행자 수표 / personal effects : 개인 소지품 / Have a nice trip! : 좋은 여행 되세요

*** Useful Expression**

I'm here for sightseeing.
I'm here on business.
Where is the luggage claim area?
I'm here to visit my friend.

Which gate should I go to?
Where can I find my baggage?
I'm here to attend the convention.
Is this KAL check-in counter?
When is the boarding time?
I've come here on business.

(5) Travel English 5

We are ready for take-off.

A May I move to another seat? I requested a non-smoking seat, but I am in a smoking-seat.

B No, we plan to have a full flight. And we are ready for take-off. Please fasten your seatbelt.

B I will.

Doesn't this bus go to the airport?

A Doesn't this bus go to the airport?

B No, you took the wrong bus.

A What should I do?

B Get off at the next stop and catch bus eight.

4 Domestic News

Crimes Surge amid Economic Slump

More and more South Koreans are turning to crime as the real economy remains in the doldrums. Fraud, embezzlement and other economy-related illegalities, in particular, are rising steadily according to the 2004 white paper published by the National Police Agency (NPA) on Monday. The fraud and embezzlement rate has surged over the past few years, alongside the growing number of individuals failing to pay fines or utility fees due to economic hardship. Also, a number of people are pretending to be jobless in order to receive unemployment allowances from the government, the paper said. "The surge in economy-related crimes has resulted from worsening economic conditions following the IMF crisis," an NPA official said, referring to the financial crisis that swept the country in 1997 and the country's subjection to an IMF bailout program the following year. "The financial crisis forced corporations to fire a number of employees as part of restructuring. Since then the number of credit delinquents and jobless people has grown." The official said that as more and more credit delinquents were banned from using banks and other financial institutions, fraud crimes also surged.

According to the white paper, fraud cases increased by 26.5 percent from 183,327 in 2002 to 231,951 last year, the highest level in 10 years. Embezzlements also jumped to 26,702 in 2003 from 22,986 in the previous year. In terms of forged checks, 19,582 cases were reported, up by 36.5 percent from 14,347 in 2002. Theft-related crimes soared by five percent from 178,457 in 2002 to 187,352 in 2003, the largest number in 10 years. Crime rates increased overall due to the growth in economy-related crimes, reaching 1.89 million cases last year, up by 3.4 percent from 1.83 million in 2002. The NPA white paper showed, since some 1.3 million crime cases were reported in 1994, crime rates have grown steadily for the past 10 years. Robbery cases also increased by 23.5 percent to 7,292 cases last year, while homicide cases rose by 4.3 percent to 998 in 2003 from the previous year. Cyber crimes also jumped by 14 percent yearly to 68,445 last year. The paper also showed the number of female criminals arrested last year also grew by 3.1 percent from the previous year to 320,859.

The NPA said as the numbers of divorced or single women are increasing, many women are attempting to make a living on their own. But a growing number of women are resorting to crime because of the difficulty to make ends meet in this male-centered society, the agency added. (from The Korea Times)

Note

economy-related illegalities : 경제관련 범죄들 / fraud and embezzlement : 사기와 횡령 / unemployment allowances : 실업수당 / credit delinquent : 신용불량자 / homicide case : 살인사건 / male-centered society : 남성중심사회

5 Abby

Dear Abby:

I'm in my 50s, have a serious heart condition–I almost died twice–and am living on borrowed time. My doctors know it, my family knows it, and I know it. We have talked about it, as well as my living will and organ donation. We have also discussed at length QUALITY of life, as opposed to QUANTITY of life. Some well-meaning people, out of a mistaken sense of kindness, would like me to do nothing but vegetate. I remind them I am still alive and able to do quite a few things. Perhaps vegetating would extend my life, but what would the "cost" be? Right now I can travel, do most of my own housework, putter in the flower garden and help my husband. While I cannot lift my grandchild or run in the yard with her, I can read to her and help her with the dishes. It is demoralizing when people refuse to listen as I try to explain quality vs. quantity of life. I know they want me to be cautious because they fear losing me. I am afraid much of the time, and am in no hurry to "meet my Maker," but when that day does come, I'll die knowing I made the best of the most precious gift there is life.

Abby, please ask your readers to encourage and help those with limitations to live life to the fullest. And urge your readers who are blessed with good health not to waste it, but to use this gift of life for the good of all.

—Living Life in New Hampshire

Dear Living Life:

I'm pleased to pass along your message. Our time on Earth is not infinite; therefore, our days should be spent the way we invest our money wisely. You're a pragmatic woman. I admire your determination to suck as much of the juice out of the fruit of life as you can. Bon appetit!

Note

serious : 심각한 / borrow : 빌리다(to take or receive for a certain time) / organ donation : 장기 기증 / at length : 드디어, 마침내, 오랫동안, 충분히 / well-meaning : 선의의, 선의로 행한(well-intentioned) / vegetate : 하는 일없이 지내다(not to do anything and feel bored) / extend : 연장하다(to spread or stretch forth or out) / demoralize : 혼란시키다, 사기를 저하시키다(throw into confusion) / refuse : 거절하다(not to accept or do to give) / cautious : 신중한(marked by or given to caution, careful, prudent) / precious : 귀한, 귀중한, 값진(of great value, greatly cherished) / encourage : 격려하다, 장려하다(inspire with confidence, give hope) / limitation : 제한, 한계(something that limits) / bless : 축복하다, 은총을 베풀다(endow, favor) / for the good of : ~을 위하여, ~의 이익을 위하여 / infinite : 무한정, 언제까지나(endless) / therefore : 따라서, 그 결과(as a result, for that reason, so) / pragmatic : 실제적인, 실용주의의(relating to practical affairs) / admire : 감복하다, 탄복하다(to have a very high opinion of someone) / suck : 빨아들이다(to draw liquid from by action of the mouth) / appetit : 식욕, 욕구(natural desire for satisfying some need for food)

⑥ Reading Comprehension

Canada's federal sales tax will rise to 8% from 7% if a bill that includes a temporary roll back in income tax is passed this week. This is expected to damage re-election prospects for the ruling conservative party, which had campaigned in opposition to sales tax hikes. Opposition parties were quick to point out the government's attempt to renege on campaign promises.

(1) By how much might the sales tax change?

ⓐ 1%
ⓑ 7%
ⓒ 8%
ⓓ 15%

(2) What will happen to sales and income taxes if the bill passes?

ⓐ The sales tax will go up and income tax will go up.
ⓑ The sales tax will go down and income tax will go down.
ⓒ The sales tax will go up and income tax will go down.
ⓓ The sales tax will go down and income tax will go up.

(3) What platform did the conservatives run on in the last election?

ⓐ Deficit reduction
ⓑ No sales tax hikes
ⓒ Controlled tax hikes
ⓓ Tax reduction

(4) What was the reaction of opposition parties?

ⓐ Support of the bill
ⓑ Announced intention to boycott the vote
ⓒ Point out Reversed the Conservative's campaign promises
ⓓ No response

Note

sales tax : 판매세 / bill : 법안 / include : 포함하다 / temporary : 일시적인 / roll back : 물가 인하책, 물가를 이전의 수준으로 하락시킴 / income tax : 소득세 / pass : (의안을) 통과시키다 / be expected to : ~일 것으로 보이다, ~일 전망이다 / renge : 약속을 어기다 / damage : 손상시키다 / re-election : 재선 / prospect : 전망, 기대 / rulling conservative party : 집권 보수당 / campaign : 유세하다 / in opposition to : ~에 반대하여 / opposition party : 야당 / be quick to : 재빨리 ~하다 / point out : 지적하다, 가리키다 / attempt : 시도, 노력 / platform : 정강, 강령 / run on : 계속하다, 줄곧 이야기하다 / deficit reduction : 적자 감축 / controlled tax hikes : 세금 인상 억제 / tax reduction : 세금인하 / support of the bill : 의안 지지, 찬성 / intention : 의도 / boycott the vote : 투표를 거부하다 / reiterate : 되풀이하다, 반복하다 / no response : 무반응

⑦ Humour in English

(1) A Wise Young Man

At a jewelry store, a young man bought an expensive locket as a present for his girlfriend. "Don't you want her name engraved upon it?" asked the jeweler. The young man thought for a moment, and then replied, "No, just engrave it : To My One And Only Love. That way, if we break up and she throws it back to me in anger, I can use it again."

Note

jewelry store : 보석점 / locket : 로켓(사진 등을 넣어 목걸이에 매다는 것) / engrave : (금속, 돌 등에) 새기다 / break up : (남녀가) 헤어지다

(2) A Brilliant Young Man

The management of a faltering corporation offered a $100 award to those employees who turned in the best suggestions as to how the company could save money. One of the first prizes went to a brilliant young man who suggested that in the future the prize money be reduced to $50.

Note

management : 경영진 / faltering : 비틀거리는, 고전하는 / award : 상, 상품, 상금 / brilliant : 총명한

Exercise

(1) Only 60% of College Grads Finding Jobs

Once again, the nation's tight job market is taking its toll on the nation's young hopefuls. Four out of ten college graduates from 36 four-year colleges in Seoul are roaming around unemployed, with only 60 percent of the graduates having found jobs, according to a report released by Rep. An Sang-soo during the assembly audit of Education Ministry yesterday. According to the report, job hunters from two-year institutions were more successful, with 67 percent of recent graduates from 11 two-year colleges in Seoul succeeding in securing a job. However, job-hunting success has been in a declining trend for the last four years for graduates of both two-year and four-year institutions. The percentage of two-year college graduates who had found jobs was 76 percent in 2001.

According to the report, among 36 universities in Seoul, graduates of only three schools–Korea University, Kyunghee University, and Sogang University–had a more than 80 percent successful labor force entry rate. At 18 universities, including the nation's most prestigious institution of higher education, Seoul National University, graduates failed to reach the 60% entry mark. Considering that graduates of universities in Seoul are considered to have a better chance of securing a job than graduates in other locations, the report suggests the nationwide unemployment among college graduates could be a lot worse. The data shows that graduates from medical schools and nursing and pharmacy colleges hold best shots in the tight job market, while graduates majoring in law have the lowest labor market entry rates. In the case of Korea University, employment among graduates in medical fields approached 100%, while that of law majors stood around 60%, far below the average of 77% for all majors. "The report proves that the saying 'one out of three college graduates in Korea are bums' is not too far from the truth," Ah said during the audit session. He called for the Education Ministry to act on issue and come up with measures to help colleges better prepare their students for the labor market. (from The Korea Herald)

(2) Actress Goh Back on TV

Goh Hyeon-jung, one of the top actresses in Korea, said yesterday she would be starring in Seoul Broadcasting System's 20-episode drama "Spring Days," confirming rumors of her returning to the entertainment business. Her appearance in the drama, which will be aired in January, comes 10 years after the Miss Korea-turned-actress performed in the much-celebrated drama "Hourglass" in 1995. Goh divorced Jung Yong-jin, vice president of Shinsegae, last November ending eight years of marriage, during which she hid from the entertainment world. Following the divorce, she was courted by the show biz industry to resume her career. Reportedly, Goh will receive the highest-ever paycheck for starring in a TV drama. The story of "Spring Days" is adapted from the Japanese drama "Heaven's Coins."

Goh will play Seo Jeong-eun, an adoptee brought up on an island who is forced to stop playing piano after an injury, which combines with another traumatic experience involving her first love which left her unable to speak. She finds hope when she meets Goh Eun-ho (played by Ji Jin-hee) and overcomes her aphasia. However, he leaves the island and suffers from amnesia after a car accident. And his stepbrother Goh Eun-seop(Zo In-sung) steps in forming a love triangle. (from The Korea Herald)

제14장

Crude Hits 21-year High on Supply Fears

① Warm-up

(1) After you have left the aircraft, please collect your luggage and clear it through customs before you exit the main airport terminal.

(2) A formal dinner will be held to honor our ex-president Mr. Lee, who dedicated himself to being the best CEO this company has ever had.

(3) An eye examination is one step in the process of being registered as a legal driver in this country.

(4) A complimentary light breakfast will be served for all participants at the conference to show the companies appreciation for their contribution to the meeting.

(5) Once one has acquired the habit, smoking is very difficult to give up.

(6) Whoever gets the highest grade point average will be the recipient of the scholarship.

(7) A considerable number of people object to the government's attitude to immigration.

(8) Having received several attractive offers from other companies, Jane decided to quit her job.

(9) Even though she had a good job, she gave it up when she got married.

(10) After closing the car door, it occurred to me that I had left my car key inside.

Note

1) clear through : 세관을 통과하다
2) formal dinner : 정찬 / dedicated : 헌신적인
3) step : 절차
4) complimentary : 칭찬의, 무료의
5) habit은 '습관이 든다'할 때 acquire, adopt, develop 등과 같이 쓰임. cf get into a habit(습관이 들다)
6) grade point average : 전과목의 평균성적(=GPA) / recipient : 수령자
7) considerable : 상당한, 적지 않은 / object to : ~에 반대하다 / immigration : 이민
8) offer : 제의
9) give something up : 자리 등을 내주다, 남의 손에 넘기다 cf give something in (제출하다, 건네주다), give something out (배부하다), give give away(거저 주다)
10) it occurred that ~ : 어떠한 생각이 떠올랐다

② Current Terms

(1) Prime Time

Many more are beginning to agree. For example, MBC, one of Korea's three major broadcasting services, recently announced that it will stop broadcasting the Miss Korea pageant real time after this year, when their contract with contest organizers, a major Korean daily, expires. MBC has aired the competition live every year for 12 years. "We agree that there may be ethical problems in broadcasting the beauty contest live like it's national news on prime time TV," MBC's Kim Taek-kwon said earlier this month. (from The Korea Herald)

(2) Company Town

The Federation of Korean Industries, a big business lobby, said yesterday that it is planning a project to build "company towns" to help create jobs. According to the federation, its Special Committee on Job Creation has decided to build the company towns, encourage corporate investment, promote peaceful labor-management relations and nurture the services industry, all aimed at creating jobs. (from The Korea Herald)

Note

Federation of Korean Industries : 전국경제인연합회 / company town : 기업도시 / corporate investment : 기업 투자 / labor-management relations : 노사관계

3 Practical English

(1) Meeting a guest 1

Excuse me, but are you Mr. McNamara of the Sunshine Traveling company?

Pardon me, sir. Are you Mr. Kennedy of the Toronto Electronics?

Hello, are you Mr. White from South Africa?

Pardon me, but are you Mr. and Mrs. San Miguel of the Columbian coffee company?

Good afternoon, Ms. Hanson. I'm here to accompany you to the company.

How do you do, Mr. Young? I will accompany you to Mr. Brown's office.

Good afternoon, Ms. Jack. I'm Tony Kim from Cel Research. I'm here to accompany you to the reception hall.

*** Related Conversation**

A Excuse me, ma'am. But are you Ms. Roland of Minnesota Trading company?

B Yes, I am. You must be Mr. Santiago of Cuban Tobacco.

A Yes, I am. How do you do? I'm here to accompany you to the company.

B Nice to meet you.

Note

Excuse me! : 실례합니다 / Mr. Kennedy of Toronto Electronics : 토론토 전자회사의 케네디 cf '전자회사'는 electronics company라고 하거나 회사 이름 바로 뒤에 ~ electronics라고 하면 된다. / from : ~ 출신 cf Mr. White from South Africa : 남아프리카에서 오신 White 씨 / Mr. and Mrs. ~ : ~ 부부 cf 김 선생님 부부 : Mr. and Mrs. Kim / to accompany ~ : ~를 모시러 왔다 cf They are here to accompany Mr. Kim.(그 사람들이 김 선생님을 모시러 왔다.) / to accompany ~ to … : ~를 어디어디로 모시고 간다 cf James is going to accompany Mr. Lee to the airport.(James 씨가 Mr. Lee를 공항까지 모시고 간다.) / the reception hall : 환영회장

(2) Meeting a guest 2

How do you do, Mr. Kim? Thank you for your kind welcome.

Thank you for waiting for me, Mr. Damskey.

Nice to meet you, Ms. Finch. How was your trip from Canada?

Hello, Mr. Park. Did everything go well during your flight from New York?

Mr. Alejandro, did you enjoy your flight from Venezuela?

How do you do, Mr. Mason? How was your flight from

San Diego? You must be tired.

It was a very pleasant trip.
It was a nice flight, but I feel a little tired.
The trip was nice, but I have jetlag.

*** Related Conversation**

A Pardon me, but are you Ms. Jack of Winnipeg Ski Resort?

B Yes, I am. Are you from Seoul Sports Equipment?

A Yes, I am. Nice to meet you. How was your trip from Canada?

B It was a very pleasant trip. Thank you for waiting for me.

Note

How do you do? : 처음 뵙겠습니다(=Nice to meet you) / Thank you for your kind welcome : 환영해 주셔서 감사하다 cf kind welcome : 진실된 환영 / wait for : ~를 기다리다 / how를 사용한 예 : How was last night?(어젯밤 어땠어?), How was Korean food? (한국음식 어땠어?) / Did everything go well ~? : 힘든 일은 없으셨나요? cf Did everything go well during your presentation?(발표회 무사히 잘 끝냈어?) / You must be tired : (공항에 막 도착한 분에게) 피곤하시죠? cf must를 이용한 다른 표현 : He must be tired.(그 사람 분명히 피곤할거야.), She must be rich.(그 여자 부자임에 틀림없어.) / jetlag : '시차'에서 오는 피로감 / Ms. Jack of Winnipeg Ski Resort : 위니펙 스키 리조트에서 오신 잭 cf Mr. Yamamoto of Toyota motor company(도요타 자동차 회사에서 오신 Yamamoto 씨)

(3) Meeting a guest 3

Ms. Parson, shall I carry your bags?
Mr. Miguel, let me help you with your luggage.
Mrs. Simpson, why don't you give me your suitcase? It looks heavy.

Oh, thank you so much, Mr. Kim.
Oh, no thanks. I can get it myself.
That's okay, Mr. Lee. Please don't bother, I can manage.

No, it's okay. I can handle it by myself. Actually, it's not heavy.

No thanks, but could you get me a baggage cart?

*** Related Conversation**

Case 1)

A How was your trip, Ms. Parson?
B It was nice, but I feel a little tired.
A Ms. Parson, let me help you with your luggage.
B Oh, thank you so much, Mr. Kim. It's very kind of you.

Case 2)

A Mr. Anderson, let me help you with your luggage, it looks heavy.
B No, it's okay, I can handle it by myself. Actually it's not heavy.
A Is this your first trip to Seoul?
B Not really, about 10 years ago I was here as a tourist.

Note

carry : 짐을 들어주다 / luggage와 baggage의 차이 : 그리 큰 차이는 없지만 luggage는 일반적으로 '영국식 표현'이고 baggage는 '미국식 표현'이라고 볼 수 있다. 물론 요즘은 서로 구별없이 쓰임. / It looks heavy : 가방이 무거워 보인다 cf heavy : 무거운, 우울한, 침울한 → a heavy night (나를 짓누르는 우울한 밤) / I can get it myself : 제가 들고 갈 수 있어요 cf Can you get it yourself?(당신 혼자 할 수 있어요?) / Please don't bother : 신경 쓰지 마세요 cf Is this bothering you?(이 물건이 걸리적거려요?), I can manage.(제가 하죠.) → manage : 일을 처리하다 / a baggage cart : (공항에 가면) 짐을 싣고 갈 수 있는 수레

(4) Meeting a guest 4

Ms. Johnson, would you wait here for a moment? Let me get a taxi for you.

Shall we stand in line at the taxi stand?

Mr. Smith, please wait here for a while. I'll page my chauffeur.

Excuse me, where can I get a taxi?

Will you show me the way to the airport limo?

I'll take you to the hotel by car.

Let me bring the car to the front. Please wait here for a moment.

Mr. and Mrs. Choi, the car is waiting for you in front of the hotel.

Please give me your bags. I'll put them in the trunk.

*** Related Conversation**

Case 1)

A Excuse me, where can I get a taxi?

B Over at the taxi stand.

A Oh, thank you.

Case 2)

A Ms. Park, please give me your bags, I'll put them in the trunk.

B Thank you very much, but let me keep this briefcase. It has very important documents in it.

Note

for a moment : 잠시만(=for a while) / wait here: 여기서 기다리세요(wait for here라고 하면 안 됨) / get a taxi : 택시를 불러오다(=call a taxi) / taxi stand : 택시 타는 곳 / stand in line : 줄을 서 있다 / page : 사람을 (방송 등으로) 불러 찾다 **cf** paging office : 사람을 찾기 위한 방송실 / airport limo : 공항버스(limo는 limousine의 준말) / show me the way : 길을 알려 달라 / take+사람+to+장소 : 어떤 사람을 ~로 모시고 가다 **cf** I will take you to the zoo.(너를 동물원에 데려갈게.) / bring the car to the front : 차를 정문쪽으로 가져오다 **cf** bring : ~를 가져오다, take : ~를 가져가다 / car is waiting for you : 차를 준비해 두다, 차가 (당신을 태우려고) 대기하고 있다

(5) Meeting a guest 5

A Excuse me, are you Ms. Sharif of Hitec Trading?
B Yes, I am. You must be Mr. Tanaka of Nippon Trading.
A Yes, ma'am. How do you do?
B I'm glad to meet you.
A How was your trip from Paris?
B I enjoyed my trip and the flight attendants' service was excellent.
A I'm glad to hear that. I have heard a lot about you from Mr. Nakamura.
He said you are one of the best salespersons in Europe.
B Oh, thank you for the compliment.
A You must be tired. Give me your bag. I'll carry it.
B No, thanks. But would you get me a baggage cart, please?
A Okay. Here you are. Wait here for a moment. I'll go get the car.
B Okay.

Note

Ms. Sarif of Hitec : Hitec사의 Sarif 양 / How was your trip? : 여행은 어땠어요? / the flight attendants' service : 기내 서비스 / compliment : 칭찬의 말 / I'll carry it : 제가 들고 가겠습니다 / a baggage cart : 화물 운반용 손수레

④ International News

Crude Hits 21-year High on Supply Fears

U.S. crude prices shot to a 21-year high as markets reacted to a threat by Russian authorities to shut down most of the production from that country's largest oil company. Yukos, which produces 2 percent of the world's oil, has been battered by a gigantic overdue back taxes bill. The company said it does not have the cash to pay its tax debt. And, with its assets frozen by court order, Yukos roiled markets Wednesday by saying it might have to halt its main production units within a few days. In Wednesday trading, September contracts of U.S. light crude spiked 3 percent to $43.05 a barrel of the New York Mercantile Exchange N the highest level since the exchange began offering the light, sweet crude contract in 1983. In London, Brent crude for September delivery reached $39.68 a barrel on the International Petroleum Exchange, beating the previous high of $39.65 on Oct. 12, 1990, when Iraqi troops invaded Kuwait. "The Yukos thing could dramatically affect global oil supplies," said Adam Sieminski, an oil price strategist at Deutsche Bank in London.

Crude supplies are already extremely tight, with Iraqi's output hampered by saboteurs and most producers already pumping as much as they can. Saudi Arabia, the only producer that still has significant spare capacity, has recently boosted its production by about 1 million barrels a day, but much of this fresh oil has yet to reach customers and replenish their depleted inventories. (from AP)

Note

authorities : 당국 / batter : 치다, 타격을 입히다 / gigantic : 거대한, 엄청난, 막대한 / asset : 자산 / contract : 계약 / hamper : 방해하다 / replenish : 보충하다, 채우다 / deplete : 비우다, 고갈시키다

5 Abby

I am not a princess

Dear Abby:

I am a 15-year-old girl from a financially secure family. My best friend, "Audrey", is in the opposite situation. Her parents are divorced. Her mother works full time to support the family. I used to get annoyed at Audrey when she'd hesitate after I'd suggest we do something fun together. She finally admitted she didn't have the money. I feel awful because money has never been a problem for me, and I thought it was not a problem for any of my friends. I love being with Audrey. I don't want her financial situation to put a damper on our friendship. I am more than willing to pay for things like admissions to amusement parks, movies and other events and even buy her clothes when we go shopping together. The problem is, she is very sensitive about money. She never takes me up on my offers. How do I get to do fun things with Audrey without making her feel she is accepting charity?

—Not a Princess in Pasadena, Calif.

Dear Not a Princess:

Stop offering to buy her clothes. Do offer to do things with her that don't cost a lot of money–listen to music, rent videos, exercise, or do homework together. Include her in some group activities(movies or amusement parks), but always let her reciprocate in some way. Respect her decisions, and remember that the burden of gratitude can sometimes hang very heavy, so try to keep a balance.

Note

get annoyed at : 짜증이 나다, 귀찮다 / put a damper on our friendship : 우리의 우정에 금이 가게 하다

⑥ Reading Comprehension

The interviews collected in "Other Voices: Immigrant Women in the U.S." are thematically related despite the wide varity of nationalities and cultures represented in the collection. From the Italian-American grandmother who recounts the story of her first week of life in New York city in 1920, to the young Cambodian refugee who describes her first experience of an American public school in 1989, all the women have stories to tell. Some are stories of economic hardship and racial prejudice encountered in American cities, while others describe joyous celebrations and community spirit. The collection is a much-needed, timely oral history.

(1) "Other Voices" is a book of interviews with

ⓐ women from Asia
ⓑ Children from war zones
ⓒ immigrant women
ⓓ refugees

(2) The Italian-American woman came to New York in

ⓐ 1989
ⓑ 1930
ⓒ 1955
ⓓ 1920

(3) This book is a(an)

ⓐ oral history
ⓑ short story collection
ⓒ novel
ⓓ scholarly investigation

Note

thematically : 주제별로, 테마적으로 / recount : ~을 이야기하다 / refugee : 난민 / hardship : 궁핍, 역경 / racial prejudice : 인종 편견 / encounter : 마주치다 / joyous : 즐거운 / community spirit : 공동체 정신 / much-needed : 매우 필요한, 소중한 / oral history : 구술 사료, 구술된 역사 / scholarly investigation : 학문적 조사(서)

⑦ Humour in English

(1) Homework

A fifth grader looked downcast, so her teacher asked, "What's the problem, Carol? I hope it's not homework again." "Well, uh, yes, it is." replied Carol. "I was stupid and made my homework paper into a paper airplane." "Carol, you're right, that wasn't a very bright thing to do," said the teacher, "but this once I'll let you just unfold the paper and hand it in." "Oh, but that won't work," said Carol, looking even sadder. "You see, the plane was hijacked."

(2) An Odd Honeymoon

A Scotsman, dressed in tartan, was standing on the platform of Kingsbridge railway station, Dublin, when another kilted Scot came along and inquired, "Where you bound for?" "I am going to Killarney on my honeymoon," was the reply. "Where is the bride?"

"Am not taking her," said the bridegroom. "She has been there before, so I left her at home."

Exercise

(1) Arafat's Health Has Worsened Sharply Again

Palestinian President Yasser Arafat's health has worsened sharply and he is slipping in and out of consciousness at his besieged West Bank headquarters. Arafat, who is 75, veteran symbol of the struggle for statehood, beloved by most Palestinians and reviled by many Israelis, was "very, very sick," a Palestinian cabinet minister said on condition of anonymity. Details of the illness were unclear. Palestinian leaders were summoned to the battered compound where Arafat has been effectively penned by Israeli forces for more than two years, accused by Israel of fomenting violence in a 4-year-uprising. Arafat denies the charge. (from ybmFM Daily News)

Note

worsen : 더 나쁘게 하다, 고약하게 되다 / slip : 미끄러지다, 놓치다, 도망가다 / besiege : 포위하다, 둘러싸다 / anonymity : 익명, 무명 / summon : 소환하다, 소집하다

(2) Cold Spell Hits Nation

After a long spell of unseasonably warm weather, the nation is now feeling the winter blues with people reaching for their heavy woollies. A cold front from Siberian region blanketed the Korean Peninsula yesterday, dropping the mercury to its lowest level so far this season. Seoul had a minimum temperature of minus 5.5 degrees Celsius while the northern city of Dongducheon was the chilliest in the nation with minus 7.2. "The Siberian high pressure is likely to influence the nation for a while, so citizens are advised to dress warm, and farmers and maintainance workers at facilities should guard against possible damage by the cold spell," the Korea Meteorological Administration said.

It will be cold on the peninsula again today, with strong winds adding to the chill factor. Seoul temperatures will touch minus 5 degrees. Tomorrow will be worse as the current spell of cold weather reaches its nadir with morning lows in Gangwon province forecast at minus 11 degrees. Seoul, too, will have a cold day with a morning low of minus 6 degrees. The nation is likely to see a few sprinkles or a light shower on Thursday, and the wet conditions will continue through Friday morning. Some areas will have snow flurries instead of rain, the KMA said. But Christmas Eve and Christmas itself will be pleasant with clear sunny skies and temperatures in the plus Celsius column throughout the day. (from The Korea Herald)

제15장 7 Former East-bloc Nations Join NATO

1 Warm-up

(1) Although decades of adverse economic conditions have led to its current dilapidated state, remnants of the resort's former grandeur still remain.

(2) The Micro Software Company attributes its recent gains in market to price cutting.

(3) The Europe trade discussions concluded with delegates unanimously supporting the call for lower tariffs.

(4) The prescription for successful negotiations requires that all parties involved listen without judging.

(5) Despite the evidence indicating otherwise, the manager still assumed that all the older employees knew their jobs.

(6) Many people believe that national identity is endangered by the many large corporations now operating globally.

(7) Many people believe in law and order, therefore many politicians make law and order a significant part of their policies.

(8) Usually, more than one teacher can be said to have contributed to the success of their students.

(9) It is more beneficial to take prescribed medicine at the times indicated by your physician.

(10) The most cost-effective way of hiring someone from out of state, may be for the employer to do a telephone interview with the candidate.

Note

1) dilapidated : 황폐한 / remnant : 잔상
2) attribute : 누구의 탓으로 돌리다
3) with … 분사 : ~하는 가운데, …가 ~하면서(분사구문에 유의) / discussion : 심의, 토의, 토론 / delegate : 대의원, 대표자 / tariff : 관세, 관세율 / unanimously : 만장일치로
4) negotiation : 협상 / require that 주어+(should)+동사원형 : ~하기를 요구한다 / prescription : 방법, 규정, 처방
5) assume : 가정하다 / indicate : 암시하다, 보여주다 / otherwise : 다르게, 달리
6) identity : 주체성, 동질성 / endangered : 위험에 처한, 멸종 위기에 놓인 / globally : 국제적으로
7) therefore : 그러므로 / believe in : ~의 가치를 믿다 / law and order : 법과 질서 / significant : 중요한
8) be said to have p.p. : 과거에 ~했었다고 얘기되어진다(완료부정사) / contribute : 헌신하다, 공헌하다
9) prescribe : 조제하다 / indicate : 암시하다, 지시하다 / physician : 내과의사 / beneficial : 유익한
10) cost-effective : 비용이 적게 드는

② Current Terms

(1) Collective Bargaining

The Korea Employers Federation advised companies yesterday to reject equal treatment of part-time or contract workers. In guidelines released for collective bargaining, the federation also recommended a reduction of paid leave when a 40-hour workweek goes into effect at member companies. The recommendations, which run counter to labor unions' demands, suggest major confrontations may occur between employers and unions in upcoming collective bargaining at many companies this year. (from The Korea Herald)

Note

The Korea Employers Federation : 한국경영자총협회 / collective bargaining : 단체교섭 / paid leave : 유급 휴가 / run counter to : ~에 상충하다, 거스르다 / confrontation : 대결, 대치 / upcoming : 다가오는 , 곧

(2) Eoljjang Syndrome

This addiction to appearance is not new to Korean society as many women have sought plastic surgery since the early 1990s. However, it seems to be getting more serious as something called the "eoljjang syndrome" has found its way into the nation's vocabulary. Eoljjang is slang, meaning pretty face in English. The term first gained popularity among teenagers. (from The Korea Herald)

Note

addiction : 몰두, 탐닉 / appearance : 외모 / plastic surgery : 성형 수술 / find one's way into : 도달하다, 들어가다 / vocabulary : 어휘 / slang : 속어, 통용어 / popularity : 인기

③ Practical English

(1) Inviting 1

John, I look forward to your visit to the company.
Please join us for Mr. Lee's retirement dinner.
Sally, I'd be happy to have you at my birthday party.
Would you come and dine with us this Saturday?
Mr. and Mrs. Ferrel, please come and visit us at six this Friday.
Mrs. Clarke, please join us for luncheon tomorrow. My husband will be very pleased to see you.
Susan, I will be at your house to pick you up at 7 tomorrow.
We hope you and your wife will be able to join us on December 28.

*** Related Conversation**

Case 1)

A Would you come and dine with us this Saturday?
B Thank you for inviting me.

Case 2)

A Sally, I'd be happy to have you at my birthday party tomorrow.
B Sorry, I have a prior engagement.

Case 3)

A Please join us for Mr. Lee's retirement dinner.
B Sure, when and where?

Note

look forward to+명사[동명사] : ~을 기대하다 / retirement dinner : 정년퇴직 저녁식사 / join : 참석해 달라 / would be happy to have you at party : 파티에 참석해 주시면 감사하겠다 **Cf** We are happy to have you at my parent's wedding anniversary.(저희 부모님의 결혼 기념일에 와주셔서 고맙습니다.) / this Saturday : 이번 주 토요일 **Cf** next Saturday : 다음 주 토요일 / come and dine with us : 오셔서 함께 식사하다 / Mr. and Mrs. ~ : ~ 부부 / at six this Friday : 이번 주 금요일 오후 6시 / luncheon : lunch보다 더 큰 규모로 차려진 점심식사 / pick ~ up : ~를 모시러 가다 **Cf** Let me pick you up tomorrow : 내일 모시러 가겠습니다

(2) Inviting 2

If you are free tomorrow, I'd like to invite you and your wife to my daughter's birthday party.

Mr. and Mrs. Morrison, would you join us for dinner tomorrow? It's our wedding anniversary.

Jim, I look forward to your visit to my promotion party tomorrow.

Tomorrow is the company's foundation day. Will you join us for dinner at 7?

Ralph, why don't you join us tonight? We're celebrating Hugh's promotion.

Mr. Goulden, do you happen to be free this evening? If so, I'd like to invite you to my son's welcome home party. He just completed his military service.

We cordially invite you to see our new facility and to attend an open house.

*** Related Conversation**

Case 1)

A If you are free tomorrow, I'd like to invite you and your wife to my daughter's birthday party.

B Sure. What time will the party start?

Case 2)

A Tomorrow is the company's foundation day. Will you join us for dinner at 7?

B Sure, thank you for inviting me.

Note

if you are free tomorrow : 내일 시간이 있으면 **cf** Are you free this weekend? : 이번 주말에 시간 있으세요? / invite you and your wife : 당신과 당신 부인을 함께 초대한다(즉 동부인하셔서) / Would you join us for dinner tomorrow? : 저녁(식사)에 초대하고 싶다(=I would like to invite you for dinner tomorrow) / wedding anniversary : 결혼기념일 / promotion party : 진급 파티 **cf** promotion : 승진시키다, 앞으로 나아가다(동사인 promote의 명사형) / company's foundation day : 회사 창립기념일 **cf** foundation : 기초(동사 found의 명사형) / be celebrating : ~기념 파티를 하다(~를 축하하다) **cf** 소유격+promotion : ~의 승진 → Mr. Kim's promotion : 김 선생님의 승진 / do you happen to ~? : (상황에 따라서) 혹시 ~하세요? **cf** Do you happen to have some change? : 혹시 잔돈 가진 것 있어요? / welcome home party : 귀향파티 / complete his military service : 군복무를 마치다

(3) Inviting 3

What time do you want me to drop by your office?

Mr. Clint, I'd like to visit your company.

What would be a convenient time to be at your party?

Charles, how about going to your place around six thirty?

Mr. and Mrs. Perry, it's very kind of you to invite us to your wedding anniversary party.

Can I come to your party with my children?

Ms. Hillary, thank you very much for inviting me to your party tomorrow.

Thank you for your kind dinner invitation on December 28. My husband and I would be happy to attend.

*** Related Conversation**

Case 1)

A What would be a convenient time to come to your

party?

B Dinner will start at seven o'clock. So, please come around six.

Case 2)

A Can I come to your party with my children?

B Of course!

Case 3)

A What time do you want me to drop by your office?

B 10:30 a.m. will be fine.

(4) Inviting 4

Mr. and Mrs. Mallory, please come this way.
Ron, please make yourself at home.
Mr. Lee, please take a seat here.
Sean, would you like to sit down here?
Linda, here is something for you.
May I open it now?
Mr. Landers, this is a little something for you from Japan.
Ma'am, let me show you around. Please come this way.
Ladies and gentlemen, may I make a toast?
Will, please help yourself to the spare ribs.
Where can I wash my hands?
Ross, why don't you have seconds?

*** Related Conversation**

Case 1)

A Ross, why don't you have seconds?

B No thanks. I've had enough.

Case 2)

A Mr. Landers, this is a little something for you from Japan.

B It's really beautiful!

Case 3)

A Where can I wash my hands?

B Come this way, please.

④ International News

7 Former East-bloc Nations Join NATO

NATO on Monday signed up seven new countries in Eastern Europe in a historic expansion that takes its military muscle to the Russian border, heightening concerns in Moscow. The prime ministers of Bulgaria, Estonia, Latvia, Lithuania, Romania, Slovakia and Slovenia deposited "instruments of accession" to the North Atlantic Treaty Organization's founding Washington treaty and brought the number of members to 26. "To the seven heads of states here assembled, I say to you and to your people: Welcome to the greatest and most successful alliance in history. Welcome," said Colin Powell, the U.S. secretary of state. He said the expansion was a "historic step" in achieving a vision to extend "Europe's zone of freedom and security from the Baltics to the Black Sea." "NATO is determined above all to prevent aggression," Powell said. "Now it is determined above all to promote freedom, to extend the reach of liberty and to deepen the peace." "Today, our alliance faces a new enemy, which has brought death to innocent people from New York to Madrid. Terrorists hate everything this alliance stands for. They despise our freedom. They fear our unity." he said. (from AFP)

Note

expansion : 확대 / sign up : 승인하다 / heighten : 높이다 / treaty : 조약 / assemble : 모이다, 집회하다 / determined : 결연한, 결의한

5 Annie

Excluding others

Dear Annie:

We moved into our house just over a year ago. In that time, my 5-year-old son, "Kyle," has made friends with three of the children who live nearby. At first, I had play dates for the kids and moms at my house, and the neighbors reciprocated. A few months ago, however, one of the mothers (I'll call her "June") began excluding my son from play dates. We can see her house from our window, and when she has the other children over, Kyle cries and asks why he isn't invited. Last Halloween, June organized the children in the neighborhood to go trick-or-treating. Kyle was never called. When I asked June about it, she said there wasn't enough room in her van to take him. June also organized an Easter egg hunt and did not invite Kyle. He was the only child in the neighborhood who was not included. I have asked the other neighbors if they know what's going on, but they don't have a clue. Kyle has ADHD and can get hyper at times, but I am always there to calm him down. The other mothers tell me that he is not a problem at all. Annie, these children have to live near one another for a very long time. June is pleasant whenever I see her. I still invite them for play dates at our house, and they always come. Should I ask her point-blank if there is a problem, or just let it go and hope for the best?

—Brokenhearted Mom in New Jersey

Dear N. J.:

It's time to ask. It's possible Kyle's behavior, while not a problem for the other mothers, is somehow too stressful for June. It also could be that her son has indicated he doesn't want Kyle over. Kids often go through stages where they exclude others. If that's the case, June ought to talk to her son about fairness and kindness, and explain that hurting others is not acceptable behavior. Meanwhile, it's time to involve Kyle in activities where he can make friends outside the neighborhood and be less interested in what goes on at June's house. Check into programs at your park district, YMCA or community center.

Note

ADHD : 주의력 결핍·과잉행동 장애, Attention Deficit·Hyperactivity Disorder(ADHD)는 아동기에 가장 일반적으로 나타나는 장애로서 지속적인 주의력 산만(Inattention) 및 과다활동(Hyperactivity), 충동성(Impulsivity)을 특징으로 함.

⑥ Reading Comprehension

It is estimated that over 3 million children starve to death in the world each year. Last year 2.7 million children starved to death in Africa and Central American alone. They are the victims of an underdeveloped economy, but you can help to prevent this tragedy. How can you help? By donating as much as you can to your local Save the Kids Foundation, you can help to feed several of the millions of starving children around the world. $1 will feed three children a day, $5 will feed fifteen children a day, and $10 will feed 30 children a day. Give what you can. Think about it–an average dinner in the United States costs more than what it costs to feed thirty children for an entire day. Please send your donations to your local Save the Kids Foundation. Call 555-KIDS for more information and for the location of the Save the Kids Foundation nearest your home. Canned food items and clothing are also accepted with your cash donations.

(1) According to the passage, how many children starve to death every year?

ⓐ 2.7 million
ⓑ Over 3 million
ⓒ Under 3 million
ⓓ 3 million

(2) How many children can be fed with $20?

ⓐ 15 children for one day
ⓑ 30 children for one day
ⓒ 60 children for one day
ⓓ 30 children for one week

(3) According to the passage, where can donations be sent to help starving children?

ⓐ Africa
ⓑ Central America
ⓒ Local restaurants
ⓓ Save the Kids Foundation

(4) How can people get more information?

ⓐ By calling the phone number given
ⓑ By writing to the starving children
ⓒ By writing to Africa and Central America
ⓓ By sending canned foods and clothing items

Note

It is estimated that ~ : ~인 것으로 추정되다 / starve to death : 아사하다, 굶어죽다 / alone : ~에서만 / victim : 희생자 / underdeveloped economy : 저개발국, 후진국 / tragedy : 비극 / donate : 기부하다(=contribute) / feed : 먹이다 / local : 현지의, 지역의 / average dinner : 평균적인 저녁식사 / donation : 헌금, 기부금, 기부 / item : 품목 / cash : 현금

⑦ Humour in English

(1) Housework

My working wife had no more vacation left, but I still had some time off. It was boring to be home alone, so one day I decided to surprise my wife by doing dishes, dusting and straightening up the house. I was sure I would get all sorts of praise from her when she came home, but she didn't say a word. Finally, I could stand it no longer. "You didn't even notice how nicely I straightened up today," I complained. Her reply opened my eyes. "Yeah," she said. "It's a thankless job, isn't it?"

Note

boring : 지루한, 따분한 / get all sorts of praise : 온갖 칭찬을 듣다 / thankless job : 감사받지 못하는 일

(2) A Mistake

Six months before they were married, the boy took his fiancee to "meet the family." 95-year-old grandmother was sweet and lively but, like many hard-of-hearing people, she spoke loudly. As the girl was admiring the pictrres of her children and grandchildren in the living room. She took her grandson to one side and discreetly shouted, "Don't worry. I put away all those pictures of you with that other girl."

Note

hard-of-hearing : 귀가 어두운, 난청의 / discreetly : 신중하게, 조심스럽게

Exercise

(1) Foreign Minister Ban Ki-moon Reiterated the Need for Seoul and Washington to Stand Side-by-side in a "Horizontal Relationship".

The Korea Herald reports that, in his first public address on the Korea-U.S. alliance since last week's presidential election in the United States, Foreign Minister Ban Ki-moon reiterated the need for Seoul and Washington to stand side-by-side in a "horizontal relationship". Pointing out that South Korea, in the past has been extremely reliant on the United States, which had overwhelming priority in the country, Ban stressed that today such a relationship is undesirable and Korea is pursuing a cooperative self-reliant national defense. Ban also repeated the government's view that Washington will take more active steps in trying to restart the stalled six nation disarmament talks, which involve the two Koreas, the United States, Russia, China and Japan. (from ybmFM Daily News)

Note

reiterate : 되풀이하다, 반복하다 / reliant : 의지하고 있는, 믿고 있는 / overwhelming : 압도적인, 대항할 수 없는 / self-reliance : 자기 의존, 자립, 독립 / disarmament : 무장해제, 군비축소

(2) Consumer Sentiment Still at Lowest Point

A leading index for consumer sentiment remained at its lowest point in three-and-a-half years during the third quarter, the latest evidence that domestic demand will continue to be a big drag on Asia's third-largest economy. The consumer confidence index, which gauges the six-month outlook consumers have on their living conditions, stood at 80 during the June-September period, compared with 84 in the first quarter. It was the lowest reading since the fourth quarter of 2000 when the figure was 68. A score below the benchmark 100 means that among the 2,500 households surveyed, the number of respondents expecting their situation to worsen was greater than those seeing an improvement. Another index measuring consumer prospects for spending over the next six months also tumbled from 102 to 98, suggesting Koreans are still reluctant to open their wallets. The central bank's sub-index of future price levels stood far below the 100 reading at 57, indicating a majority of respondents expect prices to rise going forward. Another sub-index on the employment situation during the next six-month period was unchanged at 66 in the third quarter.

Korea's economic growth more than halved to 3.1 percent last year after households borrowed beyond their means, forcing them to trim spending. About one in 13 of Korea's 48 million population are three months or more behind on debt payments. (from The Korea Herald)

Answers

제1장

1. Warm-up

(1) 1863년에 링컨 대통령은 모든 노예들이 자유를 찾게 될 것이라고 선언했다.

(2) 지뢰가 폭발해서 치명적인 파편들이 사방으로 날렸다.

(3) 테니스 챔피온의 명성 때문에 신인선수는 보통 주눅든다.

(4) 그녀는 바삐 서두르거나 행동하는 일이 없는 건강회복기의 나른함을 즐겼다.

(5) 일부 보고서들은 혈중 콜레스테롤을 낮추는 것이 심장병을 예방하는데 도움을 준다고 주장했지만, 다른 일부 보고서에서는 모호한 입장을 취해 왔다.

(6) 과장법의 한 예는 "내가 그런 말을 쓰지 말라고 백만 번이나 말했잖아"이다.

(7) 그는 그 기구가 쓸모 없어지기 전에 본전을 뽑고 싶어한다.

(8) 그의 전후 정책은 자신의 인기를 손상시킬 만한 비난을 초래하였다.

(9) 대낮에 하늘이 어두워지는 것은 보통 폭풍우가 임박했다는 것을 암시한다.

(10) 화학 공장에서 직원들은 때때로 위험한 일에 대한 추가 수당을 받는다.

2. 시사용어

(1) 핫머니

그러나 한국은 원화가 지난 1997~98년 외환위기 동안 그랬던 것처럼 핫머니의 공격 목표가 된다면, 더욱 심각한 문제에 봉착할 것이다. 단기자금의 갑작스런 유출로 유동성 위기가 생기자 펀더멘탈이 건전했던 한국

경제는 붕괴되었다. 최근 국내 주식시장에 투자된 외국 자본의 일부는 핫머니로 알려져 있다.

cf 단기차익을 겨냥해 국제금융시장(international financial market)을 이동하는 투기성 외화자금을 말함. 각국의 단기금리(short-term interest rate) 차이, 환율(exchange rate)의 차이에 의한 투기적 이익, 또는 국내통화의 불안을 피하기 위한 자본도피 등 두 가지 목적으로 주로 사용된다. 주요 투기대상은 주식(stocks), 채권(bonds) 등 환금성이 높은 자산이나 통화(currency) 등이 해당되며 목표한 수익률(earning rate)이 달성되면 급속히 빠져나가는 특징을 갖고 있다. 이에 따라 핫머니가 이동하게 되면 해당국의 급격한 유동성(liquidity) 변동으로 외환 수급관계가 크게 동요되며 국제금융시장의 안정성이 저해될 가능성이 높다. 핫머니의 대표적인 예로는 1백명 미만의 투자자(investors)로부터 자금을 모아 이자율과 환율의 예상을 교묘히 조합한 도박성 파생상품에 투자하는 헤지펀드(hedge fund)가 있는데, 지난 1997년 전 세계를 교란했던 신흥시장(emerging market) 통화위기(currency crisis)의 주범이기도 하다. 대표적인 헤지펀드로는 George Soros의 'Quantum Fund' 및 Julian Robertson의 'Tiger Management' 등이 있다.

(2) 지구 온난화

중국은 현재 지구온난화의 주범 가운데 하나로 꼽히는 이산화탄소의 배출 규모가 전세계 배출량의 14%을 차지, 세계 2위를 기록하고 있으며 오는 2020년까지 18%로 늘면서 현재 세계 1위인 미국을 앞지를 것으로 예상되고 있다. 국제에너지기구(IEA)에 따르면, 중국의 에너지 소비량은 전체 에너지소비량의 77%가 석탄에 의해 제공됨에 따라 향후 20년 동안 두 배 이상 늘어날 것으로 나타났다. 미국의 환경연구기구인 월드와치에 따르면 중국내 자동차 보급의 확대도 이같은 오염을 더 악화시키는 주요인이 될 것으로 보인다.

cf 이산화탄소가 지표에서 대기로 다시 방사되는 적외선을 흡수, 온실의 유리지붕과 같은 역할을 하게 되는 greenhouse effect(온실효과) 등으로 지구표면의 온도가 올라가는 현상. 이산화탄소는 외부 물질과의 화학적인 반응이 쉽게 발생하지 않으며 독성이 없어 그 자체는 생물에 직접적인 해를 끼치지 않으나 태양의 빛 가운데 짧은 파장은 통과시키고 긴 파장은 잡아두는 물리적 성질을 갖고 있다. 대부분의 학자들은 대기중

이산화탄소량의 증가를 global warming 현상의 주원인으로 보고 있다. 대기중의 이산화탄소량이 증가하는 것은 석유, 석탄 등 화석연료를 많이 쓰는 데 기인한다. 50년대부터 40년간 대기중 이산화탄소 함유량은 0.031%에서 0.035%로 늘어났고 지구는 지난 100년간 섭씨 0.5도 더워진 것으로 조사된 바 있다. 이런 추세가 계속되면 지구의 해수면은 매년 3.9㎜씩 높아져 바닷물에 침수되는 지역이 넓어지고 2070년에는 우리나라의 기온이 지금보다 2~2.5도 오를 것으로 예상되고 있다.

3. 실용영어

(1) 전화영어 (비서인 Kelly양과 사장님간의 대화)

A: 여보세요, 켈리양. 내 로마행 출장 서류는 어떻게 됐어요?
B: 서류준비는 완료됐습니다. 캐세이 퍼시픽 항공편으로 로마에 가실 겁니다.
A: 몇 시 비행기죠?
B: 오후 12시30분발입니다.
A: 로마엔 몇 시에 도착하나요?
B: 오후 다섯시 삼십분입니다. 나폴리 지사 소장이신 로마노씨가 공항에 마중 나오실 겁니다.
A: 잘 됐군요. 내 귀국 스케줄은 어떤가요?
B: 5일, 수요일이고 루프트한자 540기입니다.
A: 켈리양, 내 귀국 스케줄을 4일 화요일로 변경시켜 주겠어요? 수요일엔 홍콩 구룡 지사의 리드씨를 만나야 하거든요.
B: 하지만 리드씨와의 미팅은 6일 목요일인데요.
A: 맞아요. 하지만 항생주식 건 때문에 좀 더 일찍 만나야 해요.
B: 알겠습니다. 미팅은 수요일로 변경하고 비행 스케줄도 화요일로 옮기겠습니다.
A: 좋아요.
B: 다른 사항 있으신가요?
A: 흡연석으로 예약했나요?
B: 아닙니다. 사실상 캐세이 퍼시픽 항공사의 비행기는 모두 금연입니다.
A: 그럼 다섯 시간동안 담배를 참아야 한다는 말이요?
B: 네, 새로 만들어진 규정입니다.
A: 좋아요. 규정이라면 따라야겠지.

B: 사장님, 즐거운 여행 되십시오.

A: 글쎄 (담배도 못 피우니), 나도 그랬으면 좋겠소.

(2) 회사소개 1(미국에서 온 바이어 Mr. Hear Well과 '맑은 귀'社의 무역 담당 권 대리의 대화)

웰 : 어떤 회사에 근무하십니까?

권 : 저희 회사는 면봉을 생산하고 세계시장에 판매하지요.

웰 : 아, 그래요. 회사위치는 어딘가요?

권 : 경기도에 있습니다.

웰 : 연간 매출은 어느 정도입니까?

권 : 연간 백만불입니다.

웰 : 현재 임직원은 얼마나 됩니까?

권 : 현재 300명입니다.

(3) 회사소개 2

1)

A: 괜찮으시다면, 질문을 드려도 될까요?

B: 물론이죠.

A: 싱가폴 지사엔 몇 분의 이사와 부장이 근무하고 있나요?

B: 이사님 두 분과 부장님 네 분이 계시죠.

2)

A: Mr. Stevenson, 이 분이 신임 총무 부장이신 Krinston씨 입니다.

B: 만나 뵙게 되어 반갑습니다, Mr. Krinston.

A: 저도요.

3)

A: 기술담당 부장 (엔지니어링 부장)은 누구신가요?

B: Jekinson씨 입니다. 하지만 휴가중이십니다.

A: 언제 오시나요?

4)

A: 동남 아시아 지역 담당 부장님이 새로 부임하셨다고 들었는데 맞아요?

B: 사실입니다. John Randon 이란 분이죠.

A: 어디서 오셨나요?

(4) 전화 자동응답기

1) 지금은 부재중입니다.
2) 삐 소리가 나면 성함과 전화번호 그리고 메시지를 남겨 주십시오.
3) 9시부터 5시까진 567-1234로 연락 주시고 6시 30분 이후엔 224-5634로 연락 바랍니다.
4) 오늘과 내일 2:30부터 5:30분까진 진료를 하지 않습니다.
5) 비상 전화는 435-4567을 이용해 주십시오.
6) 아담스씨의 사무실입니다.
7) 4시30분 이후에 전화 주십시오.
8) 이 메시지는 싱가폴 항공사의 녹음 내용입니다.
9) 악천후로 인해 괌행 모든 노선이 일시적으로 결항입니다.
10) 다른 항공편은 연착없이 순항합니다. 감사합니다.

4. 국내뉴스

병역기피자 130명 입영 조치

일부 프로야구 선수와 연예인 등 130여명의 병역기피자들이 11월 말까지 입영조치되거나 재판을 통해 실형을 선고를 받게 된다고 어제 병무청은 밝혔다. 이들 중 송승헌, 장혁, 한재석 등 3명의 연예인들은 법무부의 협조로 10월 14일부터 출국금지 조치가 내려졌고, 나머지 병역기피자들도 화요일부터 출국이 금지되었다고 병무청 관계자는 말했다. 병무청은 경찰청에게서 병역기피자 명단을 통보 받은 후 이 같은 조치를 발표했다. 이들은 소변검사 조작을 통해 병역을 면제 받은 것으로 알려졌다. 병무청에 따르면 공시시효 만료된 52명의 병역처분을 취소했으며 11월 말까지 입영조치할 계획이라고 말했다. 이들 52명은 형법 하에서 3년간의 공소시효가 만료되기는 했지만 여전히 군복무 의무는 이행해야 한다. 18세에서 35세 사이의 한국 남자는 중대한 신체적, 정신적 결함이 있는 경우를 제외하고 24개월간의 군복무를 수행해야 한다. 신장질환을 조작한 나머지 77명의 경우는 공소시효가 지나지 않았다. 이들에 대한 병역명제 처분도 취소되었고, 이들은 실형을 살거나 군복무를 이행해야 한다고 병무청 대변인은 말했다. 법적으로 병역기피자는 1년에서 최고 3년의 실형을 선고 받을 수 있다. 병무청은 병역기피자의 최고 형량을 5년으로 늘리는 등 처벌을 강화하기로 결정했다. 그와 더불어 병무청은 병역기피자에 대한 공소시효를 현행 3년에서 5년으로 연장하는 방안을 제안하고 있다. 병무청은 신장관련 질환을 중점 관리대상에 포함시키기로 결정했다. 이 대상에 포함된 환자들은 추가로 6개월간 불시의 건강검진을 받게 된다. 중점관리 대상에 속하는 13개 질환에는 아토피성 피부염, 문신이나 자해로 인한 상처, 고혈압, 간염, 척수 또는 시각 장애, 정신질환 등이 포함된다.

5. Ann Landers

병든 아이의 부모

앤 랜더즈 여사께:

저는 자주 어린 아이가 아파서 병원에 입원시켜야 하는 부모들에게 다소나마 도움이 될까 하여 이 글을 씁니다. 저는 장기간 병 치료를 받아야 하는 아이가 있어서 매년 3, 4주일씩 병원에서 시간을 보내야 합니다. 남편과 저는 우리 둘 중 최소한 한사람은 아이 곁에 온종일 있도록 하고 있습니다. 저는 자녀를 오랜 기간 동안 병원에 입원시켜야 하는 여러 다른 부모들을 만나보고 우리를 도와주실 분들에게 바라는 "소원 목록"을 작성해 보았습니다.

1. 만약 병원이 허락한다면 우리를 방문해 주십시오. 우리는 오전 6시부터 시작하여 어린 아이가 깨어 있는 동안은 줄곧 아이들을 혼자 내버려 둘 수 없습니다. 우리는 지루함과 스트레스를 좀 덜어주실 방문객을 환영합니다.
2. 만약 우리 아이가 여러분과 친해지게 되면 저희들이 커피를 한잔 마시거나 잠깐 간단한 식사를 할 동안 아이와 잠시 함께 계셔주실 수 있으십니까? 저는 때로는 남편과 단둘이서 이야기 한마디 나누지 못하고 며칠씩 보내기도 한답니다. 단 몇분만이라도 대단히 감사하겠습니다.
3. 여러분께서 저희들을 방문하실 형편이 안되시면 아이가 입원해 있는 병원에 전화를 거시어 전화로 잡담을 하셔도 괜찮은지 물어봐 주십시오. 잡담을 나누는 그 시간이 저희들에게는 하루 중 가장 중요한 시간이 될 수 있을 것입니다. 사람들은 흔히 아픈 아이의 부모들도 이따금씩 휴식 시간이 필요하다는 사실을 잊어버립니다. 저희들을 도와주시는 것은 또한 저희 아이를 도와주시는 것입니다. 왜냐하면 그렇게 도와주시면 저희들은 침착해지고 휴식을 취하여 기운이 나게 되니까요.

–모 시에서 모 부모로부터

모 부모께:

아픈 아이들을 가지신 부모에게 뜻밖의 행운이 될 수 있는 편지를 보내주신 데 대하여 감사드립니다. 건강한 아이를 가지신 복받은 부모들께서 이 제안들을 실행해 주셨으면 합니다.

6. 독해문제

지금 잠깐 외출해야 하는데 11시 전에 이 팩스를 보냈으면 좋겠어요. 그리고 여기 찾아야 할 파일 목록이 있어요. 찾아서 책상에 놔 두면 내가 나중에 볼게요. 전화 오면 2시 30분경에 돌아온다고 말하세요. 고마워요.

【정답】

(1) ⓑ

(2) ⓐ

7. 유머영어

(1) 실직

실업수당을 받으려고 줄서서 기다리던 사람이 갑자기 몸이 이상해져서 쓰러졌다. 사람들이 주위에 모여들었지만 어떻게 해야 하는 것인지 아는 사람은 하나도 없었다. "여기 의사 없어요?"하고 젊은 여자가 애원하듯 소리쳤다. 그러자 뒤쪽에서 퉁명스러운 소리가 들렸다. "아니, 실직한 의사 어디 봤어요?"

(2) 초능력을 가진 인디언

영화제작진이 사막 한가운데서 야외촬영을 하고 있었다. 하루는 늙은 인디언이 영화감독에게 다가와서 "내일은 비가 올 것이다"라고 말했다. 다음날 비가 왔다. 일주일 후 그 인디언은 그 감독에게 다시 와서 "내일은 폭풍이 올 것이다."라고 말했다. 다음날 폭풍이 왔다. "이 인디언은 믿을 수 없는 능력을 가졌어." 감독은 말했다. 그는 비서를 시켜 그 인디언을 고용해서 날씨를 예측하게 했다. 그러나 그 인디언은 서너번 예보를 맞힌 후 2주동안 잠적했다. 결국 그 감독은 인디언을 찾아왔다. "내일 중요한 촬영이 있어요." 감독은 말했다. "나는 당신만 믿고 있어요. 내일 날씨는 어떨 것 같아요?"라고 물었다. 인디언은 어깨를 으쓱해 보이며 "모르겠네요. 컴퓨터가 고장 나서 인터넷을 쓸 수 없어요."

제2장

1. Warm-up

(1) 죄수는 체포 경찰에 의해 거친 대우를 받았다고 넌지시 말했다.
(2) 운전자는 차를 급정거하여 사고를 피하려고 했다.
(3) 많은 문화에서 의복은 주로 사교적, 종교적 행사에 장식물로 입혀진다.
(4) 모든 직원들은 회사의 새로운 방침에 익숙해져야 한다.
(5) 일주일 전에 예약을 취소하지 않으면 보증금은 환불이 되지 않습니다.
(6) 나는 적당한 속도로 운전을 했으나 경찰은 내가 속도 위반을 했다고 말했다.
(7) 내가 좋아하는 프로그램은 다른 채널에 나온다(채널에서 방영되었다).
(8) 모든 수입되는 선적물에는 반드시 정부의 공문서가 첨부되어 있어야 한다.
(9) 야영하는 사람들은 캠프 파이어의 불을 완전히 끄고 나서 캠프장을 나가야 된다.
(10) 서비스위원회는 참가자 요청에 따라 추가사본을 드립니다.

2. 시사용어

(1) 카지노

국내 최초의 내국인 상대 카지노가 강원도 정선의 옛 광산촌에 개장한 지 일주일 정도가 지났으나 벌써부터 여러 문제들이 속속 발생하고 있다고 현지 공무원들 및 주민들이 어제 밝혔다. 무엇보다도 큰 문제는 지역 주민들이 전국 각지에서 몰려든 현금을 싸든 고객들과 함께 도박장으로 몰려들고 있다는 점이다. 정부는 당초 폐광 이후 해당 자치단체 및 주민들의 경제적인 여건을 개선해 주기 위해 카지노 건립을 허가한 것이라고 이들 공무원들이 밝혔다.

cf 댄스 · 음악 등의 오락이 있는 도박장 또는 2~4명이 하는 card game을 말함. 처음에는 음악과 댄스를 위한 대중적인 사교장으로 19세기 초반부터 설립되기 시작했으나, 19세기 중반 이후부터 도박시설이 밀집되어 있는 전문적인 도박장을 지칭하는 말로 통용되었다. 고전적인 casino의 전형으로서 오랫동안 세계적인 명성을 유지해온 casino는 1861년에 개장된 Monte Carlo casino로 1879년 오늘날의 현대적인 도박장을 갖춘 casino로 자리잡았다. 미국에서는 19세기 후반부터 New York주 및 Indiana주 등지에서 불법적인 casino 영업을 시작으로 casino가 보급된 바 있다. 한편 20세기 들어 casino는 gambling, gaming, house, club 등 다양한 이름으로 불리기 시작했으며 도박꾼들이 도박장측의 banker 또는 dealer를 상대로 돈을 거는 식으로 진행되는 것이 보편화되었다. 참고로 우리나라의 경우, 외국인 상대의 casino 영업은 허용되어 있으나 내국인의 경우 태백권 지역 1개소에만 출입이 허용되는 casino 사업권을 허가해 주는 등 원칙적으로 금지하고 있다.

(2) 기러기 아빠

박씨의 두 자녀는 현재 8학년과 10학년에 재학 중으로, 지난 2000년부터 캐나다 밴쿠버 교외에서 엄마와 살고 있다. 박씨와 불운한 신씨는 소위 "기러기 아빠"라는 새로운 계층을 대변하고 있는데, 이들은 자신의 자녀와 아내를 캐나다, 미국, 호주, 뉴질랜드 등지로 떠나 보내고, 국내에서 혼자 살며 일을 해 이들의 이주 비용을 대고 있다.

cf 자녀의 해외유학을 위해 자녀는 물론 아내까지 해외로 보내고 홀로 사는 남편 가장을 지칭하는 조어. 외로움을 상징하는 기러기(wild goose)에 아빠(father)를 합친 단어로 국내에서 수년 전부터 40, 50대 의사, 변호사, 교수, 외교관 등 고소득 전문직을 중심으로 태동한 것으로 알려져 있다. 이들 기러기 아빠는 유학 자녀를 돌보기 위해 아내가 자녀와 함께 외국으로 나가게 되는 바람에 국내에 혼자 남아 회사에 계속 다니면서 생활비와 학비를 보내 준다. 최근 들어서는 국내 사교육비의 폭등, 조기유학 바람 등을 타고 중산층이나 30대까지 확대되는 추세에 놓여 있다. 특히 40~50대가 주류를 이루다 보니 건강을 해치거나 신세를 비관, 자살하는 사례까지 등장하는 등 새로운 사회현상으로 떠오른 상태이다.

3. 실용영어

(1) 내가 한턱 낼게.

A: 점심 먹으러 가자, 내가 한턱 낼게.
B: 웬일이야? 오늘 자네 생일이라도 되는 거야?
A: 사실 말이지, 지난 주에 복권에 당첨돼서 돈이 좀 생겼거든.
B: 야 대단한데, 얼마 당첨됐는데?

(2) 오늘 밤 특별 메뉴가 뭔가요?

A: 아저씨, 오늘 밤 특별 메뉴가 뭔가요?
B: 신선한 구운 감자에 티본스테이크입니다.
A: 점심때 스테이크를 먹었거든요. 혹시 해산물 특별요리 있어요?
B: 물론이죠. 무게가 2 파운드 되는 캐나다산 바닷가재 요리가 있습니다.

(3) 많이 먹었어요!

A: 자, 자, 사양하지 말고 여기 이 감자 좀 더 들어요.
B: 됐습니다. 많이 먹었는 걸요.
A: 좋아요, 그럼 디저트 어때요?
B: 딸기 아이스크림 있어요?

(4) 식당에서

A: 안녕하세요, 사모님.
B: 2인용 테이블로 주세요.
A: 이리로 오세요. 담당 웨이터가 곧 도와 드릴 겁니다.
B: 고맙습니다.

• 잠시 후

A: 안녕하십니까, 사모님. 저는 '리치'라고 합니다. 담당 웨이터입니다.
B: 안녕하세요, 리치
A: 주문하시겠습니까?
B: 등심스테이크와 구운 감자로 주세요.
A: 잘 선택하셨습니다. 스테이크는 어떻게 해 드릴까요?
B: 바짝 구워 주세요.

A: 잘 알겠습니다. 또 필요하신 건 없으세요?
B: 없습니다.

* 음식이 제공된 후

B: 웨이터!
A: 네, 뭘 도와 드릴까요?
B: 네, 스테이크를 바짝 구워 달라고 했는데 덜 구워졌어요. 여기 이 피 보여요?
A: 아, 죄송합니다. 요리사가 오늘 새로 왔거든요. 다른 스테이크로 바꿔 드리겠습니다.
B: 이해해요. 천천히 하세요. 난 별로 바쁘지 않아요.
A: 이해해 주셔서 감사합니다.

4. 국제뉴스

고이즈미 신사 참배

고이즈미 준이치로 일본 총리가 목요일 전범자들을 포함한 일본 전쟁 사망자를 기리는 야스쿠니 신사를 참배하여 새해를 맞아 중국과 한국으로부터 비난과 야당 의원들로부터 비판을 불러 일으켰다. 일본 지도자들의 도쿄 야스쿠니 신사 참배는 제 2차 세계대전 동안 및 이전 일본에 의해 침략당하고 잔인하게 점령당한 아시아 국가들을 언제나 격분하게 한다. 하지만 이번 고이즈미의 신사 참배는 일본이 근 60년만에 가장 큰 규모의 해외 군 배치인 미국 주도의 이라크 재건 지원군 파병 계획을 시작하는 때에 이루어져, 일본의 군사적 역할을 확장시키려는 고이즈미의 노력을 경계하며 지켜봐 온 이웃 국가들로부터 더욱 격렬한 항의를 불러 일으킬 수 있다.

고이즈미는 신년 축하객들 속에서 야스쿠니 신사에 도착했다. 그는 흰 옷을 입은 신토 사제의 인도 하에 신사로 안내되었으며 3만엔(280달러)의 개인 헌금을 했다. 고이즈미는 지난 2001년 4월 총리가 된 후 4번째인 자신의 참배를 "일본의 평화와 번영"을 기원하기 위해 결정했다고 말했다. 그는 기자들에게 "일본은 지금 살고 있는 사람들의 노력에만 기초하지 않는다. 일본은 과거 사람들의 희생을 바탕으로 서 있다."고 말했다.

5. Ann Landers

(1) 걱정거리

앤 랜더즈 여사께:

저는 거의 열일곱살이 되었는데도 아직 키스를 한 번도 받아본 적이 없습니다. 저는 점점 저에게 무슨 문제가 있음에 틀림없다는 생각을 하기 시작하였습니다. 사람들은 저보고 이쁘다고 하고 저는 남자애들과도 편안합니다. 그런데 무슨 문제가 있을까요? 좋은 충고 한 말씀 해주세요.

–피닉스에서 선인장으로부터

피닉스 분께:

아무런 문제도 없어요. 기다리세요, 시간이 가면 해결됩니다.

추신: 남자가 진지하다고 확신이 설 때까지는 아무에게나 키스를 허용하지 마세요.

(2) 어린아이를 때리는 것

앤 랜더즈 여사께:

어린아이 엉덩이를 때리는 것과 때릴 이유가 절대로 없다는 주장에 대한 많은 편지들을 실어주신 데 대하여 감사 드립니다. 많은 독자들이 "우리집 아이는 때렸더니 빨리 버릇을 고치게 되었다."는 말이나 "나는 절대로 화가 나서 아이를 때린 적이 없다."는 말들을 하는 데 대하여 그것은 "말도 안되는 헛소리"라고 저는 생각합니다. 어른이 화가 나지 않은 상태에서 어린아이를 때리는 법은 결코 없습니다. 저 자신이 경험을 했기 때문에 압니다. 제가 저의 두 아이들을 때릴 때 (저는 그렇게 한 것을 지금 깊이 후회하고 있습니다만) 그것은 제가 화를 참지 못하고 이것이 나의 뜻을 즉시 전달하는 방법이라고 생각했기 때문이었습니다. 이와같이 아이들을 때린 것은 불행한 결과를 낳았습니다. 첫째, 저의 큰 딸은 저를 두려워하게 되었고, 둘째, 저의 아들은 화가 났을 때는 남을 때리는 것이라는 것을 배웠습니다. 저는 아이들이 저와 같은 잘못을 다시 반복하지 않도록 하기 위하여 제 행동을 고치려고 오랫동안 열심히 노력해 왔습니다. 앤 여사님, 계속하여 비폭력 훈육을 주장하여 주십시오.

–보스턴에서 후회하며 개조된 아빠로부터

후회하며 개조된 아빠께:

귀하께서 후회하며 개조된 것 모두에 대하여 축하를 보냅니다. 이를 이룩하기 위해서는 많은 겸허함이 요구됩니다. 어린아이를 때릴 때는 자신이 통제력을 잃었다는 것을 분명히 나타내 주는 것이라고 오랫동안 저는 주장해 왔습니다. 그리고 기왕 이 문제에 대하여 이야기가 나온 김에 저는 다시 한번 강조하고 싶습니다. 혁대나 채찍이나 가죽끈이나 브러시나 회초리는 절대로 사용해서는 안된다구요. 어떤 경우에라도 이런 물건을 사용할 타당한 이유는 없습니다.

6. 독해문제

알다시피 1/4분기 수익이 좋지 않습니다. 경영 방식을 획기적으로 바꿔야 합니다. 우리 회사 제품의 가격은 업계 내 최고 수준입니다. 가격을 올리면 경쟁력이 떨어질 것이고, 가격을 내리면 채산성이 맞지 않습니다. 유일한 해결책은 제조 원가를 줄이는 겁니다. 각 부서장들은 제조공정 합리화 방안을 제출해 주십시오. 불필요한 직책 폐지도 적극적으로 검토하시기 바랍니다. 수요일 오전 9시까지 보고서를 제출해 주십시오.

【정답】

(1) ⓛ

(2) ⓒ

7. 유머영어

(1) 금발아가씨

열차편으로 도시 직장에 첫 출근했던 금발 아가씨가 집에 돌아왔다. 좀 초췌한 모습을 눈여겨본 어머니는 "얘, 괜찮어?"하고 물었다. "괜찮은게 아니에요. 기차에 거꾸로 앉아왔더니 메슥거리는 거 있죠." "왜 앞좌석 사람하고 잠시 자리를 바꾸자고 하지 그랬어?" "그럴 수가 없었어요. 앞좌석에 누가 있기를 했어야죠"라고 금발 아가씨는 대답했다.

(2) 왕의 분노

한 귀족에게 진노한 왕은 그를 투옥했다. 감옥에서 그를 못 나오게 하고 싶었던 왕은 말 한마리를 구해와야만 풀어주겠다면서 그 말은 갈색도 검정

색도 아닌 뿐더러 한마디로 말이 가질 수 없는, 그 어떤 색도 아닌 말이어야 한다는 것이었다. 그 귀족은 그런 말을 구해오겠다고 약속했다. 그래서 풀려나자 그는 말을 궁정으로 데리고 갈 날을 폐하의 편의에 따라 정해 달라면서 다만 월·화·수·목·금·토·일요일이 아닌 다른 요일로 해 달라고 애원했다.

제3장

1. Warm-up

(1) 사람이 "무엇을 해야 하는가"에 대한 역할 모델은 각계 각층의 모든 사람들이 행동을 결정하는 데 중요하다.

(2) 켄은 언젠가는 테리에게 복수를 할 것이라고 맹세하였다.

(3) 성공적인 정치가가 훌륭한 회고록을 쓰기는 불가능하다. 그 이유는 한 분야 [정치]에 관련된 기술(정치와 관련된 전략전술을 의미)이 좋은 글과는 상극을 이루기 때문이다.

(4) 국가가 그 크기에 의해서 판단되는 것이 아니듯이 개인도 마찬가지이다.

(5) 사람이 재즈 추는 기분으로 교육을 받을 수 없는 것처럼, 인생도 재즈 추는 기분으로 살 수 없다는 것은 여전히 진리이다.

(6) 나는 아주 멋진 집 따위에 마음을 뺏길 그런 류의 사람이 아니었다.

(7) 이제 이혼은 더 이상 치욕스러운 것도, 비극도, 심지어 실패로도 간주되지 않는다.

(8) 주위가 완전히 어두워진 후에야 비로소 왕자는 추적을 당하지 않았다.

(9) 모든 것에 관심을 갖기에는 인생이 너무 짧다. 그러나 우리의 나날들을 충만하게 하는 데 필요한 만큼의 일에 관심을 갖는 것은 좋은 것이다.

(10) 그가 세상을 떠난 후에야 비로소 그가 뿌린 씨는 열매를 맺었다.

2. 시사용어

(1) 로드맵

부시행정부 아래 첫 번째 공식적인 북미간 대화로서, 베이징 회담은 보도된 바에 의하면 양국이 서로간의 입장을 적극 표명할 수 있도록 할 예정이다. 이번 회담이 조만간 존립 가능한 결론에 이를 것으로 기대하는 이는 거의 없다. 그럼에도 불구하고 참석자들은 외교적인 결론에 도달하는 별개의 단계들을 가진 "로드맵" 형태로 협의 사항을 마련하는 것이 꼭 필요하다.

cf 우리 말로는 자동차 여행용 '도로 지도, 이정표'라는 의미로, 최근 들어서 '계획안, 일정표, 단계적 접근법' 등을 아우르는 의미로 통용되고 있는 유행어임. 대표적으로 국제사회가 마련한 중동평화 중재를 위한 로드맵을 들 수 있으며, 우리 정부에서 즐겨 쓰는 '대북정책 로드맵, 인사개혁 로드맵, 재정-세제개혁 로드맵' 등을 들 수 있다. 한 마디로 '계획성 있는 연도별 개혁 프로그램'을 의미한다고 할 수 있다. 이밖에 산업, 경제 부문에서는 앞으로 개발 판매될 제품의 성능 등을 미리 공개하는 것을 의미한다. 즉 로드맵에는 지금과는 비교도 되지 않는 놀라운 기능이 담겨지고, 이미 나온 제품을 초라하게 만드는 경우를 함축하고 있다. 예를 들어 미 인텔(Intel) 사의 로드맵은 Pentium series 제품을 통해, 자사의 의지대로 CPU(Central Processing Unit, 중앙처리장치) 시장을 활성화시키고 호환 칩(chip) 제조업체인 경쟁사들을 따돌리는 데 사용돼 왔다.

(2) 주민투표제

지방정부의 기능 향상을 위한 시도로서, 노무현 행정부는 오는 9월부터 문을 여는 정기 국회에 주민투표제 법안을 제출할 계획이다. 본 법안이 승인되면 중요한 지역 현안에 대한 결정권이 선거민에게 주어지게 된다. 주민들에게 자신들의 삶에 영향을 주는 중요한 제안에 대한 결정권을 허용하는 것은 우리나라의 참여 민주주의에 있어 커다란 진보가 될 것이다.

cf 지역 주민들이 쓰레기 매립장 설치, 지방 축제 개최 등 지역의 현안에 대해 직접 안건을 내고 이를 투표로 결정하도록 하는 지방자치제의 하나임. 2004년 하반기부터 도입될 예정인 행정자치부의 관련법안에 따르면 주민과 단체장, 지방의회 등이 주민 투표를 청구하면, 투표 심사(투표관리위원회), 주민투표 발의(단체장), 투표실시, 결과공표(투표관리위원회), 결과 이행(행정 · 재정 조치)의 과정을 거치게 된다. 지자체 의사결정의 최후 수단인 주민투표제는 자치단체의 고유 권한에 속하는 업무가 그 대상이다. 단 casino 허가 등 중앙 정부의 권한과 지방세 감면,

공무원 인사와 보수 등은 투표대상에서 제외된다. 또한 원자력 폐기물 처리시설 설치 등 국가업무의 추진을 위해서는 관련부처 장관이 주민투표 실시를 요구할 수 있다. 이 경우에는 투표 결과에 대한 법적 구속력이 없으며 국가정책결정의 참고자료로만 이용된다. 이 제도는 주민의 정치적 참여와 책임 의식을 높이고 지역 통합이 이루어질 수 있다는 긍정적인 측면과 함께, 지역 분열을 조장하고 정치적 악용의 소지도 갖는다는 단점도 있다.

3. 실용영어

(1-a) 성명(성함)이 어떻게 되십니까?
A: 성명(성함)이 어떻게 되십니까?
B: 저는 안토니오 E. 로페즈입니다.
A: 로페즈가 성입니까?
B: 네, 그렇습니다.

(1-b) 당신의 middle name이 뭐예요?
A: 김 선생님, 당신의 middle name이 뭐예요?
B: 우리 한국인들은 middle name이 없지요.
A: 아, 그렇군요.

(1-c) '첸'은 홍콩에서 흔한 성씨입니다.
A: 홍콩에서 흔한 성씨는 뭐죠?
B: '첸'입니다. 한국은요?
A: 한국엔 '김'씨가 흔한 성이죠.

(1-d) 이 선생님, 어째서 사모님의 성은 '김'인가요?
A: 이 선생님, 질문하나 드려도 될까요?
B: 물론이죠, 말씀해 보세요.
A: 당신의 성은 '이'씨인데 어째서 사모님의 성은 다릅니까?
B: 한국 여성들은 결혼을 해도 친아버지의 성을 계속 사용합니다. 한국의 법이지요.

(2-a) 성씨 1

1)

A: 성이 어떻게 되시나요?

B: 델리온입니다. D는 Doris, E는 Edward, L은 Love, I는 Italy의 앞자이고, 그리고 마지막으로 N은 Nancy의 앞자이지요.

A: 이름의 약자는 어떻게 되십니까?

B: T.J.입니다.

2)

A: 성이 어떻게 됩니까?

B: 제 성은 '정'입니다. C는 Charlie의 앞자이고, H는 Harry의, U는 Universe, N은 Noel, 마지막으로 G는 Great의 앞자입니다.

A: 이름의 약자를 불러 주시겠습니까?

B: 물론이죠. B.L.입니다.

(2-b) 성씨 2

A: 안녕하세요, 불러바드 호텔입니다. 뭘 도와 드릴까요?

B: 네, 방을 예약하고 싶은데요.

A: 날짜와 기간을 말씀해 주시겠습니까?

B: 이번 금요일부터 2박 3일간입니다.

A: 잘 알겠습니다. 성이 어떻게 되시죠?

B: 'Perot'입니다.

A: 철자가 어떻게 되지요?

B: P는 Peter의 앞자이고, E는 Edward이며, R은 Robert이고, O는 Oliver 이고 마지막으로 T는 Tom의 앞자입니다.

A: 감사합니다. 이름의 약자는 어떻게 되지요?

B: D.O.입니다.

A: 잘 알겠습니다. 전화 감사합니다.

B: 천만에요.

A: 좋은 하루 되세요.

B: 네, 좋은 하루 되세요.

(3) 문의

1)

A: 여보세요 506호의 '김'이라는 사람입니다. 호텔 내 가게가 몇 시에 여는 지 알 수 있을까요?

B: 물론이죠. 10시에 열지요.

A: 고마워요.

2)

A: 이태리 식당에서 아침식사를 하고 싶은데, 몇 시에 시작하죠?

B: 아침식사는 8시에서 9시 30분까지입니다.

A: 7시 30분 전에 여는 식당 있나요? 아침에 회의가 있어서요.

B: 아, 그러세요? 미국 음식은 어떠세요? 24시간 영업을 하지요.

3)

A: 여보세요, 프론트인가요?

B: 네, 뭘 도와 드릴까요?

A: 신문을 보고 싶은데요.

B: 1층에 비치되어 있습니다. 아니면 원하신다면 방으로 배달해 드릴까요?

A: 제가 로비에 가서 보죠.

4. 국내뉴스

노 대통령, 행정수도 이전을 둘러싸고 거대 언론과 공방

행정수도 이전계획을 둘러싼 논쟁은 국내 주요 일간지들이 야당 편을 거들면서 여당 대 야당간의 치열한 정치적인 일전으로 확산될 조짐을 보이고 있다. 청와대 비서실은 일요일 행정수도 이전 계획 폐기 요청을 반박하는 발언공세의 수위를 높였다. 김병준 청와대 정책실장은 일요일 "국가 정책이 조심성 없이 성급하게 맹목적인 반대에 부딪히고 있다"고 반대론자들에게 새롭게 맹공을 퍼부었다. 김 실장은 청와대가 졸속으로 행정수도 이전 정책을 강행한다는 주장을 일축했다. 김 실장은 또한 정부의 신 행정수도 건설 계획을 좁은 지역적 세력에서 벗어나 동북아 중심국가로 향해 가려는 비전으로 봐야한다고 강조했다. "그와 같은 꿈이 더 이상 짓밟히고 뭉개져서는 안 된다. 10년 뒤 서울 인구가 3백 50만 명이 더 증가한다면 어떻게 국가가 경쟁력을 강화할 수 있겠는가?" "정부 정책에 반대하는 인사들은 국가수반에 대한 뿌리깊은 불신과 2002년 대선에 불복하는 심리에서 나온 것으로 보여진다."고 했다. 이 사업의 개폐에 대해 고조되는 국민투표 요청에 관해서 김 정책실장은 국회에서 사전에 논의되었어야 할 문제라고 일축했다. 그의 이같은 발언은 청와대가 양대 주요 보수 언론사인 조선, 동아일보가 이전 계획에 반대 여론 조장을 주도한다고 비난한 지 이틀 만에 나온 것이다. 노 대통령은 일찍이 정부의 수도이전 계획에 반대하는 보수 일간지들을 비난하는 언론과의 싸움에 뛰어들면서 "행정수도 이전에 반대하는 운동은 현직 대통령에 대한 불신임과 퇴진운동"이라고 밝혔다. 여당과 야당은 지난 주 정부가 한국의 중심부에 있는 연기-공주 지역을 사실상 신행정수도지로 선정하고 난 직후 이에 대한 공방을 해왔다.

5. Ann Landers

무모한 운전

앤 랜더즈 여사께:

지난주 남편과 저는 친척들과 점심 식사를 하기 위하여 음식점으로 가고 있었습니다. 레스토랑은 우리 집으로부터 약 두시간 거리였습니다. 남편은 시속 35마일 제한 구역에서 65마일로 달리고 있었습니다. 저는 속도를 좀 늦춰달라고 조용히 말했습니다. 그러자 남편은 반대로 속도를 올려 길가에 가는 자전거 탄 사람들을 추월하여 지나갔습니다. 그 다음 우리는 커브길에 다다랐는데, 그곳은 지난 몇년 동안 여러 운전자들이 사망한 곳이었습니다. 남편은 액셀러레이터를 계속 밟았습니다. 저는 그의 이러한 무모한 운전으로 우리 둘 다 죽을 것 같아서 너무나 무서웠습니다. 결국 저는 "이렇게 속도를 줄일 수 없다면 차를 세워 저를 내려주세요."라고 말했습니다. 남편은 즉시 차 방향을 돌려 우리 집으로 되돌아 갔습니다. 그리고는 저보고 내리라고 말했습니다. 저는 남편에게 제가 점심식사에 빠지지 않게 해달라고 사정했습니다. 남편은 아무 말도 하지 않았습니다. 그리고는 차에 훌쩍 올라타서 혼자 레스토랑으로 가버렸습니다. 남편은 친척들과 식사를 했을 뿐 아니라 다른 친척들과 함께 병상에 누워 있는 저의 할머니를 뵈러 갔습니다. 남편이 집으로 돌아왔을 때 저는 너무나 화가 나서 남편에게 집에서 나가 절대로 돌아오지 말라고 말했습니다. 그는 근본적으로는 착한 사람입니다만, 그렇게 미성숙한 태도를 취한 것은 이번이 처음이 아니라 이젠 신물이 납니다. 제가 너무 화가나서 똑바르게 보지 못하는 것일까요? 어떻게 해야 할지 부디 말씀해 주십시오.

—노스 캐롤라이나주에서 화난 사람으로부터

노스 캐롤라이나주 분께:

두분께서는 결혼 생활에 관한 상담이 절대적으로 필요합니다. 그리고, 남편은 분노 관리에 대한 학습을 받으면 좋겠습니다. 물론 상담에는 돈이 듭니다. 그러나 귀하의 결혼 생활과 남편의 정신적 건강에는 남의 도움이 필요합니다. 지금이 가장 중요한 시기입니다. 여러분이 필요로 하는 도움을 받으세요. 이것은 자기 힘으로 될 수 있는 일이 아닙니다.

6. 독해문제

The Encounters지 편집진은 귀하께 새로 발행되는 창간호를 무료로 제공코저 합니다. 동봉한 카드만 보내 주시면 The Encounters지 한 부를 보내드리겠습니다. 귀하께서 이 책을 받으시고 정기구독을 신청하시게 되면 1년(12개월분) 구독료를 36달러에 받아보실 수 있으시게 되며, 이 가격은 매호 4달러씩 하는 가격에서 연간 12 달러가 절약되는 것입니다. 만약 귀하께서 이번에 정기구독을 하시게 되면 매년 계약을 갱신하실 때 시중에서 구입하시는 가격보다 25% 싸게 받아볼 자격을 얻으시게 될 것입니다. 저희들은 귀하께서 이번 기회를 놓치시지 않으시기를 바랍니다.

【정답】

(1) ⓑ ⇒ 'Simply return the enclosed reply card and an issue of The Encounters will be sent to you.'에 나와 있음.

(2) ⓓ ⇒ 'If you subscribe at this time, you are entitled to renew annually at a savings of 25 percent off.'에 나와 있음.

7. 유머영어

(1) 어떤 제안

한 백만장자가 살아 있는 악어들을 수집해서 저택의 풀장에 풀어 놓았다. 그에게는 미혼의 아름다운 딸이 있었다. 어느 날 그가 성대한 파티를 열던 중에, "친애하는 내빈 여러분, 모든 남성들께 제안 하나 하지요. 백만 달러 아니면 내 딸을 드리리다. 악어들이 우글거리는 저 풀장을 가로질러 무사히 수영하는 사람에게 말이외다."라고 말했다. 갑자기 풀장에 첨벙거리는 소리가 들렸고 모두가 놀란 얼굴로 쳐다 보았다. 한 남자가 제인을 구하려는 타잔처럼 능숙하게 풀장을 가로질러 헤엄치고 있었다. 남자가 물살을 헤치고 나갈 때마다 군중들은 환호했으며, 마침내 그는 무사히 건너편에 도착했다. 백만장자는 매우 감명을 받고 말했다. "자네, 정말 놀라운 사람이구만. 훌륭해! 가능하리라고는 생각지 못했는데 말이야. 어쨌든 약속은 지켜야지. 뭘 원하나? 내 딸인가, 백만 달러의 돈인가?" 남자 왈, "이 보슈, 난 경제적으로 양호하니 당신 돈은 필요없소. 그리고 결혼한 몸이니 당신 딸을 가질 수 없소. 내가 원하는 것은, 날 저 풀장에 떠민 자식이 어떤 놈이야, 나와!!"

(2) 축구광

쌍안경으로 경기장을 살피던 미식축구 팬은 50야드 라인에 빈자리를 발견했다. 그는 그리로 내려가서 그 좌석 옆에 앉아 있는 사람에게 "이 자리 임자 있어요?"하고 물었다. "그게 우리 마누라 자리였는데 그 사람 죽었어요. 아주 열렬한 팬이었는데…"라고 그 사람은 대답하는 것이었다. "거 참 안 됐군요. 그런데 어째서 입장권을 친구 분이나 집안 사람 누군가에게 주지 않았죠?"하고 그는 그에게 물었다. "다들 장례식에 갔습니다"라고 그 사람은 대답했다.

제4장

1. Warm-up

(1) 당신은 언제 벨기에로 떠납니까?
(2) 그의 전공은 경제학이지만, 그는 취미로 건축학을 공부한다.
(3) 꼼짝말고 여기서 기다려, 조지. 난 곧 돌아 올거야.
(4) 에드 번스틴은 그 당시에 가장 뛰어난 전사(戰士)였다.
(5) 만일 도매업자를 통해 구입한다면 항공권을 큰 폭으로 할인하여 살 수 있을 것이다.
(6) 우리는 이 어려운 과제를 우리의 마케팅 기술에 대한 도전으로 간주하고 있다.
(7) 그는 영화상영 내내 내게 너무 많은 질문을 했기 때문에 내 자신도 무슨 일이 일어났는지 거의 모르고 있다.
(8) 그들은 은행의 출납 계원으로 일하는 것을 즐긴다.

(9) 작년에 연예계에 흥미로운 새 스타가 몇 명 탄생했다.
(10) 어떤 생산품들은 1, 2년 후에는 낡아서 쓸 수 없도록 만들어진다.

2. 시사용어

(1) 종합토지세

2006년부터 일정수준 이상의 부동산을 소유하고 있는 개인은 세금 부담이 더 늘어날 것이라고 행정자치부가 어제 밝혔다. 이같은 움직임은 부동산 가격의 상승을 억제하고 빈부간의 소득격차를 줄이려는 정부 노력의 일환이라고 행자부가 밝혔다. 현재 국민들은 주로 종합토지세와 재산세의 2가지 형태로 자신의 부동산 보유분에 대한 세금을 부담하고 있다.

cf 지방세법에 의거하여 토지를 보유한 납세 의무자에게 부과하는 대표적인 토지 관련 지방세임. 전국에 있는 모든 토지를 소유자별로 합산한 다음, 그 합산한 토지가액에 누진세율을 적용하여 산출한 세액을 토지의 소재지인 관할 시·군에 납부한다. 부동산 투기와 과다한 토지 보유를 억제하여 지가 안정과 토지 소유의 저변 확대를 목적으로 1990년부터 시행되었다. 국가·지방자치단체·지방자치단체조합·외국정부 및 주한국제기구의 소유에 속하는 토지 등 일정한 요건을 갖춘 경우에 한정하여 비과세라는 규정이 주어진다. 과세표준은 토지의 종류에 따라 종합합산과세표준, 별도합산과세표준, 분리과세표준으로 구분하는데 종합합산과세표준의 경우 과세기준일 현재 납세의무자가 소유하고 있는 전국의 모든 토지 중 대통령령으로 정하는 건축물의 부속 토지를 제외한 토지가액을 합한 금액으로 한다. 해마다 6월 1일 과세기준일 현재의 토지 소유자에게 부과하며 10월 16일부터 31일까지 납부해야 한다.

(2) 사외이사제

시민단체는 인터뷰를 한 사외이사 163명 가운데 51명과 그들이 사외이사로 활동 중인 기업체 경영진 사이의 관련성을 발견했다. 7명은 전-현직 경영진이었으며, 33명은 전-현직 금융기관 간부, 그리고 11명은 기업체와 밀접한 연관이 있는 정부기관 또는 연구소의 전-현직 관리였다. 사외이사 제도는 1998년 우리나라에 처음 도입된 바 있다.

cf 회사의 경영을 직접 담당하는 이사 이외에 외부의 전문가들을 이사회(the board of directors) 구성원으로 선임하는 제도임. 대주주와 관련이 없는 사람들을 이사회에 참가시킴으로써 대주주의 전횡을 방지하려는

데 목적이 있다. 미국과 영국에서는 예전부터 사외이사제를 채택하고 있었으며, 일본도 이와 유사한 기능을 갖고 있는 외부감사제를 도입하였다. 우리나라의 경우 1998년부터 상장회사(listed companies)에 한하여 사외이사를 의무적으로 두도록 하였다. 이 규정에 따라 상장회사에서는 다른 기업체 임직원 출신이나 교수 · 공무원 등을 사외이사로 임명하고 있다. 사외이사제도의 도입은 주식회사의 3대 기관인 주주총회(shareholders meeting) · 감사(auditor) · 이사회(the board of directors) 가운데 2개 기관에 대한 임원 선임과 기능을 크게 바꾸는 결과를 가져오게 되나, 미국 기업의 경우에서 볼 수 있듯이 우리나라에서도 사외이사가 회사의 경영에 대하여 감시 활동을 제대로 할 수 있을지 그 실효성을 기대하기는 어렵다는 것이 일반적인 지적이다.

3. 실용영어

(1) Wall Mart에 가본 적 있어?

A: 월마트에서 물건 사 본 적 있어? (Wall Mart에 가본 적 있어?)
B: 응, 있어.
A: 어때(물건 값이 어때?)? 샤퍼스 빌(마트이름)보다 더 싸?
B: 내 생각에 비슷한 거 같더라고.

(2) 일주일치 식료품을 사야 해요.

A: 린다, 이번 주말에 다른 계획 있어?
B: 별로, 장보러 가야 해.
A: 뭐 살 건데?
B: 일주일치 식료품.

(3) 저는 매주 일요일에 쇼핑가요.

A: 매주 일요일엔 보통 뭘 하세요?
B: 매주 일요일엔 쇼핑을 합니다.
A: 저두요, (괜찮으면 또는 시간이 되면) 같이 갑시다.
B: 좋지요. 가실 때 연락 주세요.

(4) 가장 가까운 편의점이 어디에요?

A: 실례지만, 가장 가까운 편의점이 어디에 있나요?
B: 미안합니다만, 전 이곳에 사는 사람이 아니어서 잘 모르겠어요. 하지만 다음 거리에서 본 듯합니다.
A: 대단히 고맙습니다. (그런데) 어디서 오셨나요?
B: 일본에서 온 관광객입니다.

(5) 쇼핑 가시면 버터 좀 사다 주세요.

A: Jane, 나 쇼핑가요. 뭐 살 거 있어요?
B: 버터 좀 사다 줄래요?
A: 물론이죠, 다른 건?
B: 그게 다예요, 고마워요.

(6) 지루하기 짝이 없었어.

A: 미팅 어땠어?
B: 지루하기 짝이 없었어. 처음엔 그녀가 재미있다고 생각했는데 아니었어.
A: 무슨 말이야?
B: 그게 말이지, 시간이 좀 지나고 나니 고루하고 지루한 질문들만 하는 거였어. 내 말은, 여가 시간에 뭘 하길 좋아하느냐고 세 번이나 물어봤다구.

(7) 호텔에서

A: 안녕하세요. 프론트입니다.
B: 안녕하세요, 1203호입니다.
A: 네, 뭘 도와 드릴까요?
B: 네, 머리 손질을 하고 싶은데요.
A: 네, 사모님. 미용실은 10시부터 6시까지 영업을 하지요.
B: 몇 층에 있나요?
A: 지하에 있습니다.
B: 그리고 이 호텔에 칵테일 바가 있나요?
A: 네, 오후 5시부터 자정까지 영업합니다.
B: 고마워요.

A: 천만에요.

(8) 호텔을 예약해 주시겠습니까?

10월 18일에 귀사를 방문합니다. 호텔을 예약해 주시겠습니까?
하얏트나 쉐라톤을 희망합니다.
일정은 아래와 같습니다.
10월 18일 싱가포르 도착 체크 인
19일 간 씨와 면담
20일 체크 아웃 싱가포르 출발
협조에 감사 드립니다.

• 관련 표현
인터콘티넨탈 호텔에 싱글 룸 하나를 예약해 주시겠습니까?
제 숙박비 예산은 1박에 100달러입니다.
공항 근처의 호텔을 희망합니다.
귀사 근처에 권할 만한 호텔이 있습니까?
공항에서 호텔까지의 교통수단을 미리 준비해 주시겠습니까?

4. 국제뉴스

이라크

공격의 구실은 아주 사소한 것이라도 충분하며 때로는 아예 필요 없는 것 같기도 하다. 지난 3월 자살폭탄 테러범들은 카르발라와 바그다드에서 아슈라 축제에 평화적으로 참석하고 있던 2백여명의 시아파 신도들을 학살했다(아슈라 축제는 후세인 통치 시절에는 금지됐다). 이라크 시아파 중에서 가장 존경받는 지도자 알리 시스타니는 그런 폭탄 테러를 막지 못한 미국의 허술한 보안 상태를 비난했다. 이제 미군 당국은 4월 12일 시아파의 또다른 대규모 축제를 앞두고 터져 나올지 모르는 폭탄 테러 위협에 대비하고 있다. 그날 카르발라에는 시아파 신도 약 1백만명이, 나자프와 바그다드에는 각각 약 75만명이 운집할 것으로 예상된다. 가장 우려되는 점은 더 많은 사상자가 날 경우 시아파와 과거 시아파를 다스렸던 소수 수니파간에 성전(聖戰)이 촉발될 수 있다는 것이다.

5. Abby

딸 아이를 집 안에 감금해야만 안심하는 남편

에비 여사께:

제 사랑스러운 15살난 딸 "베키"는 고등학교 2학년에 재학 중이지요. 그 앤 우등생이며, 예의도 바른데다가 정말 좋은 애랍니다. 제 고민은 바로 제 남편 때문이랍니다. 아이 아버지가 좀 지나칠 정도로 엄격하거든요. 제 딸은 언제나 저에게 마음을 터놓고 솔직하게 얘기하는 편이에요. 올해 그녀에게 멋진 남자 친구들이 생겼으며, 이 때문에 남편은 아이를 더욱 과보호하지요. 남편은 아이가 전화로 수다떠는 것조차 못하게 한다니까요. 또 신기하게도 저희한테 항상 들키지요. 아이는 저희없이 어떤 곳에도 혼자 갈 수 없답니다. 가는 것조차 허락이 안됩니다. 그 앤 치어리더 연습에 참여하는 것 외에 어른 지도하의 파티를 가거나, 다른 단체활동에 참여할 수 없답니다. 참으로 불쌍한 제 딸은 전혀 사회 생활을 할 수가 없지요.

베키의 죽마 고우들은 이젠 어딘가 함께 놀러 가자고 그녀에게 전화도 걸지 않아요. 남편이 절대 허락하지 않을 것을 알거든요. 더구나 아예 저희 집에 오지도 않는걸요. 고작 소파에 앉아서 저나 제 남편과 함께 TV를 보는 것이 전부인 걸 아니까요. 베키도 저희의 간섭을 받지 않고 그녀만의 사생활이나 사회활동을 즐길 권리가 있을 텐데…. 한번은 그녀에게서 17살의 선배가 자기를 좋아한다는 말을 한적이 있지요. 물론 남편은 아이가 그 남학생 부모님과 함께 영화를 보러 가는 것은 물론이고, 그 남학생이 저희를 차로 상점 앞까지 데려다 주는 것조차 허락하지 않지요. 에비씨, 어떻게 하면 남편이 좀 더 여유로워질 수 있을까요?

－텍사스 어느 중부지역에 갇혀 있는 사람이

중부지역에 갇혀 있는 분에게:

남편 분에게 당신이 얼마나 그를 사랑하는지, 그리고 아이를 보호하려는 그의 마음은 이해하지만 너무 지나친 것 같다고 말해 주세요. 더구나 그는 사랑이라는 이름으로 아이를 망치고, 결국 아이는 부모님 품에서 벗어나려 할 거란 사실을요….

6. 독해문제

미래가 보장되지 않은 세상에서 가장 확실한 투자는 훈련과 교육입니다. 지금은 기술이 다양한 사람이 출세하기 유리한 세상입니다. 애버딘 대학교에는 이런 현실을 감안해서 만든 경영자 MBA 프로그램이 있습니다. 재무나 마케팅과 같이 한 분야를 정해 전공하는 것이 아니라 비즈니스의 전 분야를 총망라해서 배우게 됩니다. 그 외에도 컴퓨터 실력을 키워 주며, 언어능력이 부족한 분을 위해 일본어와 중국어 중 한 가지 언어를 유창하게 하도록 공부시킵니다. 이 프로그램은 소극적인 사람을 원치 않습니다. 이 프로그램은 국제 비즈니스 무대에서 정상에 도전하기로 결심한 남녀 여러분을 위한 것입니다. 이 프로그램은 18개월의 정규 코스로 학비는 교재와 일일 점심을 포함해 3만 5천달러이며, 기타 학습자료와 생활비는 별도입니다. 더 자세한 내용을 알고 싶으신 분은 애버딘 대학교 경영자 MBA 프로그램 학장 앞으로 편지를 보내시기 바랍니다.

【정답】

(1) ⓒ
(2) ⓓ
(3) ⓒ

7. 유머영어

(1) 천생연분

빌과 힐러리가 차를 타고 힐러리의 고향 마을 부근 시골길을 달리고 있었다. 연료가 떨어져가자 빌은 한 주유소에 차를 댔다. 주유원이 나와서 대통령 부부의 차에 휘발유를 채우기 시작했다. 그러던 중 그는 창문을 들여다보고 이렇게 말했다. “어이, 힐러리. 우린 고등학교 때 데이트를 즐겼잖아. 생각 안나?” 둘은 몇 분 동안 그렇게 이야기를 주고 받았다. 빌이 기름값을 지불하고 차는 주유소를 떠났다. 운전하면서 의기양양해진 빌은 힐러리를 건네다 보며 뽐내는 말투로 이렇게 말했다. “그래 저 작자와 데이트를 했다고? 생각해 봐, 나랑 결혼 안했으면 어떻게 되었을지 말야.” 힐러리가 빌을 쳐다보며 대답했다. “뭐, 당신이 저기서 기름을 넣고 있고, 저 작자는 대통령이 되었겠죠.”

(2) 99번째 생일

99세된 노인의 생일을 맞아 인터뷰하러 간 기자가 "백년이 되는 명년 돌잔치 때 다시 찾아뵐 수 있기를 간절히 바랍니다"라고 했다. 그러자 노인은 대답하는 것이었다. "이봐요 젊은이, 보아하니 멀쩡한데 내년에 또 다시 못 올 것도 없잖아."

제5장

1. Warm-up

(1) 당신은 이 제안을 반대하는 데 설득력 있는 이유가 있어야 한다.
(2) 회계는 매우 힘든 직업이다. 오류의 여지가 없다.
(3) 승객의 말은 너무 불분명해서 나는 그 말을 이해할 수 없었다.
(4) 아니, 됐습니다. 그 밖의 다른 것은 원하지 않습니다.
(5) 이 상품은 1년 동안 재료나 기술상의 모든 결함에 대해 보증을 해드립니다.
(6) 손실액은 보험이 보상하는 것으로 추정되었다.
(7) 다리가 폐쇄되어서 운전자들은 다른 길로 가야 했다.
(8) 저가 컴퓨터 기술이 위조지폐 유통량을 증가시켰다.
(9) 그들은 월 생산 목표를 달성할 뿐 아니라 심지어 능가할 것이라고 장담했다.
(10) 분석가들에 의하면 그 회사는 가격을 인하함으로써 판매를 촉진시키려 할 것이다.

2. 시사용어

(1) 펜션

펜션은 호텔보다 가격이 저렴해 1박에 6만~15만원 선이고, 시설은 민박보다 고급스럽다. 야릇한 조명과 무료 콘돔이 갖춰진 방을 찾는 커플들이 주로 찾는 소위 "러브 모텔"은 모든 관광지에 저렴한 선택 사항으로 확산된 상태이나, 가족들이나 자연스러운 휴식 분위기를 선호하는 커플들한테는 인기가 없다.

cf Hotel의 합리성과 민박의 가정적 분위기를 갖춘 새로운 숙박 시설임. Pension은 원래 연금 · 장려금 등의 의미를 가지며, 유럽(Europe)에서 노인들이 여생을 연금과 민박 경영으로 보내는 데서 그 이름이 붙여진 것으로 알려져 있다. 유럽에 오래 전부터 있었던 민박풍의 작은 hotel은 가족 경영에 의한 전 가족의 서비스가 특징이다. 최근 들어 펜션은 승마장, 수영장, inline skate rink 등 각종 운동 시설은 물론, 황토 찜질방이나 온천(spa) 등 건강 시설을 설치하는 게 기본일 정도로 고급 민박 수준을 넘어서고 있는 추세이다. 가족 여행자의 장기 체류에 대한 편의 제공을 목적으로 하고 있으며, 방 10개 정도의 양실 위주로 유럽풍의 민박 분위기를 느끼게 하는 호텔에 가까운 시설로, 청결하며 사생활(privacy)이 보장된다. 요금은 hotel보다 싸지만 민박보다 비싼 편이며 독일과 프랑스 등지에서는 휴양지(leisure area)만이 아니라 도시 및 농어촌까지 번져 숙박시설의 35% 이상을 차지하고 있다.

(2) 적대적 인수합병

정부는 조흥 및 외환은행에 대해서도 노조 동의서가 없을 경우 이들의 개선안을 거부할 방침이다. 두 은행은 경영개선 및 무수익 여신 축소를 조건으로 독자운영을 유지하기로 허용된 바 있다. 정부의 고위 관계자는 "은행측이 노조의 동의서가 없는 개선안을 제출할 경우 이를 절대 받아들이지 않을 것"이라며 정부의 승인을 얻지 못할 경우 그에 따른 결과를 감수해야 할 것이라고 덧붙였다. 그는 "은행 경영진은 부실경영의 책임을 묻게 될 것이며, 또한 적대적 인수합병이나 금융지주회사로의 강제합병도 감수해야 할 것"이라고 밝혔다.

cf 기업소유 지분의 인수 및 합병 가운데 기존 대주주와의 협의 없이 행해지는 기업지배권 탈취 행위 내지는 전략. M&A 관련 주체가 상호합의와 정해진 절차에 따라 기업인수 혹은 합병을 추진하는 경우를 우호적 M&A라 한다면, 어느 한편이 상대기업의 의사에 반하여 강제적으로 managerial right(경영권)를 탈취하고자 하는 경우를 hostile M&A라고 한다. 우호적 M&A는 협상을 통해 진행되므로 그 진행 과정이 공개되는 반면, hostile M&A에서는 매수자가 대상기업의 managerial right를 완전히 장악한 뒤에야 전면에 등장한다. 특히, 최근 들어 기업인수 전략으로 자주 등장하고 있는 hostile M&A 경우에는 managerial right를 탈취하려는 측과 이를 방어하려는 측 사이에 필사적인 전쟁을 벌이게 되는 사례가 많아 양자가 동시에 막대한 손실을 입어 공멸할 수 있다.

3. 실용영어

(1) 블랙으로 하겠어요.

M: 휴식을 취하는 게 어때요? 마실 거 드릴까요?
W: 예, 커피로 할게요.
M: 설탕과 프림 넣을까요?
W: 블랙으로 할게요.

(2) 메뉴 어디 있어요?

A; 미안하지만, 메뉴 어디 있어요?
B: 벽에 붙어 있습니다.
A: 아, 그렇군요. 고마워요. 참치 샌드위치(a tuna sandwich) 주세요.
B: 음료수는 뭘 드릴까요?

(3) 점심식사하면서 토론합시다.

A: 몇 시인가요?
B: 11시 30분입니다.
A: 그럼 점심식사하면서 토론을 마치지요.
B: 잘 아시는 곳 있어요?

(4) 오늘 밤 외식할까?

A: 오늘 밤에 할 일 있어요?
B: 별로.
A: 그럼 저녁 외식 할래요?
B: 좋지. 이곳 근처에 해산물 요리 잘하는 식당이 한 곳 있어. 그리로 가자고.

(5) 크리스마스 카드

1) 당신의 Christmas가 이 세상 모든 기쁨으로 가득차길 원해요.
2) 친한 친구(동성 또는 이성)에게, "기찬 크리스마스 보내!!! 내 생각도 좀

하고 말야!!! ”

3) (약간 격식을 차릴 필요가 있는 상황) 당신의 인생을 Christmas의 빛으로 채우세요.
4) (친구끼리 부담없이 쓸 수 있는 표현) 즐거운 시간이 또 찾아 왔어! Christmas 잘 보내!
5) (친구끼리 또는 부모가 자녀들에게) Christmas의 기쁨이 모두 너의 것이 되기를!
6) (특히 어느 정도 나이가 있는 친구들끼리) 가장 즐거운 인사를 당신과 아는 모든 이에게! Christmas 뿐 아니라 일년 내내 기쁨이 넘치기를…
7) (친구끼리 또는 약간의 격식을 필요로 하는 경우) 즐거운 성탄절을 맞이하여 당신을 생각하는 우리가 있다는 걸 기억해요.
8) 앉으나 서나 당신이 즐거운 Christmas 맞기를 바래요.
9) (친한 친구 또는 연인에게) 진실로 당신의 생에 축복을!
10) (가족끼리 쓸 수 있는 표현) 당신의 집에 즐거움과 기쁨이 넘치길…
11) (친구에게) 벽난로처럼 따뜻하고 기쁜 마음을…
12) (부모가 아이에게 혹은 친구들끼리) Christmas와 다음 일년 내내 마음을 기쁘게 해 줄 수 있는 마술같은 시간이 왔어.
13) (멀리 있는 친척이나 가족에게) 항상 이맘 때면 함께 있지 못함을 유감으로 생각합니다. 하지만 가까이 있지 않아도 항상 기쁨이 넘치길 바랍니다.
14) (남자친구[남편]가 여자친구[부인]에게) 당신은 언제나 내 맘속에 있어요.

4. 국제뉴스

베이징서 사스 의심환자 발생

지난 7월 사스 여파가 진정 기미에 접어든 후 처음으로 베이징에서 사스(SARS · 중증 급성호흡기증후군) 의심 환자가 발생했다고 중국 언론이 전했다. 중국 관영 신화통신은 중국 위생부 발표 내용을 인용, 지난 4월 5일 20세 여자 간호사가 사스 증세를 보였고, 그로부터 이틀 후 병원에 입원했다고 보도했다. 이 여성은 감기, 발열, 기침 증세를 보였으며, 그 외 5명 역시 검사 차원에서 격리된 상태라고 신화통신이 전했다. 신화통신은 위생부 발표 내용을 인용 “이 여성과 가까이 지냈던 5명 역시 발열 및 다른 증세를 보이고 있다”고 보도했다. 그밖에 어떤 형태로든 이 여성과 접촉했던 1백71명에 대해서도 검사를 벌이고 있다고 신화통신은 보도했다.

사스는 2002년 말 중국 남부 지역에서 처음 발발해 세계 전역으로 번져 나가면서, 8천명이 감염되고 7백70명 이상이 사망했다. 하지만 지난 7월 이후로 중국에서 보고된 사스 환자 발생 건수는 단지 4건뿐이었으며, 4건 모두 중국 남부 광둥성에서 발생했다. 이후 환자 4명은 모두 완쾌되었다. 대만과 싱가포르에서 사스를 연구하던 과학자 2명 역시 사스에 감염됐다가 회복됐으며, 이후 다른 사스 감염 환자는 보고된 바 없었다. 작년 7월, 세계보건기구(WHO)가 사스 사태 종결을 선언한 이래 사스 감염 환자로 확인된 경우는 6건뿐이었다. 사스 발발로 중국 본토에서는 3백49명이 사망했으며, 당시 가장 큰 피해를 입은 도시 중 하나가 바로 베이징이었다.

5. Ann Landers

자랑하는 것

앤 랜더즈 여사께:

남편과 저는 18개월 전 새 집으로 이사를 왔습니다. 우리는 아름답게 집을 꾸미고 가구를 갖추었습니다. 우리집에 손님이 올 때면 언제나 남편은 손님들에게 온 집안을 구경 시켜줘야 한다고 주장하는데, 거기에는 화장실, 세탁실, 청소 도구 넣어두는 광까지도 포함되는 것입니다. 저는 그것이 불필요하다고 생각합니다. 집안에는 사람들이 자세히 보면 만족하지 않을 곳이 있기 때문에 남에게 보여주고 싶지 않은 곳들이 있는 것인데 남편은 그것은 바보같은 생각이라는 것입니다. 누구를 저녁 식사에 초대한다는 것은 온 집안을 구경시킨다는 것을 의미하나요? 여사님께서 답변해 주시면 효과가 있을 것입니다.
–알라스카주에서 여사님께 기대하며

알라스카 분께:

귀하께서 편들어줄 사람을 찾으신다면 저를 잘 찾으셨습니다(in은 여기서 〈~이라고 하는, ~라는〉의 동격관계를 나타내는 의미임. → "당신은 나라고 하는〈나라는〉 사람을 갖고 있다" 혹은 "나는 당신의 바로 그 사람이다"라는 의미임). 남편이 들으시면 쇼크를 받으시겠지만 대부분의 사람들은 남의 집 화장실이나 청소 도구를 넣어두는 광에는 관심이 없습니다. 남편이 주장하는 그러한 자세한 관광은 정말 남편 자신만을 위한 것이지 방문객들에게는 너무나 지루하기 짝이 없는 것입니다.

6. 독해문제

저는 닐 영입니다. 교통 상황을 말씀 드리겠습니다. 시내로 들어오는 교통은 잘 소통되고 있습니다. 다만 트루먼 터널은 30분간 정체되고 있습니다. 링컨 터널은 10분 정도만 정체되기 때문에 운전자들께서는 그쪽을 이용하시는 것이 좋겠습니다. Second 애브뉴와 Third 애브뉴 사이 57번가에서 지하 수도관이 터졌습니다. 가능하면 이 지역을 피해주십시오. 저희들은 20분 후에 다시 새로운 소식을 가지고 뵙겠습니다. 닐 영이 전해드렸습니다.

【정답】

(1) ⓓ

(2) ⓒ ⇒ "a water main break on 57th Street between Second and Third Avenue. Avoid this area," 즉 지하 수도관이 터졌다는 말이 나옴.

7. 유머영어

(1) 죄수의 편지를 가로채는 간수

감옥에 갇힌 한 죄수가 부인의 편지를 받았다. "사랑하는 당신에게. 제가 뒷마당에 상추를 키우기로 했어요. 언제쯤 파종하는 게 좋을까요?" 간수가 죄수들의 편지를 모두 읽는 걸 알고 있는 이 죄수는 이렇게 답장을 했다. "사랑하는 당신에게. 뭘 해도 좋지만 뒷마당은 손대지 마시오. 그곳에 돈을 모두 묻어두었거든." 일주일 정도 지난 뒤 그는 부인으로부터 또 편지를 받았다. "사랑하는 당신에게. 무슨 일이 벌어졌는지 상상도 못하실 거예요. 사람들 몇이 삽을 들고 와서 뒷마당을 몽땅 파헤쳤어요." 죄수는 다시 이렇게 편지를 띄웠다. "사랑하는 당신에게. 지금이 바로 상추씨를 뿌리기에 가장 좋은 때라오."

(2) 어떤 막일꾼 노인

항공학박사인 킨볼 교수가 아이들의 그네를 사 가지고 와서 조립작업을 시작했다. 설명서를 읽어가면서 A볼트를 B슬롯에 끼워보는 등 이리저리 만지작거리기를 몇 시간… 그는 마침내 손을 들고 말았다. 옆집 마당에서 일하고 있는 막일꾼 노인을 불렀다. 교수 집에 온 노인은 설명서를 집어

던지고 잠시 만지작거리더니 그네를 완전히 조립했다. 박사는 탄복했다. "설명서를 보지도 않고 그렇게 해낼 수 있다니 도무지 이해할 수 없군요." "실은 나 글을 몰라요. 글을 모르다 보니 머리를 쓰지 않을 수가 없단 말씀이야."라고 노인은 대답했다.

제6장

1. Warm-up

(1) 우리가 무엇을 제공하는지를 이해하도록 하기 위하여 잠재고객과의 회의 약속을 가능한 한 곧 정하는 것이 필요하다.

(2) 시간을 절약하기 위하여 합의사항을 가능한 한 많이 복사해 둬라. 그래야 회의 중에 사본이 떨어져도 여분이 있게 된다.

(3) 추천은 세 가지 특별한 섹션으로 나뉜다. 각 섹션은 도심 슬럼가의 심각한 문제의 다른 측면들을 다룬다.

(4) 이 새로운 근육단련 기구는 고객들이 살을 빼면서 동시에 TV도 보면서 긴장을 풀 수 있게 해 준다.

(5) 당신이 방금 구매하신 제품에 관해 문제가 있거나 질문사항이 있으시면 영업 직원에게 연락 주세요.

(6) 개막 연설에서 역사학과 교수는 자기 강연에서 상세히 설명하고자 하는 기본 이론을 설명하려 했다.

(7) 이 새로운 CD 플레이어는 내구성이 있고 사용하기도 쉬우며 모든 가능한 상황하에서 고장나지 않고 계속 작동되는 것이 보장된다

(8) 이 비행기의 비상시 대피 절차는 여러분 앞좌석 주머니에 있는 팜플렛에 상세히 설명되어 있다.

(9) 이번 토론이 경제협력을 통해 긍정적인 국제관계를 조장하는데 도움을 줄 것이라고 이 국제 무역회의 대부분의 대표단원들은 믿고 있다.

(10) 회사 안내 책자에 명시된 대로 안전규정을 지켜서 모든 직원들은 한 달에 한 번 의무적인 소방훈련에 참가해야 한다.

2. 시사용어

(1) 조류 독감

지난 주 2만 마리가 넘는 닭이 치명적인 조류 독감에 걸려 폐사한 닭농장 근처의 한 농장에서도 오리들이 조류독감에 감염됐다고 농림부가 어제 밝혔다. 농림부는 서울에서 130km 떨어진 충청도 음성군 소재 문제의 농장에 있는 오리 3,300마리 전체를 폐사시키도록 명령했다고 밝혔다. 농림부의 한 관리는 "오리들이 지난 1997년 홍콩서 발견됐던 고병원성 가금 인플루엔자와 같은 변형 조류 독감에 감염됐을 가능성이 높다"고 말했다.

cf 일반적으로 닭, 오리 등의 조류가 걸리는 독감(Influenza)임. 일부 유형은 사람에게도 전염되며 폐사율 등에 따라 고병원성, 약병원성, 비병원성 등 크게 3가지 종류가 있고 혈청형에 따라 135종으로 분류된다. 현재까지 사람에게 감염된 사례를 보면 지난 1996년 Britain에서 H7N7형에 1명이 감염됐다는 보고가 있고, 지난 1997년 Hong Kong bird flu(H5N1)의 경우 18명이 감염돼 6명이 사망했다. 국내에서는 지난 1996년 약병원성이 처음 발견된 뒤 약병원성은 올들어서만 9건의 발생 보고가 있을 정도로 흔한 가축질병(livestock disease)이 됐지만, 2003년 12월 충청북도 음성군에서 발생한 Hong Kong 조류독감은 물론 고병원성 바이러스(Virus)가 발견되기는 처음이다. 주요 증상은 고열과 기침, 전신 근육통 등 일반 독감과 증상이 유사하다. 심해지면 폐렴으로 사망하는 경우도 생긴다. 1997년 Hong Kong 조류독감 발생시 18명의 환자가 발생, 이 중 6명이 사망할 정도로 치사율이 높다. 증상이 의심될 경우 바이러스 증식을 막는 독감치료제를 투여 받으면 합병증(complications) 등을 현저히 떨어뜨릴 수 있다. 조류 독감은 철새 분비물 등에 의해 전파되는 만큼 전세계적으로 발생되고 있으며, 최근 고병원성 발생국들을 보면 미국(1983년), 호주(1985년과 1994년), 멕시코(1995년), 홍콩(1997년, 2001년, 2003년), 이탈리아(1999년), 칠레(2002년), 네덜란드(2003년) 등이다.

(2) 브릭스

현재 브라질, 러시아, 인도 및 중국의 주식시장은 미국, 영국, 일본 및 독일의 주식시장 총 가치의 5%에 불과하다. 비록 브릭스 시장에서 견실한 성장이 예상되나, 전세계 주식 시장 총가치의 약 45%를 차지하는 미국은 오는 2050년까지 최대 규모의 시장 지위를 유지할 것으로 예상된다. 하지만 중국은 25%로 세계 두 번째 규모의 시장으로 올라설 것이며, 인도가 10%선을 넘어 3위에 자리잡게 될 것이다.

cf Brazil, Russia, India, China 의 영문 머리글자를 딴 약어로 경제 중심축으로 떠오르는 신흥성장국을 지칭하는 조어임. 이들 나라는 국토가 넓고 자원과 인구가 많으며, 세계 경제가 전반적으로 어려운 데도 불구하고 경제가 상승세를 타는 국가라는 공통점이 있어 최근 국내외 언론에서 현재 G7 선진국(developed countries)을 대체해 향후 20~30년 후 세계 경제를 주도할 충분한 성장 잠재력을 가진 경제 대국이라는 평가를 받고 있다. 특히 우리나라 입장에서 볼 때 중국은 지난해 미국을 제치고 우리 나라 최대 수출국으로 부상했고, 인도는 휴대전화 및 가전제품 등 IT에 대한 소비가 늘고 있는 추세이다. 러시아와 브라질도 우리나라 수출기업들의 새로운 수출 시장으로 부상할 가능성이 큰 국가들이다.

3. 실용영어

(1) 버스 혹은 택시 타기

(Michael이 Julie에게 지하철역에 어떻게 가냐고 묻자 Julie는 81번 버스를 타거나 바쁘면 택시를 타라고 얘기하고 있다.)

마이클: 여기서 지하철역에 어떻게 가지?
쥴리 : 81번 버스를 타면 돼.
마이클: 81번 버스 정류장이 어디에 있는데?
쥴리 : 대학 정문 길 건너편에 있어.
마이클: (찾기)쉬울 것 같네.
쥴리 : 물론, 만약 급하면 택시를 타는 것이 가장 좋아.
마이클: 택시 요금은 얼마나 하는데?
쥴리 : 여기서 1500원 정도 들거야.

(2) 택시 안에서

A: 미안합니다만, 택시 정류장이 어디죠?
B: 이 건물 뒤에 있습니다.
A: 감사합니다.

(택시 안에서)

A: 안녕하세요? 어디로 모실까요?

B: 힐튼 호텔로 가주세요.

A: 어디에 있는 Hilton을 말씀하시나요? 두 군데가 있는데요.

B: 아, 미안해요. 바닷가쪽에 있는 곳으로 가 주세요.

A: '힐튼 파빌리온' 말씀이군요. 그렇죠?

B: 맞아요.

A: 휴가차 오셨나요?

B: 아니요, 사실은 사업 설명회차 왔습니다.

A: 어디서 오셨나요?

B: 스위스에서 왔습니다.

(3) 지하철 타기

(Michael이 신촌에서 친구를 만난다고 하자 Julie가 지하철을 타고 신촌에 가는 방법을 설명해 주고 있다.)

마이클: 신촌에서 친구 좀 만나려고 해.

쥴리 : 신촌에 가려면 먼저 1호선을 타야 해.

마이클: 1호선에서 어느 방향으로 가야 하는데?

쥴리 : 플랫폼에 섰을 때 의정부라고 쓴 표지를 찾아봐.

마이클: 그리고 나서 무엇을 해야 하는데?

쥴리 : 시청역에서 갈아타야 해.

마이클: 시청역에서 내리라고?

쥴리 : 응. 그리고 2호선으로 안내하는 표지를 따라가. 2호선을 타면 신촌으로 갈 수 있어.

(4) 회신 : 김포공항

김포공항을 이용한 적이 없는데, 종합전시장까지는 어느 전철로 가는 것이 가장 좋습니까?

종합전시장으로 가려면 공항에서 리무진 버스가 가장 편리합니다. 리무진 버스는 팔레스 호텔, 노보텔 호텔 종합전시장에 섭니다. 소요 시간은 40분입니다. 지하철이 쌉니다만, 김포공항에서 종합전시장으로의 직행편은 없습니다. 바꿔 타도 좋다면, 당산역까지 버스로 가서 종합전시장까지

지하철로 갈 수도 있습니다.

그 외에 궁금한 사항이 있으면 알려 주십시오.

4. 국제뉴스

칸, 클럽 이적에 관심

독일의 골키퍼 올리버 칸이 바이에른 뮌헨을 떠나는 것을 고려하고 있다. 그는 유럽 최고의 팀으로 이적하는 데 관심을 보이고 있다. 독일 국가대표팀 주장 칸(34세)은 "뮌헨에서 10년 동안 뛰어오면서 그동안 15번의 우승컵을 차지했다. 이제 새로운 도전이 필요하다"고 밝혔다. 독일 축구협회 홈페이지에 오른 인터뷰에서 칸은 "새로운 시즌에 때맞춰 이적이 필요할 것"이라고 말했다.

칸은 고액의 이적료가 자신의 이적에 방해가 될 것인가에 대해 의문을 두고 있다. 현재 칸은 곧 포르투갈에서 열릴 유로 2004 결승전을 준비하기 위해 프라이부르크 인근의 빈덴 임 엘츠탈에서 독일 국가대표팀에 합류하고 있다. 이번에 새로 바이에른 뮌헨의 사령탑을 맡게된 펠릭스 마가트 감독은 "칸의 의사에 대해 아무것도 아는 바가 없다"고 말했다. "나는 올리버 칸이 다음 시즌에도 여전히 바이에른 뮌헨의 골문을 지킬 것이라고 생각한다"고 마가트 감독은 말했다.

5. Abby

떠드는 애들과 전혀 말리려 하지 않는 부모의 꼴불견

에비 여사께 :

어젯밤 저희 부부는 동네 가까운 곳의 유일한 "고급" 레스토랑에서 저녁 식사를 했답니다. 저희 뒤쪽의 테이블에서는 세 명의 어린 자녀들과 함께 온 부부가 앉아서 식사를 하고 있었답니다. 저희가 식사를 하는 동안 내내 그 애들이 계속 소리 질러대며 떠드는데도 그 부모들은 말릴 생각도 안하고 가만히 있더군요. 그 애들이 하도 요란하게 법석을 떨어대는 바람에 또 다른 테이블에 앉아 있던 어떤 커플은 아예 식사도 마치지 않고 그냥 나가 버리더라구요. 레스토랑 매니저는 자리를 다른 곳으로 옮겨 주었습니다만, 그 애들의 째지는 목소리는 레스토랑 전체에 쩡쩡 울려 퍼지더군요. 저희는 계속해서 그 부모들을 째려보면서 눈치를 주었지만 내 참, 기가 막혀서 그 아버지란 사람은 제가 불편해 하는 것은 저에게 문제가 있어서라고 빈

정거리며 쏘아대더군요. 만일 당신이 그 레스토랑의 매니저였다면 어떻게 하셨겠어요?
—불쾌하게 느끼는 사람이

불쾌하게 느끼는 사람에게:
제가 만일 그 레스토랑의 매니저였다면 그들에게 다가가서 부부 중 한 명이 그 어린 꼬마 녀석들을 밖으로 잠시 데리고 나가 그들이 레스토랑 안에서 예절 바르게 행동하도록 대답할 때까지 꾸짖도록 부탁하겠어요. 레스토랑 안의 손님 전체를 잃느니 한 가족 손님만 잃는 것이 낫겠죠?

6. 독해문제

대기 중의 꽃가루 수가 오늘 기록적으로 높았습니다. 이것은 지난 10년 전 최고치를 기록한 이래 처음입니다. (10년전 마지막으로 이렇게 높은 기록을 나타냈었습니다.) 비가 오지 않아 꽃가루가 대기 중에 더 오래 머무르게 되었기 때문입니다. 이로 인하여 이 지역 주민들은 호흡에 어려움을 느끼게 되고 감기나 기관지염과 비슷한 증세를 경험하게 될 것입니다. 앞으로 2주간은 비가 오지 않을 것이기 때문에 이 영향하의 지역 주민들은 에어컨을 켠 채 집안에 머무르시고 외출시에는 보호 마스크를 하시기 바랍니다. 내일 대기 중의 꽃가루 수는 한층 더 올라갈 전망입니다.

【정답】

(1) ⓐ ⇒ 대기 중의 꽃가루 때문에 주민들이 호흡에 고통을 받는 등, 대기 중의 높은 꽃가루 수가 문제가 됨.

(2) ⓒ ⇒ 'No new rain is expected for the next two weeks'라는 말로 볼 때 2주일이 지난 뒤 비가 와서 대기 중의 꽃가루 수가 줄어들 때까지는 문제가 해결되지 않을 것임. abate : 감소되다

(3) ⓓ ⇒ 'wear a protective mask when outside'라는 말에 나와 있음.

7. 유머영어

(1) 악몽 치료법

한 남자가 몇 년 동안 악몽으로 고통받고 있었다. 잠이 들 때마다 끔찍하게 생긴 동물이나 파충류가 자신의 침대 밑을 들락거리는 꿈을 꾸는 것이

었다. 그러던 그가 마침내 친구에게 자신이 치유되었다고 말했다. "우리 형한테 말했더니 형이 그걸 멈추게 했어." "자네 형님이 정신과 의사이신가?" "아니, 목수야."하고 그 남자가 대답했다. "형이 내 침대 다리를 톱으로 잘라내 버렸다네."

(2) 훌륭한 경영방식

두 여자가 작은 기업을 운영하는데 따르는 어려움에 관해 이야기를 나누었다. "나는 작년에 새 방법을 도입했어요. 데리고 있는 사람들에게 석 달에 한번씩 최소한 1주일의 휴가를 주고 있습니다." "아니 대관절 어쩌자고 그렇게 하십니까?" "누가 불필요한 사람인가를 알아내는데는 그보다 좋은 방법이 없답니다."

제7장

1. Warm-up

(1) 그린컴의 목적은 우리의 자연 환경의 보호와 멸종에 직면한 많은 동물들의 보호에 대한 공공연한 옹호자가 되는 것이다.
(2) 편의상 여분의 담요가 여러분이 겨우내 확실히 따뜻하고 편안하게 머물도록 하기 위해 모든 호텔 객실에 마련돼 있습니다.
(3) 정부는 최근에 갑자기 밀어닥친 홍수의 희생자들에게 그들의 집, 농장, 가축에게 가해진 피해를 보상하고자 모든 노력을 기울일 것이다.
(4) 대부분의 판지로 만든 상자와 박스들은 신제품으로 변해 다시 팔릴 수 있기 때문에 수지가 맞게 재활용될 수 있다.
(5) 그녀가 사람들을 만날 때마다 항상 화장을 짙게 하는 것을 좋아하기 때문에 본래의 안색을 알기는 어렵다.
(6) 당신이 구입한 물건이 결함이 있다는 것을 발견하면 우선 해야 할 일은 교환받기 위해 상점으로 되가져 가는 것이다.
(7) 위원회의 위원들이 그 문제의 해결 방법에 관하여 서로 의견일치를 이루지 못하는 것이 문제를 더욱 어렵게 만들었다.
(8) 그 프로그램은 경쟁력을 높이기 위하여 고안된 것이다. 더욱이 그것은 더 높은 수입을 얻을 가능성도 높여 줄 것이다.

(9) 마르코위츠씨는 자기의 호텔 체인점을 세우기에 적당한 소도시를 찾아 전국을 돌아다닌다.

(10) 그 분석가는 회사가 파산하지 않고 심지어 수익을 낼 것이라고 예측했다.

2. 시사용어

(1) 기동부대

정부는 어제 기획예산처 산하 테스크포스팀이 다소 힘든 일인 국내 금융감독체계의 합리화에 대한 일련의 방안을 내 놓음에 따라 금융체계개편에 대한 첫번째 조치를 발동하게 됐다. 금융감독원과 상급 정책결정기구인 금융감독위원회는 구조개혁에 초점을 맞춤으로써 하루아침에 불경기로 이어진 외환위기에서 국가경제를 벗어나게 하는 데 일조했다고 폭넓게 인식되어 왔다.

cf 특정의 작전구역 없이 주어진 특별한 작전임무 수행을 위해 자유롭고 기민하게 행동하는 작전부대를 일컫는 용어. 1940년대초인 제2차대전 때 일본해군이 aircraft carrier(항공모함) 중심의 작전부대에 이 이름을 붙인 데서 비롯되었으며 미국에서는 이를 임무부대라고 부른다. 그 뒤에도 aircraft carrier는 함대전력에서 주력의 지위를 유지하게 됨에 따라 이를 중심으로 순양함, 구축함 등 호위함정으로 편성된 항모전투그룹을 task force로 부르게 되었다. 영국에서는 특별 수사대, 조사단 등을 일컫기도 한다. 한편, 오늘날에는 공공기관이나 일반 기업체 등에서 특별한 임무나 사업을 수행하기 위해 한시적으로 구성된 전담 부서나 팀을 일컫는 말로 널리 쓰이고 있다.

(2) 국제에너지기구

에너지 비용이 올라가면 소비자들은 경제 회복이 힘들어질까 두려워한다. 26개 선진국들의 에너지 부문 조언기구인 국제에너지기구(IEA)는 화요일 에너지 가격이 너무 높다며 석유수출국기구(OPEC)가 시장을 식히기 위한 행동에 나서야 한다고 밝혔다. IEA의 아시아 태평양 및 라틴 아메리카 비회원국 지부의 에하라 노리오 대표는 "현재의 수준은 너무 비싸다"라며 "석유수출국기구의 2월 회의에서 OPEC이 시장 과열을 식히길 희망한다. 우리는 어느 정도의 가격 안정이 필요하다"고 말했다.

cf 1974년 9월 벨기에 브뤼셀에서 석유소비국간 합의를 거쳐 같은 해 11월 Organization for Economic Cooperation and Development (OECD, 경제

협력개발기구) 이사회에서 설립을 결의하여 1976년 1월 발족한 국제적인 에너지 계획 기구임. 제1차 석유파동 이후 산유국 모임인 Organization of Petroleum Exporting Countries(OPEC, 석유수출국기구)의 석유공급 삭감에 대항하기 위하여 주요 석유소비국에서 만든 에너지 계획의 실천기관이며 OECD 산하기관이다. 회원국간의 석유 긴급운용 시스템으로 국제석유시장에 대한 정보 공유를 통해 석유공급 위기에 대비하고, 대체에너지 개발 및 석유수급 비상시 회원국간 공동대처 방안 등을 마련하는 것을 주요 기능으로 하고 있다. 최고 결정기관은 이사회이고 그 밖에 사무국과 상설위원회, 에너지연구개발위원회가 있는데, 상설위원회는 석유시장, 장기정책, 산유국과 소비국과의 관계 등을 다룬다. 투표권은 각 참가국 3표씩과 참가국의 석유소비량 전체를 100표로 하고, 각국의 소비량에 따라 분배한 표로 이루어져 있다. OECD 회원국에 한해 가입 자격이 부여되며, 한국은 2001년에 가입하였다. 2002년 현재 26개국이 가입해 있다. 본부는 프랑스 파리에 있다.

3. 실용영어

(1) 상업영어 1 [Taiwan에 있는 Mr. Tan(B)과 미국의 Mr. Smith(A) 사이의 전화내용]

A: 제가 9월 10일부터 9월 25일까지 타이완의 전자관련 세미나에 참가할 예정입니다. 그 기간에 뵐 수 있을까요?

B: 타이완에 오신다고요? 잘 됐군요. 언제쯤 뵐까요?

A: 9월 12일쯤 어떨까요? 그땐 제가 시간을 낼 수 있습니다.

B: 잘 됐습니다. 타이완에 도착하셔서 전화 주세요. 혹시 어느 호텔에서 묵을 예정이신가요?

A: 만다린 호텔에 묵을 예정입니다.

B: 잘 됐군요, 저희 회사는 만다린에서 그리 멀지 않습니다.

A: 정말 다행이네요. 타이완에 도착한 후 연락을 드리지요.

B: 좋습니다, 그때 통화하지요.

(2) 상업영어 2 [Taiwan에 있는 Mr. Tan(B)과 미국의 Mr. Smith(A) 사이의 전화내용]

A: 안녕하세요. 탄 차오씨 계십니까?

B: 전데요. 스미스씨인가요?

A: 네, 이틀 전에 타이완에 도착했지요. 뵐 수 있을까요?

B: 물론이죠. 전화 기다리고 있었습니다. 내일 아침 10시 30분 정도 어떠세요?

A: 잠깐만요. 제 세미나 스케줄을 확인해 보겠습니다. 아, 죄송하지만 제가 내일 아침엔 세미나에 참가해야 하는군요. 내일 오후는 어떠세요?

(3) 상업영어 3 [Taiwan에 있는 Mr. Tan(B)과 미국의 Mr. Smith(A) 사이의 전화내용]

B: 내일 오후 말씀이죠? 좋습니다.

A: 어디서 뵐까요?

B: 호텔 로비 어때요? 제가 말씀 드렸죠? 저희 회사가 지금 계시는 호텔에서 넘어지면 코 닿을 곳이라고요.

A: 맞아요. 좋습니다. 괜찮으시다면, 제가 오후 3시 30분 경 로비에서 기다리겠습니다.

B: 알겠습니다. 그때 샘플이나 안내 책자를 보여드릴까요?

A: 호텔 로비에서 뵙고 제품을 회사에 가서 직접 보면 어떨까요? 회사가 제가 묵고 있는 호텔에서 가깝다고 하셨잖아요.

B: 그게 더 좋겠군요. 내일 오후에 뵙겠습니다.

(4) 상업영어 4 [Mr. Smith와 Mr. Tan이 직접 만나서 대화하는 내용]

B: 실례합니다만, 미국에서 오신 Mr. Smith시죠?

A: 네, 혹시 Mr. Tan Chow인가요?

B: 네, 그렇습니다. 처음 뵙겠습니다.

A: 이렇게 만나게 되어 반갑습니다.

B: 여행 어떠셨어요? 시차 때문에 힘드시죠?

A: 네, 그래요. 여행 피로감을 제외하곤 다 좋습니다. 특히 대만 분들이 참 친절하시네요.

B: 아, 감사합니다. 회사로 가실까요?

A: 그러죠.

4. 국제뉴스

(1) 코피 아난, 사담 사형 안된다

코피 아난 유엔 사무총장은 월요일 사담 후세인의 사형을 지지하지 않는다고 밝혔으며, 이라크 옛 대통령의 재판 법정은 국제적 기준을 충족시켜야 함을 강조했다. 재판 절차에 있어 UN의 도움을 제안한 아난 사무총장은 '비록 이것이 부시가 과거에는 자기 손에 들어온 사람들에게 용인하지 않았던 대우이긴 하지만' 사담 후세인을 인도주의적으로 처리할 것이라는 부시 행정부의 말에 고무되었다고 말했다. 하지만 그는 UN은 이전에 있었던 어떤 재판에서도 사형을 지지하지 않았다고 말했다. "따라서 사무총장으로서 나는 지금 방침을 바꿔서 사형을 지지하지는 않을 것"이라고 말했다. 압델라지즈 알-하킴 이라크 과도통치위원회 의장은 파리에서 사담이 사형에 처해질 것이라고 말했다. 또한 그는 그 과정에서 국제적인 역할의 필요성을 인정한다고 말했지만 자세한 사항은 밝히지 않았다.

아난 사무총장은 사담의 다소 긴 그림자 없애기가 이라크의 화합을 촉진시키길 바란다고 밝혔지만 지난 8월 19일 바그다드 본부가 폭탄 테러를 당한 유엔이 언제 이라크로 돌아갈 것인지에 대해서는 신중한 입장이었다. 이라크 주재 영국 수석 특사인 제레미 그린스톡 경은 아난 사무총장이 폭탄 테러로 숨진 서지오 비에라 드 멜로를 대신할 특별 대표를 봄이나 여름까지 지명할 것으로 예상되지 않는다고 말했다. 뉴욕에 잠시 머무른 아난 사무총장을 만난 그린스톡은 미국 점령이 7월에 끝난 후까지 이라크에 UN 대표를 두지는 않을 것 같다고 밝혔다.

(2) 우리의 감자를 살리자

[미국 아이다호(Idaho)주의 감자농부들이 과잉생산으로 감자 값이 폭락하자 자구책을 강구하고 있다는 내용]

Idaho주의 감자농부들은 연방정부가 과잉 생산된 감자를 매입할 것을 요구하는 운동을 중단한 후 감자의 과잉생산 분을 줄이기 위한 새 계획을 추구하고 있다. 그 재배농부들의 집단은 Potato Management Co.라는 협동조합의 구성을 원하는데, 그 조합은 감자를 사들여 유통시키지 않게 하여 과잉생산 분을 적어도 10퍼센트 줄이려고 할 것이다. 과잉생산은 가격을 하락시키고 있다.

5. Annie

장모님 모시기

애니에게:

아내와 저는 결혼한지 3년째로 6개월된 아들이 있습니다. 그런데 무슨 문제가 있냐고요? 장모님이 저희와 함께 살고 계신다는 것입니다. 작년에 저희는 장모님(큰 개 두 마리와 함께)의 자립을 돕기 위해 저희 집으로 옮겨오시도록 했습니다. 장모님은 실업보조금으로 생활하고 계셨기 때문에 직업을 찾을 때까지 저희 집에서 계시도록 한 것입니다. 장모님은 매달 약간의 임대료를 주십니다. 아내가 임신을 하자 저는 장모님께 9개월 후에는 이사를 나가셔야 한다고 말씀드렸습니다. 그게 벌써 15개월 전 쯤인데 장모님은 꿈쩍도 하지 않으십니다. 지난 주에 아내는 쇼핑을 하던 중에 아르바이트 구인 광고가 걸린 상점을 보게 되었습니다. 아내는 장모님의 등을 떠밀어 그 상점에 들어가 지원 신청서를 한 부 받도록 했습니다. 다음 날 장모님은 상점 지배인에게 지원서를 제출했어야 했는데, 그 쇼핑몰에 다시 가려고 하지 않았습니다. 임시직원을 구하는 사람이 있으면 이웃들이 저희한테 자주 알려주지만 장모님은 절대 알아보지를 않습니다.

장모님이 저희 집에 가져온 짐이 하도 많아 저희는 이제 지하실이나 차고에 들어갈 수가 없습니다. 그리고 데리고 온 개들은 우리 카펫이나 문에 엄청난 피해를 끼쳤습니다. 아내와 저는 우리 애를 평화롭게 키우고 싶습니다. 장모님께 나가 달라고 하면 저희가 나쁜 인간일까요? 제가 이삿짐 차를 대절해서 장모님의 짐을 실어 창고로 옮겨도 괜찮을까요?

– 캐나다에서

캐나다 분께:

당신 집이 돈도 저렴하고 안전하다 보니 장모님이 자신의 거처 찾기를 꺼리는 게 분명합니다. 자신의 어머니이기에 부인이 이 문제를 논의해야겠지요. 부인은 어머니가 환영받기에는 너무 오래 머물렀다는 점을 분명히 밝혀야 합니다. 장모님은 감정적인 면에서 자립능력을 해치는 문제가 있는 것 같군요. 그녀는 카운셀링을 받을 수 있으며(YMCA나 유나이티드웨이 또는 동네 여성센터에 알아 보세요), 만약 일자리를 찾는 진지한 노력을 하지 않으면 이삿심 차를 부르겠나는 협박을 실행에 옮길 수 밖에 없을 것이라는 최후통첩도 함께 하세요.

6. 독해문제

승객 여러분께 알립니다. 오전 시카고행 셔틀버스가 심한 눈보라 때문에 취소되었습니다. 유감스럽게도 기상청에서는 이번 눈보라가 최소한 하루 종일 계속될 것이라고 예상하고 있어 항공편은 무기한 연장되었습니다. 승객 여러분께 불편을 끼쳐 드리게 되어 죄송하오며, 환불이나 항공편의 변경에 관한 자세한 사항은 고객 안내 카운터에 문의해 주시기 바랍니다.

【정답】

(1) ⓑ ⇒ 'due to a blizzard'란 말이 나오는데 blizzard는 snow임.

(2) ⓓ ⇒ 'report to … on refunds'란 말이 나오는데 refund는 get the money back임.

7. 유머영어

(1) 마음 아픈 진실

어느 화창한 봄날 아침 네 명의 고등학교 남학생들이 수업을 빼먹기로 작정했다. 소년들은 점심 시간이 끝난 후에 학교에 와서는 선생님께 오는 길에 버스 바퀴가 펑크나서 그렇게 늦었노라고 둘러댔다. 천만 다행히도 선생님은 조용히 웃으며 말씀하셨다. "너희들 오늘 아침에 시험을 못 치렀으니, 각자 떨어져 앉아서 종이와 연필을 꺼내도록." 아이들이 자리잡고 앉자 선생님이 말씀하셨다. "딱 한 문제만 푸는 거다. 펑크난 바퀴가 어느 쪽이었지?"

(2) 주정꾼들의 대화

두 주정꾼이 거리를 걷고 있었다. "참으로 아름다운 밤이로군. 저 달을 보게"하고 한 사람이 말했다. "자네 잘 모르는군. 저건 달이 아니라 태양이야"라고 동료 주정뱅이가 대답했다. 한참 옥신각신하던 두 사람은 또 한 사람의 주정뱅이와 마주쳤다. "형씨, 우리 시비를 좀 가려 주시오. 하늘에서 반짝이는 저게 뭡니까, 달입니까? 태양입니까?" 그 사람은 하늘을 쳐다보더니 "미안합니다만, 난 이 동네에 사는 사람이 아니라서…"

제8장

1. Warm-up

(1) 화성 착륙이라는 이 역사적인 임무를 수행하는 가운데 그가 항상 미 항공우주국의 지상 통제소와 연락을 유지해야 하는 것이 절대적이다.
(2) 지난 몇 년간 특권있는 직책을 이용해 온 사람들이 아니라 헌신성을 보여준 직원들에게 우선권이 주어질 것입니다.
(3) 증권거래소는 아침에 활발하게 거래를 시작했다 그 원인은 새로운 투자 자신감과 지난주의 높은 주가 때문이다.
(4) 작년 오빠의 죽음에 대해 언급할 때마다 그녀는 한없이 울어 위로 받을 필요가 있게 된다.
(5) 당신이 이번 학기에 대부분의 수업을 듣지 않았으므로 빼먹은 시간을 보충하여 주말에 보충 수업을 좀 들어야 한다.
(6) 그 달 나머지 기간이 협정을 검토하는 데 쓰일 것이고 양국간의 정전 협정을 마무리하는 데 쓰일 것이다.
(7) 두 국가가 땅 소유권과 국경선 긋기에 대한 많은 의견상의 불일치 때문에 서로 돈독하지 못한 관계를 늘 가져왔다.
(8) 대부분의 사람들 생각에 프랑스는 다음 월드컵에서 우승할 가망성이 매우 희박하다. 그 이유는 그들이 훈련과 국제경기 참가에 충분한 관심을 기울이지 않기 때문이다.
(9) 어느날 내가 버스에 올라탔을 때 포켓에 돈을 하나도 가지지 않고 집을 나섰다는 것을 알게 되었다.
(10) 나는 그녀가 어떻게 그렇게 낮은 월급으로 살아갈 수 있는지 궁금하다.

2. 시사용어

(1) 정치자금에 관한 법률(정치자금법)

만약 김영삼 전 대통령이 강 의원한테 대선운동서 남은 자금을 건넸다면, 이는 정치자금에 관한 법률을 위반한 것이다. 그러나 관련 법에 의거 김 전 대통령을 사법 처리할 수 있는 공소시효가 이미 만료된 상태이다. 그러나 그 자금이 만약 1992년 총선 승리 후 정보기관이나 기업체 기부금으로 조성된 자금으로 밝혀진다면, 김 전 태통령은 국고 자금의 유용 혐의를 여전히 적용받을 수 있다.

cf 정치자금의 적정한 제공을 보장하고 그 수입과 지출 상황을 공개함으로써 민주 정치의 건전한 발전에 기여함을 목적으로 하는 법률임. 총 34조와 부칙으로 구성되어 있는 정치자금에 관한 법률에 의하면 정치자금은 임의로 기부하거나 받을 수 없으며, 공명정대하게 운용하고 회계를 공개하며, 정치적 행위(political activity)를 위하여 소요되는 경비 이외에 사적 경비나 부정한 용도로 지출할 수 없다. 정당은 후원금 및 기부금 형태로 당비를 받을 수 있다. 후원회는 정당의 중앙당과 시·도지부, 지구당 등이 각각 하나를 지정하여 둘 수 있으며 후원회의 대표자는 관할 선거관리위원회에 등록을 신청하여야 한다. 후원회 회원 등의 납입한도와 후원회의 기부한도에는 제한이 있으며 후원회는 집회·우편·통신·광고와 정치자금 정액 영수증과의 교환 등의 방법으로 금품을 모집하고, 금품을 납입 또는 기부받은 때에는 영수증을 교부하여야 한다. 기부금은 기부하고자 하는 자가 기명으로 선거관리위원회에 직접 기탁하여야 한다. 외국인·언론기관·노동단체 등의 기부는 금지된다. 중앙선거관리위원회는 기탁된 정치자금을 기탁 당시의 국고 보조금 배분율에 따라 배분·지급한다. 적법하게 정치자금을 납입 또는 기부한 자와 납입 또는 기부받은 자에 대하여는 그에 대한 법인세·소득세 및 증여세를 면제한다. 정당의 회계 책임자는 회계장부를 비치하여야 하며 회계장부는 관할 선거관리위원회에 회계보고를 마친 후 3년간 보존하여야 한다.

(2) 아킬레스의 뒤꿈치(치명적 약점)

이산가족 상봉은 남한이 북한과의 협상에 있어서 가장 끊임없이 추진해온 의제 가운데 하나였다. 그러나 남북은 지난 85년 한 차례 이산가족 상봉 행사를 가졌을 뿐, 이후 내내 북한은 남한의 자본주의에 자신들의 통제된 주민들이 노출되는 것을 노골적으로 우려, 이산가족 문제를 회피해왔다. 동국대 강성윤 교수는 “이산가족 상봉문제는 북한으로선 아킬레스의 뒤꿈치처럼 치명적인 약점에 해당한다. 중요한 것은 북한이 이러한 과거에 금기시해 왔던 영역으로 발을 들여놓았다는 점이다”라고 말했다.

cf 고대 Greece의 전설적인 영웅 Achilles의 고사에서 유래된 말로 ‘치명적인 약점’을 가리키는 단어. Achilles는 세계 최고의 서사시인 Homer의 Iliad(일리어드)에 나오는 Greece 영웅으로 어릴 적부터 어머니가 강물에 목욕을 시켜 불사신이 되었으나 강물이 닿지 않은 발뒤꿈치에는 치명적인 급소를 갖고 있었다. B.C. 13세기경 당시 Greece는 지중해 진출의 교두보인 소아시아 공략에 나서 Trojan War를 벌였는데 Achilles는 불사신으로서 전선에서 맹위를 떨쳤다. 그러던 중 Sparta 왕비 Helen을 빼앗음으로써 Trojan War의 원인을 제공했던 Troy 왕자 Paris가 Achilles의 약점에 대한 정보를 얻어내 화살로 그의 발뒤꿈치를 명중시켜 그를 숨지게 했다. 이 전설에 의해서 Achilles tendon(아킬레스 건)은 신체에서 가장 두껍고 튼튼하지만 끊어지면 달리거나 높이 뛸 때 다리를 사용하지 못하는 발뒤꿈치 위에 있는 세로형의 힘줄을 뜻하게 되었으며 이 힘줄이 위치한 발뒤꿈치인 Achilles' heel과 함께 '유일하고 치명적인 약점'이라는 의미로도 널리 통용되고 있다.

3. 실용영어

(1) 나 좀 도와줄래?

M: 거기 옮겨야 할 짐이 꽤 많네.

W: 응, 좀 도와줄래?

M: 어떡하지. 지난 주 허리를 다쳤는데, 의사가 무리하지 말래. 하지만 문이 안 닫히도록 내가 잡고는 있지 뭐.

W: 정말, 고맙기도 하군.

(2) 예약이 다 찼습니다.

M: 다음 달에 4인용으로 방 두 개를 예약하고 싶은데요.

W: 며칠에 오시겠습니까?

M: 7월 17일부터 26일까지요.

W: 죄송합니다. 그 기간에는 예약이 전부 찼습니다. 섬 반대편에 있는 자매호텔을 알아봐 드릴까요?

(3) 이랬다 저랬다 하는

W: 테니스 경기 어떻게 돼 가?

M: 엎치락 뒤치락이야. 처음엔 샘프러스가 앞서더니, 그 다음은 매켄로가 이기고 있어.

W: 재밌겠는데.

M: 응, 정말 막상 막하야. 아무도 결과를 예상할 수 없어.

4. 국제뉴스

지진, 소중한 이란 문화 유산 파괴

참혹한 지진으로 완전히 무너져 내린 역사의 중심 밤시는 세계 최대의 진흙 건축물인 2천년 된 성채를 자랑하는 이란의 불가사의한 문화유산 중 하나였다. 전체가 진흙 벽돌, 점토, 짚, 그리고 야자수 줄기로 지어진 밤시의 고대 유적지는 이슬람 시대 이전까지 거슬러 올라간다. 하지만 유적들 중 대부분은 16세기와 17세기 사파비드 통치 하에 있던 이란의 근대 전성기 때의 것들이다. 당시 밤시는 6평방 킬로미터를 차지했으며 38개의 탑을 가진 성벽으로 둘러싸여 있었고 9천~13,000명 사이의 인구가 거주했다. 바레즈와 가부디 산악지역 사이의 넓은 평원 지대에 위치한 밤시는 조로아스터교 불꽃 신전을 방문하는 순례자들 때문에, 그리고 극동과 유럽을 잇는 그 유명한 실크로드의 상업 무역 중심지로 번영했다. 전체적으로 굽지 않은 벽돌로 지어진 그 5층짜리 성채는 여러 해 동안 자주 보수를 했지만 원형은 그리스도 때인 파르티아 시대까지 거슬러 올라간다. 밤시의 대 모스크 사원은 10세기의 것이다. 메마른 다쉬-에 카비르 지역에 있는 사막의 에메랄드로 알려진 오아시스인 밤시는 많은 야자수 숲과 감귤 농장을 가능하게 만든 풍부한 지하수를 자랑한다.

5. Annie

취업 지원자의 불만

애니에게 :

건물 관리에 23년간 종사해 왔습니다. 3년 전에 저는 변화를 모색할 때라고 결심했습니다. 아직 직업이 있기 때문에 저는 여유를 가지고 회사를 골라가며 지원을 했습니다. 최근 저는 면접을 받으러 오라는 연락을 받았습니다. 인터넷에서 지원서를 다운로드했기 때문에 좀더 멋있게 보이도록 재작성했습니다. 제 꼼꼼함을 보여주고 싶었기 때문입니다. 면접관은 제가 시간을 들여 지원서를 재작성한 점을 인상깊어 하며 면접이 아주 좋았다는 표시를 했습니다. 저는 그 여성 면접관에게 감사의 편지를 이메일로 보냈습니다. 그게 2주일 전의 일입니다. 그 이후 저는 아무런 연락을 받지 못하고 있으며 근무 개시일은 사흘 남았습니다. 시간을 내어 이력서를 작성하고 소정의 지원서를 다운로드하여 기재한 후 옷을 챙겨 입고 면접을 받으러 한 시간을 운전해 오도록 했다면 고용주는 다른 사람을 채용했다는 사실을 알리는 통지 정도는 최소한 할 수 있는 것 아니겠습니까.

실망했다는 표현으로는 정말이지 성이 차지 않습니다. 더 나쁜 것은 네 번이나 면접을 봤는데 다 똑 같았다는 점입니다. 5분만 시간을 내고 우표 한 장이면 되는 것을, 왜 회사들은 제가 채용되지 않았다는 사실을 알려줄 수 없는 것일까요? 하다 못해 이메일이나 전화 한 통화라도 괜찮았을 것입니다. 너무나 실망스러워 차라리 포기하고 싶습니다.

– 시애틀에서 실망한 사람이

시애틀 분에게 :

채용되지 않았다는 사실을 지원자에게 통지할 필요성을 느끼지 못하는 회사가 너무나 많습니다만 당신의 말이 옳습니다. 다른 사람이 채용되었다고 필히 통지해야 합니다. 1차 면접을 한 후 나흘이나 닷새 후에 전화하여 결정이 되었는지 여부를 문의하는 것도 도움이 됩니다. 그렇게 하면 당신의 관심도를 보여주어 항상 당신을 염두에 둘 것입니다. 마음만 끓이지 말고 면접관에게 전화하여 경과를 물어 보세요. 손해 볼 건 없고 어쩌면 유용한 정보를 얻을 수도 있을 테니까요.

6. 독해문제

Nevada주는 1930년대의 대공황 기간 동안 현대 경제 체제로의 전환을 시작했다. 1931년 도박의 합법화와 결혼한 부부가 이혼을 하기 위한 동거 의무기간을 6주로 줄인 후에, Nevada는 결혼, 이혼, 유흥의 중심지가 되었다. 주요 유흥 지역은 Las Vegas, Reno, Laughlin, 그리고 Lake Tahoe이다. Las Vegas는 남부 캘리포니아와 외국으로부터 많은 여행객들을 끌어들이고 또한 비즈니스와 전문 집회를 주최한다. Reno는 샌프란시스코만 지역과 태평양 북서부로부터 많은 행락객들을 끌어들인다. Laughlin은 1980년대 여행 중심지로 떠올랐고, Lake Tahoe는 계속해서 현대풍의 행락지 역할을 해 오고 있다. Colorado강에 Hoover댐의 건설은 남부 Nevada 경제를 실질적으로 도왔고, 여기서의 값싼 수력발전은 생산의 길을 열어주었다. Columbia강 Bonneville댐으로부터의 수력전기와 파이프를 통해 보내지는 천연가스의 수입이 또한 북서지역에서의 산업발달을 가져왔다. 1950년대 연방정부에 의한 Nevada Test Site의 설립은 고용기회를 확대했고, 그 주 내부의 기술산업의 발달을 자극했다. 그 새로운 산업화를 무색하게 하고 본질적으로 현재의 번영을 가져다 준 것은 관광산업의 다양화와 확대라고 할 수 있다.

【정답】

(1) ⓓ

(2) ⓓ

7. 유머영어

(1) 힘 對 영리함

밀크 쉐이크를 주문한 한 소년이 전화를 걸기 위해 잠시 자리를 비워야 했다. 자신의 음료수가 사라질 것을 염려한 소년은 잔 밑에 종이 냅킨을 깔고 그 위에 "세상에서 가장 힘센 사람"이라고 써 놓았다. 그리고 나서 전화를 걸러 갔다. 소년이 자리로 돌아오자 잔이 비어 있었다. 그리고 잔 밑에는 새 냅킨에 이렇게 씌어 있었다. "덕분에 잘 마셨네. 세상에서 가장 빠른 사람이."

(2) 엉뚱한 의사

어떤 남자가 주말에 스키를 타다가 다리를 다쳤다. 주치의는 뜨거운 물에 다리를 담그라고 지시했고 그는 의사의 지시대로 했다. 그런데 다리가 더 심하게 부어오르고 통증은 더 심해지기만 했다. 그의 가정부가 다리를 저는 그를 보더니 "붓기 빼는 데는 더운물보다는 찬물이 훨씬 좋다고 알고 있거든요"라고 말했다. 그는 그녀의 말에 따라 찬물로 바꿨더니 붓기가 금새 가라앉았다. 그는 의사에게 다시 전화를 걸어 불평을 늘어놓았다. "당신이 하라는 대로 뜨거운 물에 다리를 담갔는데 더 심해졌소. 그런데 가정부 말대로 찬물에 담갔더니 훨씬 좋아졌지 뭐요" "정말입니까?" 의사가 대답했다. "거참 이상하군. 우리 집 가정부는 뜨거운 물에 담그라고 했는데…"

제9장

1. Warm-up

(1) 이 회사가 이제껏 가졌던 최고 경영자 중에 가장 훌륭한 최고 경영자로 헌신했던 이 전 회장님을 기념하여 정찬이 있을 것이다.

(2) 1급 살인의 결과를 피할 가능성은 법으로 금지되어 있다. 그래서 법정

에서 유죄판결을 받은 사람은 그들의 범죄에 대한 대가를 치러야 할 것이다.

(3) 이 나라에서는 법에 따라 허가 받은 술집이나 레스토랑에서 술을 사려면 신분증이 필요하다.

(4) 올해 우리 회사의 생산 축소 때문에 우리는 직원들에게 어떤 봉급 인상도 제공하지 않을 것이다.

(5) 마라톤에서는 건강상태가 양호한 사람만 출전할 수 있다. 그렇지 않으면 다칠 염려가 있다.

(6) 장래에 대한 사장의 낙관적인 태도는 종업원 전원의 자신감을 회복시켜 주었다.

(7) Ms. Chung은 이 회사에 10년간 근무하고 있다.

(8) 사회의 어떤 양상을 설명하기 위하여 사회학자는 사회적인 맥락에서 인간 행동에 영향을 주는 법칙을 결정해야 한다.

(9) 경제 운동의 여러 요소들에 있어서 한 가지 어려운 점은 이 요소들이 서로서로 완전히 독립적이지는 않다는 데 있다.

(10) 한 해 중 대부분의 기간 동안 눈 속에 갇혀 있는 그 만 지역은 숲, 강, 호수로 이루어진 황야이다.

2. 시사용어

(1) 배드 뱅크

어제의 정부 대책은 국영 자산관리공사 및 금융기관들이 "배드 뱅크"로 불리는 새로운 기관에 펀드를 조성하도록 요구하고 있다. 자산관리공사는 이같은 프로그램에 최대 5천억원의 자금을 조달할 것으로 보인다고 재경부의 김석동 국장이 말했다. 자산관리공사는 3개월 또는 6개월 동안 적어도 2개 금융기관에서 5천만원 미만의 빚을 지고 있는 채무자들을 상대로, 최장 8년에 걸쳐 신규 대출을 하게 된다.

cf 다중 채무자의 연체 채권을 한 곳으로 모아 처리하는 기구임. 과거 대우 등의 기업 구조조정 과정에서 부실 자산을 모아 기존 기업과 분리하기 위해 설립했던 bad company를 차용한 구상으로서, 금융기관들이 다중 채무자에 대한 채권을 개별적으로 회수하기 어렵기 때문에 bad bank에서 연체 채권을 넘겨 받아 대표로 채권을 추심하는 것이다. 채권자들로서는 채권에서 일부라도 건질 수 있다는 점, 채무자들은 신용불량자에서 벗어나는 데다 장기 분할 상환과 이자 경감 등의 채무 재조정을 받을 수 있다는 점에서 긍정적이다. 소액 자본금은 KAMCO(자산관리공사)와 은행 등 각 금융기관이 갹출하고, 공사는 이와 별도로 채권을 발행해 최대 5천억원의 유동 자금을 조달한다. 2004년 6월 경 설립 예정인 bad bank는 각 금융기관에서 연체 채권을 넘겨받고 공사에서 빌린 돈으로 연체 채권 액면가의 9~15% 정도를 현금으로 해당 금융기관에 지급하는 역할을 수행한다. 채무자는 bad bank로 채무가 이전되면 신용불량자 신분에서 벗어나는 대신, 채무 재조정을 받는 기록이 개인신용평가회사로 넘어가게 된다. Bad bank의 채무 재조정 대상은 연체기간이 3개월 혹은 6개월 등 일정기간 이상 여러 금융기관에 빚을 진 다중채무자로 채무액이 5천만원 미만인 경우이다. 채무의 3%를 선납해야 신청이 가능하며, 나머지 채무는 최장 8년에 걸쳐 연 6% 이자로 분할 상환하게 된다.

(2) 베드 타운

서울시 교육청의 한 관리는 "비록 학급당 학생수가 미국, 일본의 학교들보다는 여전히 상대적으로 더 높은 편이지만 이는(학생수 감소) 환영할 만한 조짐"이라고 말했다. 이 관리는 "서울 근교 신도시로 이주하는 사람들이 늘고 젊은 부부들 사이에 적은 자녀를 갖는 경향으로 인해 이같은 저밀 학급 현상이 나타나고 있다"고 덧붙였다. 서울 남쪽의 베드 타운인 분당시의 한 관리는 "과밀 학급은 학습환경에 있어서 부정적인 영향을 주고 있다,"고 전제하면서 "교사들은 모든 학생들에게 충분한 주의를 기울이기가 힘들며 학생들의 심화 학습도 어렵게 된다"고 덧붙였다.

cf 모도시에 대해 주택지역으로 특화된 satellite town(위성도시)을 일컫는 용어. 밤에 잠자기 위해서만 귀가하는 곳으로 마치 침실 지대와 같다는 뜻에서 bed town이라는 이름이 생겼다. 대도시권의 일부로서 지역내의 소비수요를 충족하는 이상 별다른 기능을 갖지 않고 주로 잠자기 위해서만 귀가하는 주거형 도시로 쾌적한 주거환경 제공 등 여러 순기능에도 불구하고 직장과 주거의 분화로 출퇴근시의 러시아워 현상을 초래, 교통에 큰 부담을 주고 있으며 도시 경영상 재정부족이라는 문제를 야기하기도 한다. 수도권에서는 성남시 · 부천시 등이 이에 해당한다. 1923년 Chicago 대학의 E.W. Burgess는 도시 내부의 지역을 중심업무지대 · 점이지대 · 노동자 주택지대 · 중류 주택지대 · 정기 통근권자 지대 등 5개 지대로 분류하였는데 bed town은 정기 통근권자 지대에 속한다.

3. 실용영어

(1) 소개 1

(자신을 소개할 때)
제 소개를 하겠습니다.
제 소개를 해도 될까요?
(아주 겸손하게) 제 자신을 소개합니다.
제 소개를 하도록 허락해 주시겠습니까?
제 소개를 하도록 허락해 주십시오.
(명함을 보여 주면서)
제 명함 여기 있습니다.
제 명함을 드리죠.
제 명함입니다.
제 명함입니다. 제가 도울 일이 있으시면 언제라도 연락 주십시오.
제 명함입니다. 필요한 게 있으시면 주저말고 연락하십시오.
명함 한 장 주세요.

• 관련 대화

A: 제 소개를 하겠습니다. 저는 데이비스 전자 회사의 폴 피터슨입니다. 만나 뵙게 되어 반갑습니다.
B: 만나서 반갑습니다, 피터슨씨. 저는 이곳 부사장인 실비아 스톤입니다.
A: 제 명함입니다. 혹시 필요한 게 있으시면 알려 주십시오.

(2) 소개 2

(~를 소개하고 싶을 때)
당신을 네오 타이완 전자회사 사장이신 탄뉴 씨께 소개하고 싶습니다.
Mr. Lee와 Mr. Park을 소개해도 될까요? 그들은 서울 테크의 공동 이사입니다.
도쿄 산업의 부사장이신 사이사키 씨를 소개하겠습니다.
여러분, 이스라엘 메카닉의 연구 개발팀 이사인 에드워드 키이브 씨를 소개하겠습니다.

(성함을 알고 싶을 때)
성함이 어떻게 되십니까?

죄송하지만, 성함이 뭐라고 그러셨는지요?
실례지만, 이름의 철자가 어떻게 되십니까?
성함을 알려주시면 영광이겠습니다.

• 관련 대화

A: 벨라폰테 씨를 소개하겠습니다. 파리에 있는 네오 프랑소와의 수출입 업무를 총괄하고 계시는 분입니다.
B: 죄송합니다만, 그 분의 이름이 어떻게 된다고요?
A: 벨라폰테 씨입니다.

(3) 소개 3

(동료와 점심 시간을 이용해 만남을 가지는 주인공. 그곳에서 우연히 만나게 된 사업상 파트너에게 서로를 소개시키는 상황)

이 부장	안녕하세요, 잭슨 이사님. 이렇게 우연히 만나게 되다니, 반갑습니다. 잘 지내세요?
잭슨 이사	저도 반갑습니다. 전 잘 지내고 있어요, 이 부장님은 어떠세요?
이 부장	좋습니다. 아, 여기는 제 친구이자 동료인 토니 김입니다. 베스트 & 에버 컴퓨터 회사에서 일하고 있지요. 토니, 여기는 퓨처 & 미디어社의 스티브 잭슨씨 입니다.
잭슨 이사	안녕하세요, 뵙게 되어 반갑습니다.
김 부장	저도 반갑습니다, 잭슨 이사님.
이 부장	저희와 함께 식사하시지 않으시겠어요?
잭슨 이사	감사합니다만, 먼저 선약이 있습니다. 이곳에서 손님을 만나기로 했거든요. 참, 그리고 나중에 제 사무실로 전화 좀 주시겠습니까? 물어볼 것이 있습니다.
이 부장	그러지요. 이렇게 뵙게 되어 반가웠습니다.
잭슨 이사	저도 그렇습니다. 그리고 김 부장님도 만나 뵙게 되어 정말 반가웠어요. 점심 맛있게 드세요.
김 부장	감사합니다, 이사님도 좋은 시간 되세요.
이 부장	저 쪽 회사랑 계약을 하려는 중이야. 저 분은 마케팅을 담당하고 있는 이사이시고. 이제 곧 최종 판매 계약서가 완결될 거야. 내 생각엔 이 계약으로 판매 면에서 좋은 성과를 올릴

수 있을 거 같아.

김 부장 잘 됐네! 행운을 빌어. 아, 그건 그렇고, 괜찮다면 우리 처가 자네를 저녁식사에 초대하고 싶다는군.

이 부장 그거 정말 고맙네. 기꺼이 가고 말고.

김 부장 좋아! 자, 그럼 이제 주문해 볼까?

• **유용한 표현 1**(갑작스러운 만남을 대할 때 쓸 수 있는 표현)

이렇게 우연히 만나게 되다니 반갑습니다.
여긴 웬일이야?
이거 정말 반갑구나!
널 여기서 만나게 될 줄이야.
정말 반갑다!
이게 누구야?
널 여기서 만나게 되다니 정말 기쁘다.
여긴 웬일이야?

• **유용한 표현 2**(안부를 부탁하는 방법)

당신 가족들에게 안부 전해 주세요.
그에게 안부 전해 주세요.
그에게 안부 전해 주세요.
그녀에게 안부 전해 주세요.
어머님께 안부 전해 주세요.
부모님께 감사 말씀 전해 주세요.
제인에게 안부 전해 주세요.
김씨에게 안부 전해 주세요.

(4) 인사 1

("귀사를 방문하게 되어 반갑습니다."에 대한 표현들)

무라카미 씨, 만나 뵙게 되어 반갑습니다. 귀사를 방문하게 되어 영광입니다.

귀사와 일할 수 있는 기회를 갖게 되어 매우 기쁩니다.

귀사와 거래하게 되어 기쁩니다.

피터슨 씨, 귀사를 방문하게 되어 기쁩니다.

("다시 만나서 반갑습니다."라는 내용의 표현들)

필립스 씨, 오랜만입니다. 다시 뵙게 되어 반갑습니다.

안녕하세요, 터너 씨. 다시 뵙게 되어 반갑습니다. 어떻게 지내세요?

전에 뵌 적이 없었나요? 저는 자동차 판매원인 아놀드 닉슨입니다.

실례합니다만, 저를 기억하시는지요? 작년 부산 국제 무역 박람회에서 만났는데요.

• 관련 대화

A: 캐나다에 오신 걸 환영합니다. 이 곳에 계시는 동안 즐겁게 지내시기 바랍니다.

B: 반갑습니다, 로우 씨. 귀하의 나라를 방문하게 되어 영광입니다.

A: 안녕하세요, 관 씨. 오랜만이군요. 다시 뵙게 되어 반갑습니다.

B: 안녕하세요, 카슨 씨. 어떻게 지내셨어요?

(5) 인사 2

("말씀 많이 들었습니다."의 표현들)

만나 뵙게 되어 반갑습니다, 더브너 씨. 오사카 제휴사에서 귀하에 대한 말씀은 많이 들었습니다.

칸츠 씨, 귀하를 만나 뵙기를 고대했습니다. 프란시스코 씨께 귀하에 대한 말씀을 많이 들었습니다.

처음 뵙겠습니다. 제가 런던에 갔을 때, 이브 씨가 귀하를 찾아 뵈라고 말씀하셨어요.

(비즈니스 후)

이제 그만 가봐야 하겠습니다.

맥더먼드 씨, 죄송하지만 이제 가봐야 하겠습니다.

죄송하지만, 다른 약속이 있어서 그만 가봐야 하겠습니다.

타나카 씨, 방문해 주셔서 감사합니다.

만나주셔서 감사합니다, 라세터 씨. 귀하의 친절에 정말 감사합니다.

감사합니다. 정말 유익한 시간이었습니다.

• 관련 대화

A: 처음 뵙겠습니다. 저는 피터 더브너라고 합니다. 만나 뵙게 되어 반갑

습니다.

B: 반갑습니다, 더브너 씨. 캣멀 씨가 귀하에 대해 자주 말씀하셨습니다.

A: 죄송하지만, 이제 가야 할 것 같습니다.

B: 좀 더 계시면 안되나요?

4. 국내뉴스

양심적 병역거부 문제

대법원은 국방의 의무가 양심의 자유보다는 우선이라며 양심적 병역 거부자에 징역 1년 6월을 선고한 하급심의 원심을 확정했다. 12명의 대법관 가운데 오직 한 명만이 "종교적 양심의 자유와 국방의 의무가 충돌할 때에는 개인 양심의 자유를 더 존중해야 한다"는 반대 의견을 냈다. 사상, 양심, 종교의 자유를 허용하면서도 헌법은 법 규정 하에서 모든 국민이 국방의 의무를 이행할 것을 요구하고 있다. 그러나 헌법은 이 중 두 가치가 충돌할 경우 어느 것이 우선해야 하는지에 대해서는 언급하지 않고 있다.

목요일 내려진 대법원의 확정 판결은 징벌적이지 않는 성격의 대체복무 제도를 마련해야 한다는 1998년 유엔인권위 결의안 권고에 반하는 것이었다. 대법원의 판결은 양심적 병역거부자는 물론 국가가 양심적 병역거부를 인정할 것을 요구해 온 수 많은 시민단체에게도 실망스런 일이었다. 대법원이 양심적 병역거부에 유죄를 판결한 것은 이번이 처음은 아니다. 1969년과 1992년 종교적 이유로 입영을 거부한 자에 대해 "유죄" 판결이 내려졌다. 그러나 지난 5월 서울지법이 종교적 신념에 따라 군복무를 거부한 3명의 젊은이에게 무죄를 선고함에 따라 이번에는 과거 판결이 뒤집어질지 모른다는 기대감이 있었다. 이론상 이 사안을 심리하고 있는 헌법재판소가 대법원의 판결을 뒤집을 가능성도 있기는 하다. 그러나 법률 전문가들은 헌재 재판관 다수가 대법원의 의견에 동조하는 것이 확실하기 때문에 그럴 가능성은 거의 없다고 말하고 있다. 또한 대법원이 양심적 병역거부와 관련된 재판을 또다시 심의하려면 몇 년은 더 지나야 할 것이다. 그렇다고 해서 이제 양심적 병역거부 문제를 고려할 여지가 없다는 말은 아니다. 그와는 반대로 이번 대법원의 판결은 정부와 정치권을 상대로 대체복무제를 합법화하려는 시민단체의 병역법 개정 압력을 더욱 거세게 만들 것이 분명하다. 실제로 반대 의견을 제시한 대법관을 포함하여 12명 중 6명의 대법관은 대체복무제 도입 필요성을 보충 의견으로 제시했다.

상당히 많은 수의 젊은이들이 다양한 이유로 군복무를 면제받고 있는 현실을 감안할 때 양심적 병역거부자들이 신체적으로나 정신적으로 건강하다고 판정받더라도 이들을 현역 근무에서 제외시키는 것이 그렇게 어려운 일은 아닐 것이다. 이들 중에는 일종의 대체근무 형태로 민간 기업에서 일정기간 복무하는 공학도들도 포함되어 있다.

매년 '여호와의 증인' 신도를 포함해 약 600여명의 젊은이들이 군대 대신에 교도소를 선택하고 있다고 한다. 이들을 교도소로 보내는 것은 유엔 인권위가 지적한 바와 같이 이들로부터 "사상, 양심, 종교 자유의 적법한 행사권"을 빼앗는 일이다. 정부와 정치권은 이들이 처한 어려움에 관심을 갖고 서둘러 병역법을 개정하여 이들에게 대체복무제를 허용하는 것이 현명할 것이다.

5. Annie

애인 고르기

애니에게 :

스물 한살의 제 딸 "미스티"는 사람을 사귀는 데 서툽니다. 그 애가 혹하는 남자들이라고는 꿈도, 의욕도, 직장도, 자동차도, 가족도 없는 "덜 떨어진" 녀석들뿐입니다. 넘치는 사랑과 관심 속에서 자란 미스티가 어떻게 해서 이런 부류들에게 끌리는지 도저히 이해할 수 없습니다. 그 애가 앞날이 짱짱한 남자와는 어울리지 않는다고 생각할 이유가 없습니다.

미스티가 가장 최근에 사귄 사람은 이 동네에 친척도 없이 커피숍에서 웨이터로 있는 25세의 남자입니다. 자동차도 없고 아마 친구 집에 얹혀 사는 것 같습니다. 다시 말하자면 그는 노숙자나 별반 다름없는 신세입니다. 약혼을 했다는 말은 들은 적도 없는데 미스티는 그 녀석을 자기 약혼자라고 말하기 시작했습니다. 더 나쁜 것은 그 애 언니와 제가 그 녀석에 대해 직감적으로 두려움을 느낀다는 것입니다. 미스티가 과거에 사귀던 남자친구들 중에는 이런 느낌이 없었는데 물론 우리의 두려움을 확인할 증거는 없지만 그가 선량한 사람은 아닌 것 같습니다. 미스티에게 저희의 느낌을 이야기해 보았지만 그 망나니가 자기를 여왕처럼 모신다는 외곬수 대답만 들었습니다. 이제 그는 우리 애 집에 들어와 살게 해 달라고 늘어붙고 있습니다.

저는 약혼이나 결혼을 하기 전에 신중히 생각하고 또 그를 집에 들여놓기 전에 그와 좀 더 시간을 두고 사귀어 보라고 미스티에게 부탁했습니다. 다른 좋은 방법이 있을까요? 걱정이 되어 죽을 지경입니다.

—눈물 고인 엄마가

엄마에게:

현재 따님이 사귀는 애인이 망나니일 것이라는 당신의 직감을 믿습니다만, 그것만으로는 미스티가 그와의 관계를 끝내기에는 부족할 것입니다. 자신감 있는 젊은 여성으로 양육되었겠지만, 그럼에도 불구하고 건전한 자긍심이 부족합니다. 어머니가 자신을 사랑할 뿐만 아니라 신뢰한다는 생각을 미스티에게 불어 넣어야 합니다. 당신의 걱정이 정당할지 모르지만 자신이 선택한 연인을 비난하면 미스티는 바른 결정을 내리지 못하고 당신에게서 등을 돌릴 것입니다. 이 문제에 대해 미스티가 말을 들을 만한 누군가가 없습니까? 아버지는 어떤가요? 여자친구나 직장 사장 또는 교회 목사님은요? 그러는 동시에 그 망나니에 대해서도 알아 보세요. 도움이 될 수도 있습니다.

6. 독해문제(TEPS)

알코올 중독에 관한 많은 오해가 있다. 예를 들어 많은 사람들이 알코올 중독자들은 부주의하고 쾌락을 추구하는 사람들이라고 생각한다. 사실은 알코올 중독자들도 대개가 술을 마시는 것에 대해 죄의식을 느끼고 주변 사람들을 매우 의식한다. 흔히들 잘못 생각하고 있는 것 중의 또 다른 하나는 알코올 중독자들이 늘 술에 취해 있다는 것이다. 사실 알코올 중독자들은 세 부류로 나뉘어진다. 예를 들어 일시적인 중독자의 경우는 이따금씩만 술을 마신다. 습관적으로 과음을 하는 사람들은 가끔씩만 술을 마시지만, 그 횟수가 일시적인 중독자보다 훨씬 더 잦다. 상용자는 계속 술을 마셔야 뭔가를 할 수 있는 사람이다. 술에 대한 의존으로부터 벗어나기 위해 의료지원이 필요한 사람은 바로 이 상용자이다.

【정답】 ⓑ ⇒ 이 문제에서는 처음부터 끝까지 알코올 중독에 대한 오해와 잘못 알려진 사실을 들고 그 진실을 밝히고 있다.

7. 유머영어

(1) 수면제

톰은 아침에 늦잠 자는 버릇이 있어서 항상 지각을 했다. 그의 상사는 화가 나서, 톰이 무언가 조치를 취하지 않으면 해고해 버리겠다고 협박했다. 결국 톰은 의사를 찾아갔고 의사는 그에게 알약 한 알을 주면서 잠자리에 들기 전에 복용하라고 했다. 톰은 숙면을 취했고 실제로 아침에 알람시

계와 함께 잠에서 깨어났다. 그는 여유있게 아침식사를 하고 신나게 차를 몰고 직장으로 갔다. "부장님, 약이 정말 효과가 있던데요!" 그가 말했다. 부장 왈, "그거 잘됐군, 그런데 자네 어제는 어디 갔었나?"

(2) 죽은 자는 말이 없다.

"자, 신사 숙녀 여러분," 사기꾼 약장수가 장터에서 외쳤다. "제가 지금까지 이 굉장한 만병통치약을 백만 병이 넘게 팔았지만 이 약에 대한 불평은 한마디도 못 들었습니다. 이 사실로 보아 무엇을 알 수 있겠습니까?" "죽은 자는 말이 없다는 사실을 알 수 있죠," 구경꾼 중 한 사람이 외쳤다.

제10장

1. Warm-up

(1) 정당한 증명카드를 소지한 경우에는 근무 외 시간에도 전산실에 출입할 수 있게 됩니다.

(2) 제3세계 국가들의 발전에 대한 최근 보고서는 이들 국가들에게 제공되어지는 식량 원조와 관련된 중요한 문제들을 제기하였다.

(3) 우리 회사의 자동차부는 훌륭한 협동성과 엄격한 경영으로 매우 성공적이다.

(4) 파괴되어지기로 올해 초에 계획이 잡힌 이후 이 건물은 사람들이 거주하지 않게 되었다.

(5) 우리는 현재 진행되고 있는 경제 개혁이 21세기에도 꾸준히 계속되어야 한다고 믿고 있다.

(6) 월급 인상은 공식적인 지침에 따라 계산되었다.

(7) 그는 나에게 비행기표를 당장 사지 않으면 늦을 것이라고 충고해 주었다.

(8) 그 매니저는 한 컨설턴트의 조언에 따라 가스 유출이 있는 지역에 100명의 일꾼을 파견했다.

(9) 새 프로그램과 전시회로써 박물관의 그 교육담당 직원들은 우리에게 이 지역의 과학기술 역사를 발견하도록 권하였다.

(10) 작업장에서의 안전은 계속해서 산업의 주요한 문제이다, 그리고 오늘날 대부분의 기업들은 위험 방지와 안전 장비에 큰 중요성을 둔다.

2. 시사용어

(1) 인저리 타임

지난해 우승팀 바이에른 뮌헨은 수요일 밤 독일컵 8강전에서 2부리그 알레마니아 아헨에 2대 1로 져 탈락했다. 81분 경 에릭 마이어는 경기를 앞서가는 헤딩골을 뽑아냈다. 이에 앞서 전반 33분 알레마니아 아헨의 스테판 블랑크가 올리버 칸을 뚫고 선취골을 뽑아 냈으나 뮌헨의 미하일 발락이 전반전 인저리 타임에 동점골을 만들었다.

cf 축구경기에서 전 · 후반 45분의 정규시간 이후 주심이 재량에 따라 추가로 허용하는 시간임. loss time, lost time, extra time 등 여러 용어로 불리지만, 현재는 injury time을 사용하고 있다. 경기 도중 선수가 부상을 당하거나 선수 교체로 인해 경기가 지연될 경우, 기타 반칙 · corner kick · free kick · penalty kick 등 각종 지연 행위로 정상적인 플레이를 하지 못할 경우, 주심이 이 지연 시간을 추정해 재량에 따라 임의로 시간을 허용한다. 즉 경기 도중에 발생한 시간 낭비를 보충하기 위해 인정되는 시간으로, 이를 위해 주심은 경기 진행을 위한 시계 외에 별도의 시계를 차고 나와 지연 시간을 측정한다. 과거에는 주심이 경기 종료를 알리는 호루라기를 불고 나서야 injury time이 얼마였는지를 알 수 있었으나 1998년 제16회 월드컵축구대회(France) 때부터 후반전이 끝나는 시점에 대기심이 선수 교체판에 injury time을 표시하도록 하고 있다. 보통 2~4분 정도가 주어지지만, 1990년 Italy에서 열린 제14회 월드컵축구대회(Italy) 당시 Italy와 Argentina의 4강전에서는 연장전 전반에 정규시간 15분의 반이 넘는 8분의 injury time이 나온 적도 있다.

(2) 무노동 무임금 원칙

한편 한국경영자총협회(경총)는 어제 대기업 노사문제 간부회의에서 전국민주노동조합총연맹(민주노총)에 의해 오는 6월 12일 예정된 총파업을 반대하기로 결의하였다. 경총은 이를 불법 파업으로 규탄하면서 대체인력 활용은 물론 무노동무임금 원칙 고수, 노조 지도부에 대한 민 · 형사상 소송제기 그리고 공장 폐쇄 등을 포함, 모든 가능한 수단을 동원하여 이에 맞설 것을 대기업들에 촉구하였다. 또한 불법 파업의 대처에 있어서 사측에 도움을 줄 수 있는 이들 방안과 기타 조치들에 대한 가이드라인을 제시하였다.

cf 근로를 하지 않는 파업기간 중의 근로자 및 노조 전임자에 대해서는 임금을 지불하지 않는다는 원칙. 재계는 파업기간중 임금 지불에 따른 파업 장기화를 내세워 이를 지지하는 반면 노동계는 노동쟁의 기금이 적립되지 않은 데다가 사회보장제도마저 미약한 상태에서 no-work-no-pay는 노동운동의 탄압이라며 이를 반대하고 있다. 이 때문에 실제로는 같은 임금을 지불하더라도 생산장려금, 상여금 등의 명목으로 지불함으로써 이 원칙이 지켜지고 있는 실정이다. 1997년 3월 개정된 노동법에는 no-work-no-pay principle를 명확히 규정하고 있으나 "노조전임자에게 임금지급을 금지하며 이를 어기는 사용자는 처벌한다"는 조항은 노조 재정사정 등을 감안하여 5년간의 유예기간을 두어 시행시기가 2002년으로 미뤄진 바 있다. 그러나 최근 들어 노동계가 근로자 생존권을 들어 노조전임자 임금지급에 대한 처벌조항 폐지를 요구하고 있어 no-work-no-pay원칙을 시행에 상당한 진통이 예상된다. 한편 우리나라 대법원 판례에서는 no-work-no-pay원칙을 인정하고 있으며 일부 외국의 경우 이 원칙이 철저히 지켜져 파업기간중의 임금은 노조에 적립된 파업기금으로 지급되고 있는 상태이다.

3. 실용영어

(1) 호텔 1('안내소에서 호텔 안내'를 받고 호텔에 도착한 후 '프론트 데스크(front desk)'에서 일어날 수 있는 상황)

("호텔 좀 소개해 주세요."와 관련된 내용)
괜찮은 호텔을 소개해 주실래요?
시내 근처에 숙박료가 적당한 호텔을 부탁드려도 될까요?
(안내소 직원) 호텔 객실예약을 하셨나요?
호텔 예약을 마치셨나요?
원하시는 가격처럼 적당한 호텔을 안내해 드리지요.
(호텔 front desk에서 일어날 수 있는 상황)
오늘 밤에 묵을 빈 방 있어요?
오늘 밤에 빈 방 있나요?
3일간 숙박하고 싶습니다.
전망 좋은 일인용 방을 원합니다.
조용한 방 있나요?
바다가 보이는 방 있나요?
방을 하나 예약하고 싶습니다.

* **관련 대화**

A: (front desk 직원) 안녕하세요, 뭘 도와 드릴까요?
B: 네, 3일간 숙박할 방을 원합니다.
A: 아, 그러세요. 원하시는 전망이라도 있으신가요?
B: 바다가 보이는 방이면 좋겠어요.

(2) 호텔 2

(호텔에서 front desk 직원과 나눌 수 있는 대화)
예약하셨나요?
전 오이시토 사사키입니다. 오늘 밤 예약을 했는데요.
객실료 리스트를 좀 볼 수 있을까요?
아침 식사가 포함된 객실료입니까?
객실료엔 세금과 모든 봉사료가 포함되어 있지요.
이틀 정도 더 머물고 싶습니다.
미안하지만, 하루 먼저 체크 아웃하고 싶은데요.
다른 방으로 바꿔 주실 수 있나요? 엘리베이터가 너무 시끄러워요.
방 열쇠 여기 있습니다. 종업원을 따라 가십시오.
입실할 수 있나요?

* **관련 대화**

A: 뭘 도와 드릴까요?
B: 객실료는 얼마입니까?
A: 객실료는 65달러입니다. 종업원을 따라가 주세요.
B: 객실료엔 아침 식사비가 포함되어 있나요?
A: 죄송하지만, 아침 식사는 별도로 계산하셔야 합니다.
B: 아, 그렇군요. 고맙습니다.

* **심화 학습**

아침식사는 몇 시부터 할 수 있나요?
식당은 어느쪽인가요?
제 방으로 아침을 갖다 주세요.
식당은 몇 시에 닫나요?
화장실 물이 잘 빠지지 않아요.

여보세요, 뜨거운 물이 안 나와서 샤워를 할 수 없어요.
문이 안에서 잠겼어요.
객실료는 얼마인가요?
일박에 150달러입니다. 객실료엔 유럽식 아침 식사가 포함되어 있습니다.

(3) 호텔 3 (체크인)

(잦은 해외 출장! 투숙하는 동안 불편함이 없도록 기본적인 대화와 함께, 체크인할 때 알아두어야 할 표현들)

직원 안녕하세요. 글로리아 호텔에 오신 걸 환영합니다. 예약하셨습니까?
이 부장 네, 이름은 스캇 에이치 리입니다. 킹사이즈 침대 방으로 12일간 예약했습니다.
직원 잠시만 기다려 주시겠어요? 예, 여기 있습니다. 금연실로 예약하셨지요?
이 부장 맞아요. 경치가 좋은 방이면 좋겠습니다.
직원 물론입니다. 15층에 아주 전망 좋은 방이 있습니다.
이 부장 좋아요!
직원 숙박비는 어떻게 지불하시겠습니까?
이 부장 신용카드로 지불할게요.
직원 알겠습니다. 여기 숙박계 좀 써주시겠어요?
이 부장 그러지요. 정오까지 체크 아웃해야 되나요?
직원 그렇습니다. 시간을 연장하고 싶으시면 하루 전에 미리 말씀해 주세요.
이 부장 고마와요.
직원 열쇠는 여기 있습니다. 벨 보이가 방까지 안내해 드릴 겁니다.
이 부장 아, 그리고 매일 아침 5시 30분에 모닝콜 좀 부탁합시다.
직원 알겠습니다. 그밖에 필요하신 게 있으시면 언제든지 저희를 불러주십시오.

* **유용한 표현**(호텔 서비스를 이용하지 못해 당황해서야 국제적인 비즈니스맨이라고 할 수 없을 것임)

5시 30분에 깨워주세요.
귀중품을 맡길 수 있을까요?
7시에 모닝콜 부탁해요.
룸서비스를 주문하고 싶은데요.
사람 좀 올려보내 주시겠어요?
세탁물을 맡길 수 있나요?
방에 열쇠를 두고 나왔어요.
숙박을 연장하고 싶은데요.
제게 메시지 온 거 있나요?
방 좀 바꿀 수 있을까요?
여행자 수표 받아요?
택시 좀 불러주시겠어요?

(4) 호텔 4

(호텔 내에서 발생할 수 있는 실제 상황에 대한 추가적인 표현들)
여보세요, 외부 전화를 하고 싶습니다. (외부 전화란 일반적으로 우리가 9번을 누르고 쓰는 시내전화를 의미합니다. 시외전화는 long distance call이라고 합니다.)
짐 나르시는 분을 좀 보내 주세요.
택시를 불러 주시겠어요?
호텔 금고에 귀중품을 맡기고 싶습니다.

• 관련 대화

A: 프론트입니다.
B: 여기 301호인데요, 짐을 운반해 주실 분을 보내 주세요.
A: 알겠습니다. 다른 일은 없으신가요?
B: 있습니다. 택시를 한 대 불러 주세요.
A: 알겠습니다. 택시는 약 15분 후에 도착합니다.
B: 감사합니다.

(5) 호텔 5

(호텔과 관련된 대화의 총정리)
A: 빈 방 있어요?

B: 네, 스위트 룸이 2개 있습니다. (suite는 우리나라의 콘도 미니엄 스타일로 방과 거실이 붙어 있는 시설이죠.)

A: 객실료는 얼마인가요?

B: 일박에 150달러입니다. 객실료엔 유럽식(대륙식) 아침 식사가 포함되어 있습니다.

A: 세금과 모든 봉사료도 포함되어 있나요?

B: 네, 그렇습니다.

A: room service도 되나요?

B: 물론이죠.

A: 발코니가 붙어있는 스위트 룸으로 주세요.

B: 죄송하지만, 그런 방은 모두 예약이 되어 있습니다.

A: 그럼 바다가 보이는 방 있어요?

B: 죄송하지만 벌써 다 나갔어요.

A: 좋아요. 남아 있는 방으로 아무거나 주세요.

B: 알겠습니다. 열쇠 받으시고, 종업원을 따라 가세요. (bellman을 redcap이라고도 하지요.)

A: 참, 내일 아침 9시 30분에 제 가방을 운반해 줄 사람을 보내 주세요.

B: 물론이죠.

A: 그리고 아침 7시에 모닝콜 부탁드릴게요.

B: 알겠습니다.

A: 고맙습니다.

4. 국내뉴스

교원 연령 제한 철폐는 젊은이들의 실직을 더욱 가중시킬 것이다.

요즈음에 점점 악화되는 사업환경을 극복하기 위한 회사의 가혹한 구조조정 때문에 실직당한 40대 초반의 사람들을 보는 것은 드문 일이 아니다. 또한 30살이 넘은 나이로 개인회사에 들어가는 것은 거의 불가능하다. 민간분야의 취직이 그렇게 어려운 추세임에도 불구하고, 정부는 고용인의 수를 늘리고 있는데, 이는 정부가 구조조정을 하겠다는 처음의 약속을 위반하는 것이다. 공공분야에서 인력의 확대는 납세자들의 재정적인 부담을 가중시키는 것이다. 공무원들이 법적인 정년까지 자신들의 직업 유지를 보장받으면서, 불안한 노동시장에서 가장 큰 피해를 당하는 젊은이들은 정부부서에 일자리를 잡으려고 노력하고 있는 중이다. 정부가 공공근로자들의 채용 규제를 더욱 완화시키는 것은 민간분야에서 인력운용을 더욱 줄이는 것과 정반대이다.

또다른 예는 전국의 초중등학교 교원 시험을 볼 자격이 있는 사람들의 연령 제한을 철폐한다는 교육부의 계획이다. 현재 40세 이상의 교사 지망생들은 시험을 보지 못하게 되어 있다. 그러나 전문지식이나 기능을 필요로 하는 공석인 자리에는 예외로 되어 있다. 교육부는 인권위원회가 연령 제한에 반대한 뒤에, 2006년부터 교원 모집에서 연령 제한을 철폐할 것을 결정하였다. 인권위원회는 연령 제한은 평등권의 보장 원칙을 침해하는 것이라고 기술하였다. 연령 제한을 없애는 것이 그럴듯하게 보이지만, 이는 민간 분야는 물론이고 정부 쪽에서도 거센 반대의 회오리를 몰고 올 것으로 예상된다. 교사들은 공무원과 같은 지위를 가지고 있으므로 무엇보다 다른 국가 부처들과 공기업들도 같은 요구의 압력을 받게 될 것이다. 두 번째로 이번 조치는 실업률이 전국 평균의 두 배인 8% 대에 있는 젊은이들의 취업기회를 더욱 악화시킬 것이다. 세 번째로 나이든 교사를 채용하게 되면 인터넷에 능통한 학생들의 요구를 이들이 맞춰주지 못하므로 초・중등 학교 교육제도의 발전에 저해를 가져올 것으로 우려된다. 이런 관점에서 교육부는 교원 채용시험에서 연령 제한을 없애려는 계획을 재고해야만 할 것이다.

5. Abby

에비 여사에게:

제 편지가 다른 사람들에게 도움이 되었으면 좋겠군요. 저는 내년이면 나이가 50세인데, 최근에 22층 짜리 빌딩에서 일하기 시작했습니다. 저는 운동할 생각을 가져 본 적이 없었습니다. 그런데 최근에 사무실 빌딩 계단을 이용하여 규칙적인 운동을 해야겠다는 생각을 했습니다. 그리고 그것은 매우 효과가 있었어요. 저는 30분 일찍 출근을 해서 화장실에서 반바지와 티 셔츠로 갈아입습니다. 그리고 계단으로 가서 22층을 걸어 올라갑니다. 그런 다음 화물 엘리베이터를 타고 아래로 내려와서 다시 한번 더 올라갑니다. 시간과 힘이 허락하면 세 번씩 할 때도 있습니다. 계단을 오르면 정말 심장 고동이 빨라집니다. 그래서 당신의 독자들도 이렇게 하는 것을 좋아할 것이라는 생각이 들었습니다. 돈도 들지 않고 편리하며 퇴근 후에 클럽에 가지 않아도 되니 시간이 허비되지도 않습니다.

저는 땀이 많이 나는 체질이 아니기 때문에 젖은 수건으로 몸을 닦아낸

후, 마른 수건으로 다시 닦고 속옷을 갈아입고, 옷을 입은 후에 사무실로 가지요. 하루를 이렇게 시작하면 상쾌하고 활기찹니다. 그래서 누구에게나 권하고 싶어요. 매일매일의 도전은 제가 그 전날보다 더 빨리 할 수 있느냐 하는 것이며 맨 위층에 도달하면 진정한 성취감이 있습니다. 동네를 몇 바퀴 도는 것과는 기분이 정말 다르답니다.
−토론토에서 건강하고 행복한 사람이

F AND H 분에게:

체력 단련을 위해 그렇게 열심이시니 정말 대단하시군요. 그러나 당신과 같은 방법은 심장 상태가 어떤지 잘 모르는 사람들에게 위험할 수 있습니다. 시도해보겠다고 결심하는 분들은 먼저 압박 테스트를 받는 것에 대해 주치의와 상담해야 합니다. 그리고 강도 높은 운동을 하는 대부분의 사람들은 (당신이 생각하는 것 이상으로) 땀을 많이 흘리는 경향이 있으며 그런 사람들은 종이 물수건으로 닦아내는 것만으로는 충분치 않을 것입니다. 당신의 동료들을 배려해서, 혹시라도 누군가에게 불쾌감을 줄 수도 있으니, 그런 운동은 일을 시작하는 아침보다 일을 마친 후에 하는 것이 어떨까요. (어휴!)

6. 독해문제 (TEPS)

시속 100마일로 자동차를 모는 것이 어떤 느낌인지 상상해 보라. 시속 55마일 이상으로 가속기를 밟으면 당신은 긴장이 고조되어 운전대를 잡는 힘이 팽팽해짐을 느낄 수 있다. 잠시 후, 보통 때의 시속 55마일로 돌아가면 당신은 이상한 현상을 감지하게 된다. 시속 55마일의 속도가 훨씬 더 느리게-거의 시속 40마일의 느린 속도처럼 느껴지는 것이다. 이런 심리적 원리를 보다 빠른 독서 속도를 개발하는 데에 이용하라. 여러분이 보통 분당 250 단어의 속도로 글을 읽고 있다면 얼마동안 분당 350 단어의 속도로 글을 읽는 연습을 하라. 그러면 분당 300단어의 속도에서도 더 편한 기분을 느끼게 될 것이다. 이런 방법이 최대한의 발전을 보장해 준다.

【정답】 ⓓ ⇒ 자동차 주행의 예를 비유로 들어 읽기의 속도를 늘리는 법을 제시하는 글이다.

7. 유머영어

(1) 편리한 계산

자기 딸과 사귀고 있는 젊은이에게 아버지가 수입을 물어 보았다. "연봉이 어느 정도 되나?"하고 아버지가 물었다. "5만 달러입니다." 젊은이가 대답했다. "썩 나쁘지는 않군. 우리 딸애의 4만 달러 연봉을 합치면 상당한 액수겠는데." "아, 이 5만 달러에 이미 포함시켰습니다!"

(2) 냉정한 사장

한 직원이 사장에게 가서 말했다. "월급 좀 올려 주셔야겠어요. 저의 어머니가 많이 편찮으세요. 애들을 학교에 계속 보내기 위해서는 바닥까지 긁어모아야 하구요. 차를 수리할 돈도 없습니다. 집은 낡아서 무너질 판국이구요. 퇴근하고 집에 돌아가면 집안 일이 한 다스나 쌓여 있어요." 사장이 대답했다. "자넨 해고야. 업무 이외의 활동이 너무 많아."

제11장

1. Warm-up

(1) 더욱 자세한 정보가 필요하시면 이 서식을 작성하여 뉴욕주 뉴욕시 사서함 105호 ARCO 인터내셔널로 보내주십시오.
(2) 그들은 내년에 뉴욕시에 지점을 개설하고자 한다.
(3) 이 고속도로 지도에는 주요 고속도로와 대도시만 나와 있다.
(4) 조만간 모든 사람들이 성공할 기회를 얻게 될 것이다.
(5) 세계의 가장 심각한 문제들 중 일부는 지도자들이 서로서로 대화를 하기만 하면 해결될 수 있다.
(6) 그 회사는 매년 공원에서 환상적인 야유회를 가진다.
(7) 여행을 갈 때에는 현금보다 여행자수표를 갖고 있는 편이 안전하다.
(8) 3월의 훈련은 1월에 했던 것보다 더 어렵고 기간도 길었다.
(9) Mr. Lee는 승진할 것이라고 너무 자신을 갖고 있었다.
(10) 러시아워에 시가지에 차를 타고 갔더니 고속도로는 통근차로 혼잡했다.

2. 시사용어

(1) 보스정치

하지만 좀 더 포괄적인 시각에서, 현재의 혼란은 한국 민주주의의 진화 단계에 있어서 중요한 과도기로도 볼 수 있다. 이 나라에서 민주적 제도는 매우 충실한 지역 지지 기반을 가진 몇몇 카리스마적인 파벌의 우두머리에 의해서 지배된 수 십년간의 "보스 정치"에서 이제 막 벗어났다. 국민은 시대 변화의 요구를 충족시키는 새로운 지도력을 찾고 있는 중인데, 아직 나타나지 않은 상태이다.

cf 사회집단(A social group) 내부에서 은연중 영향력을 지닌 비공식 지도자인 boss가 실권을 장악하는 정치임. 좁은 의미에서는 미국 정치에서 정당(political party)의 지방 조직을 장악하는 실력자가 공식적인 책임을 지지 않으면서 정치적 영향력을 발휘하는 것을 말한다. 미국에서 boss가 대두된 것은 'Jackson Democracy' 아래에서 선거권과 정당의 지방 조직이 확대되면서부터이다. Boss는 선거에서 표를 기업가적 수단으로써 얻는다. 그에 대한 보수는 공적인 명예가 아니고 사사로운 이익의 형태를 취하는 것이 보통이다. Boss는 전국적인 영향력을 가진 자도 더러 있지만, 대개 지방정치에서 영향력을 발휘한다. 특히 대도시에서는 새로 이민 온 사람에 대한 지방 조직의 침투력을 기반으로 하여 boss가 시정을 좌우하며 그것이 시정을 부패시키는 경우도 있다.

(2) 베를린 국제영화제

한국의 김기덕 감독이 2월 14일 제 54회 베를린 국제영화제에서 10대 소녀의 성 매춘과 형사 아버지의 복수와 용서를 다룬 그의 영화 "사마리아"로 감독상을 수상했다. 이번 수상은 한국 감독으로서 베를린 영화제에서 감독상을 받기는 처음이다. 한국에서 가장 논쟁거리가 되고 있는 영화제작자 중 한 명인 김감독은 지난 2002년에도 "나쁜 남자"로 감독상 후보에 오른 바 있다.

cf 1951년 독일 통일을 기원하는 차원에서 시작된 Berlin에서 매년 개최되는 국제 영화제임. Italy의 Venice · France Cannes · Russia Moscow와 더불어 국제영화제작자연합에서 공인한 A급 영화제의 하나로, 매년 2월 중순경 10일간 개최된다. 독일의 국영 베를린 영화사가 주관하며, 매년 약간씩 차이가 있기는 하지만 보통 개막작을 시작으로 전세계에서 초청된 400여 편의 장단편 영화가 포츠담광장 일대의 10여개 상영관에서 상영된다. 주요 시상 부문은 최우수작품상인 금곰상, 감독상인 은곰상, 심사위원 대상, 남녀 연기상, 예술공헌상, 최우수 유럽영화상 등이 있으며, 10명의 심사위원단이 공식 경쟁부문 출품작 가운데서 부문별로 선정해 시상한다. 한국에서는 1958년 제8회 영화제 때 동아영화사의 '시집가는 날'을 처음으로 출품한 이래 거의 매년 극영화와 문화영화를 출품하고 있으며 2003년 제 54회 대회에서 김기덕 감독이 영화 '사마리아'로 감독상인 은곰상을 수상한 바 있다.

3. 실용영어

(1) 약속하기 1

("언제 뵐 수 있나요?"에 적당한 표현)
언제 방문할까요?
편안한 시간을 알려 주세요.
언제 저를 만나실 수 있으세요?
편리하신 시간이 언제인가요?
야마구치 양, 이 문제에 대하여 만나서 토론하고 싶습니다.
오늘 오후 편한 시간에 전화 주시겠어요?
베이징 계획안에 대해 토론할 시간을 좀 만들어 주시겠습니까?
시간 나면, 연락 주세요.
내일 아침 일찍 뵈러 가도 되요?

• 관련 대화

A: 라모스 씨, 편하신 시간이 언제인지 알려 주실래요?
B: 이번 주 금요일 오후 어때요?
A: 야마구치 양, 이 건에 대해서 토론할 시간을 좀 마련해 주실래요?
B: 물론이죠, 내일 아무때나 제 사무실로 오세요.

(2) 약속하기 2

("~ 용건으로 --- 하고 싶습니다."에 적당한 표현)
오늘 저녁에 로저스 씨와 시간 약속을 정하고 싶습니다.
해외 마케팅 전략에 관해서 토론할까요?
힐 양, 당신과 중요한 토론을 하고 싶소.
레인 씨, 오늘 밤 저희가 당신을 뵐 수 있을까요?

엘포드 씨가 오늘 아침에 전화하셔서 당신과 이야기하고 싶대요.
윌킨스 양이 새 프로젝트에 대해 토의하고 싶다고 했다고 탄 씨에게 말 좀 전해주시겠어요?
저를 만나고 싶으신 이유가 뭔가요?
왜 저를 만나고 싶으신가요?
스티브가 왜 저를 만나보고 싶어하는지 한번 여쭤 보실래요?

*** 관련 대화**

A: 팬 양, 오늘 저녁에 로저스 씨와 시간 약속을 하고 싶어요.
B: 알겠습니다. 몇 시가 좋으세요?
A: 톰, 저를 보자는 용건이 뭐예요?
B: 새로운 프로젝트에 대해서 의논 드리고 싶습니다.

(3) 약속하기 3

(상대방과 약속날짜 정하기)
내일은 어떠세요? (내일 괜찮으세요?)
12월 20일 괜찮으십니까?
이번 주 금요일에 뵐 수 있을까요?
11월 3일 몇 시가 적당하십니까?
수요일이나 목요일 괜찮으세요?
슈먼 씨, 몇 시에 저를 만나실 수 있나요?
박 양, 목요일 저녁에 저를 만나실 수 있나요?
가능하면 저는 금요일이 좋겠어요.
다가오는 금요일 (이번 주 금요일) 어떠세요?
저는 내일 괜찮은데 어떠세요?

*** 관련 대화**

A: 신디, 11월 1일 괜찮나요?
B: 죄송하지만, 그날 선약이 있습니다.
A: 월요일이나 화요일 괜찮으세요?
B: 저는 화요일 오후가 좋겠어요.

(4) 약속하기 4

(구체적인 '약속시간' ⇒ "몇 시가 좋을까요?"라는 표현)
존, 3시 30분 어때요?
3시 30분이라고요? 좋아요, 저도 그때 괜찮아요.
미안합니다. 아침엔 시간을 낼 수 없습니다. 오후 두 시 이후 어떠세요?
저도 4시 30분은 좋습니다.
샐리, 목요일 오후 3시쯤 뵐게요. 괜찮으세요?
금요일 2시 30분쯤 제 사무실에 들르세요.
내일 4시쯤 방문하면 괜찮으세요?
금요일 몇 시에 만날까요?

* **관련 대화**

A: 만나기 편한 시간이 언제인가요?
B: 3시 30분이 좋습니다.
A: 몇 시에 뵐까요?
B: 오후 5시 경에 들르세요.

(5) 약속하기 5

(부득이한 사정으로 (선약 등) 약속 시간이나 장소를 변경하는 경우의 표현)
밀튼 씨, 죄송하지만 월요일에 선약이 있습니다.
스미스 씨, 다른 날로 변경할 수 있을까요?
제 생각에 다음 주에는 할 수 있습니다.
제 사무실로 오시는 게 어떠세요? 주차 공간도 충분하거든요.
맥스웰 양, 전 내일 오후에 무척 바쁩니다.
그 일을 점심식사하면서 토의할까요? 제가 이 근처에 좋은 식당 한 곳을 알고 있습니다.
내일 아침 대신 오후에 뵐 수 있을까요? 아침엔 제 스케줄이 꽉 잡혀 있거든요.
금요일에 어디서 뵐까요?

- **관련 대화**

A: 버나드 씨, 내일 이 건에 관해서 논의할 수 있을까요?
B: 죄송하지만, 내일은 제가 바쁩니다. 이번 주 금요일은 어때요?
A: 언제 절 만나실 수 있나요?
B: 제 생각에 다음 주가 괜찮을 것 같군요.

(6) 약속하기 6

(총정리)
A: 편안하신 시간을 알려주시겠어요?
B: 이번 주 금요일 오후 어때요?
A: 언제 절 만날 수 있으세요?
B: 그 건에 대해서 토의하게 제 사무실로 오세요.
A: Mr. Tan에게 Ms. Wilkinson께서 새로운 프로젝트에 대해 토의하자고 했다고 전해 주시겠습니까?
B: 시간을 언제로 잡을까요?
A: 왜 저를 만나고 싶어하는지 여쭤봐도 될까요?
B: 베이징 계획안에 대해서 의논 드리고 싶어요.
A: 12월 20일 괜찮으세요?
B: 죄송하지만, 그때 선약이 있습니다.
A: 이번 주 금요일에 뵐 수 있을까요?
B: 목요일로 하면 안될까요? 금요일은 스케줄이 잡혀 있거든요.
A: 내일 4시쯤에 방문해도 괜찮으세요?
B: 죄송하지만 내일 오후는 제가 바쁩니다. 내일 오전 11시쯤이 어떠신가요?
A: 금요일 몇 시에 뵐까요?
B: 저는 아무때나 좋습니다.
A: 스미스 씨, 다른 날로 변경해도 될까요?
B: 다음 주 수요일만 빼곤 아무때나 좋습니다.

4. 국제뉴스

필리핀군 인질 구하려고 이라크 철수

필리핀 평화유지군이 그들 정부가 자국민 인질을 참수하겠다고 위협하는 이라크 저항 세력의 요구를 들어주기 위해 군 철수를 약속한 후 월요일

이라크를 떠나 고국으로 향하고 있다. 필리핀 트럭 운전수 안젤로 드 라 크루즈를 억류중인 납치범들은 이에 앞서 모든 필리핀 평화유지군이 이달 말까지 철수한다면 그를 풀어주겠다고 말했다. 델리아 알버트 외무장관은 일요일 성명에서 최초 51명의 배치병력 중에서 남아 있는 22명의 평화유지군이 월요일 이라크 바빌주에 있는 캠프 찰리에서 신임 폴란드 사령관에게 "철수 통고 예방"을 할 것이라고 말했다. 그들은 드 라 크루즈의 석방을 확실하게 하도록 이라크 주재 필리핀 외교관들을 돕고 있는 글로리아 마카파갈 아로요 대통령 특사 로이 시마투와 동행할 것이다.

"예방 후, 이 나머지 부대원들은 쿠웨이트로 향할 것이며 그곳에서 민간 항공편으로 마닐라로 돌아오게 될 것이다"라고 알버트는 말했다. 쿠웨이트 주재 필리핀 대사관이 마닐라 귀국 항공편을 마련하고 있다고 그녀는 말했다. 이보다 일찍 이라크를 떠난 일부 평화유지군은 월요일 고국에 도착할 예정이라고 관리들이 말했다. 최근 시위에서 필리핀 군의 철군을 요구했던 유명한 좌익 단체 미그란테는 사태 발전을 환영했다.

5. Abby

에비 여사에게:

저는 은퇴한 80세의 일반 외과 의사입니다. 제가 이 글을 드리는 이유는 친구가 암으로 죽었는데 그 친구는 자신이 말기 암이라는 사실을 전혀 몰랐다는 "Grieving in L.A."라는 분께 당신이 해준 답변과 제 생각이 다르기 때문입니다. 그 글을 쓴 사람은 죄책감을 느꼈다고 했지요. 질병이나 상해로부터 회복하고 살아나는 데 있어 제일 중요한 요소는 살고자 하고 낫고자하는 환자의 결단입니다. 그것은 최상의 진료나 간호, 치료보다도 훨씬 더 중대한 요소입니다. 희망을 포기하는 것은 절망을 심는 것입니다. 집에서나 전문 치료소에서는 환자를 격려해 주고 적극적인 자세를 갖도록 유도해야 합니다. 그러므로 "당신은 곧 죽을 것"이라고 말하는 것은 완전히 역효과적인 말입니다.

– 켈리포니아주 티부론에서 의사 킬고리가

킬고리 박사에게:

총명한 사람의 생각은 다를 수 있습니다. 계속 읽어보세요.

에비 여사에게:

1960년, 첫 번째 아내가 암으로 죽기 전에, 아내의 주치의가 저를 병원으로 불렀습니다. 의사는 제게 아내에게 모든 사실과 얼마나 살 수 있는지에 대해 말해주어야 한다고 하더군요. 그래서 저는 제가 알아서 하겠다고 했습니다. 의사는 아내가 가족에게 하고 싶은 말이나 세상을 떠나면서 마무리하고 싶은 일이 있을지도 모르니 아내도 알고 있을 권리가 있다고 하였습니다. 그 의사 선생님 말씀이 옳았습니다! 제가 아내에게 그 사실을 알려주자, 아내는 우리 목사님께 세례를 받고 싶다고 하더군요. 에비씨, 정말로 아내는 병원에서 침례를 받기 위해 임종의 자리에서 일어났습니다. 죽음에 임박한 사람들은 모두 자기가 죽는다는 사실을 알 권리가 있습니다. 저는 아내에게 말한 것을 후회한 적이 한번도 없습니다. 에비씨, 이 문제로 고민하고 있는 당신의 독자들에게 감추지 말고 사실대로 말해 주라고 하세요.
－아칸소주 포트 스미스에서 L.L.이란 사람이

L.L. 씨에게:

당신은 고의적인 논쟁거리를 만들었군요.

6. 독해문제

오늘날 가족이 무너지고 있다는 불안이 대중들 사이에 만연하고 있다. 그 걱정의 대부분은 과거 가족의 본질에 대한 근본적인 오해와 폭넓은 사회 경제적 변화에 반응하는 가족의 탄력성에 대한 이해의 부족에서 비롯되고 있다. 가족에 대한 일반적 견해는 그것이 역사적으로 비교적 변하지 않는 안정된 제도였으며, 지금에 와서야 비로소 변화를 겪고 있다는 것이다. 사실 가족은 언제나 변화해 왔다.

【정답】 ⓒ

7. 유머영어

(1) 결혼의 의미

"여보, 저녁식사에 친구 한 명을 초대했어." 남편이 아내에게 말했다.
"뭐라구요? 당신 제정신이에요? 집은 엉망진창인데다 장도 안 봤고 설거지도 하나도 안했어요. 게다가 난 지금 거창한 음식을 만들고 싶은 기분이 아니라구요." "다 알고 있어." "그런데 왜 친구를 저녁식사에 초대한 거죠?" "그 불쌍한 바보같은 녀석이 결혼할까 생각중이라잖아."

(2) 온몸이 아픈 여자

한 젊은 여자가 진찰을 받으면서 아프다고 투덜거렸다. "어디가 아프십니까?"라고 의사가 묻자, 여자의 대답, "온몸이 다 아파요." "온몸이라뇨?" 의사가 물었다, "좀더 구체적으로 말씀해 보세요." 여자가 집게손가락을 오른쪽 무릎에 대더니 "아이고, 아파!"라고 소리쳤다. 그러고는 왼쪽 뺨에 손가락을 대더니 다시 "아이고, 여기도 아파요!"하며 소리쳤다. 오른쪽 귓볼에 손가락을 갖다 댄 다음에도 "여기까지 아파요!"라고 울먹거렸다. 잠시 동안 여자를 꼼꼼하게 진찰해 본 다음 의사가 내린 진단, "손가락이 부러졌습니다."

제12장

1. Warm-up

(1) 회사에서는 수입 감소를 막기 위하여 모든 간부들에게 원가를 통제할 것을 요구하였다.
(2) 저는 제가 엑손사에 상당한 공헌을 할 수 있으리라고 믿습니다.
(3) 장래의 경제 추세에 대한 우리의 분석에 여러분이 동의하신다면 국채에 돈을 투자하셔야 합니다.
(4) 연금 계획은 국내 직원들만 해당됩니다. 그 결과, 해외 직원들은 별도의 준비를 해야만 합니다.
(5) 직원 모두가 경영층의 이해와 결정에 깊이 감사하였다.
(6) 사업 투자가 점차 증가함에도 불구하고, 약한 국내 수요가 많은 회사들을 압박하고 있다.
(7) 방문객들은 정문에서 로댕의 위대한 두 작품을 보게 된다.
(8) 월요일 오후에 정상회담이 합의에 도달했다.
(9) 유로화가 월요일에는 미화 85센트 보다 못한 가치로 추락했다.
(10) 두 회사가 합병을 하게 되면, 모든 경쟁사를 따돌릴 것이며 아시아 최대의 간이음식점 망을 구축하는 데 힘을 모으게 될 것이다.

2. 시사용어

(1) 이머징 마켓

한국은행 전철환 총재는 어제 모든 국내 금융기관 들에게 국제결제은행이 권고한 자기자본비율을 준수하도록 요구하는 것은 문제가 있다고 밝혔다. 전 총재는 이날 경영인클럽 강연에서 "모든 국내 금융기관에 BIS기준을 일률적으로 적용하는 것은 문제가 있다"며 "이머징 마켓의 금융기관에게 이 기준을 준수하도록 요구할 필요가 없다"고 밝혔다. 농협처럼 국제시장과 업무상 별다른 접촉이 없는 금융기관 들은 자기자본비율을 BIS기준에 꼭 맞출 필요가 없다는 것이다.

cf 말 그대로 떠오르는 시장으로 주로 금융시장, 더욱 좁게는 자본시장 부문에서 새로 급성장하는 시장을 의미하는 용어. 자본시장에 있어 emerging market이 중요한 이유는 개발도상국이나 저개발국 자본시장의 발전 정도를 반영하고 있기 때문이다. 자본시장이 급성장한다는 것은 해당 국가의 경제력이 급성장하고 개방화가 급진전되고 있다는 것을 반증한다. 국제자본의 관점에서는 emerging market의 고수익성을 노려 금융자본이 이 지역으로 이동한다는 것을 의미한다. 현재 세계적으로 신흥 자본시장으로 관심을 끌고 있는 지역은 한국을 포함한 동남아시아, 라틴아메리카, 동유럽 등으로 대별해 볼 수 있다. 특히 중국과 말레이시아 등 10% 이상의 지속적인 경제성장을 유지하고 있는 국가를 비롯하여 싱가포르, 홍콩, 대만 등의 자본시장은 모두 emerging market으로 각별한 주목을 받고 있다.

(2) 태평양 전쟁

일본 정부의 교과서 승인 움직임은 한국 정부는 물론 언론 그리고 시민단체에 이르기까지 거센 반발을 불러 일으켰다. 한국정부 관계자들에 따르면 한국정부는 다음달 도쿄에서 열리는 제 3차 한일각료회의에서 교과서 왜곡 문제를 의제로 삼을 계획인 것으로 알려졌다. 지난 1982년 일본 역사 교과서 문제가 처음으로 제기되었을 때, 일본의 지식인들은 태평양전쟁을 찬양하고 일제 한반도 강점(1910~1945)을 정당화하는 교과서에 반대하는 운동을 성공적으로 수행한 바 있다.

cf 세계 제2차대전중 미국과 일본 사이에 벌어진 전쟁(1941~45). 1941년 일본이 미국의 Hawaii 진주만을 기습 공격함으로써 미·일간 행해진 전쟁으로 1942년 6월 Midway 해전을 고비로 미국이 승세를 잡았으며, 이어 1945년 8월 Hiroshima와 Nagasaki에 atomic bombs(원자폭탄) 투하로 일본측의 무조건 항복으로 종전된 바 있다. 참고로 Pacific War를 일본에서는 '대동아전쟁'이라고도 일컬었는데, 여기서 대동아란 대동아 공영권이라는 말에서 유래한 것으로 미국과 같은 서양 열강세력에 맞서 아시아국가들이 힘을 합쳐 하나의 세력이 된다는 논리를 앞세운 일본측의 침략 야욕이 숨어 있는 표현이다. 특히 일본 군부는 Pacific War 당시 식민국가였던 한국민들의 대규모 강제 징용 및 징발을 통한 전쟁투입으로 수많은 한국인들의 목숨을 잃게 하는 아픔을 주기도 했다.

3. 실용영어

(1) 전화영어 1

(간단한 자기 소개)
저는 (여기) 존입니다.
여기는 윈글리쉬입니다.
윈글리쉬의 토니 김입니다.
("~와 통화하고 싶다"라는 표현)
스미스 양과 통화하고 싶습니다.
해외 업무부로 연결을 부탁 드립니다.
영업부로 돌려주시겠습니까?
밀러 씨 부탁합니다.
해외 업무부요.
("실례지만 어디시죠?"라고 물을 때)
누구신지 여쭤봐도 됩니까?
누구세요?

• 관련 대화

Case 1)

A: 여보세요, 윈글리쉬입니다. 뭘 도와 드릴까요?
B: 네, Smith 양과 통화할 수 있을까요?
A: 실례지만, 어디신지 여쭤봐도 될까요?

Case 2)

A: 안녕하세요, 뭘 도와 드릴까요?

B: 저는 John 입니다. '해외부'로 돌려주시겠습니까?
A: 잠시만 기다리십시오. (끊지 말고 기다리십시오.)

(2) 전화영어 2

("~씨는 지금 안 계십니다."와 관련된 표현)
스미스 씨는 지금 안 계시는데요.
그녀는 잠깐 외출했어요.
죄송합니다만, 로드리게스 씨는 지금 안 계시는데요.
미안합니다만, 그녀는 지금 회의 중이십니다.
그 분은 오늘 결근이십니다. 대신 무어 씨와 통화하시겠습니까?
죄송하지만 지금 안계십니다. 2시 30분 경에 돌아오십니다.
("~씨에게 메시지를 좀 전해 주세요."와 관련된 표현)
메시지를 남겨도 될까요?
서머빌 씨께 메시지 좀 부탁 드립니다.
오시면 전화 부탁 드릴까요?
로마 행 항공편이 확정됐다고 전해 주실래요?

• 관련 대화

Case 1)
A: 올랜도 양과 통화하고 싶습니다.
B: 실례지만 어디신가요?
A: 저는 윈글리쉬의 존이라고 합니다.
B: 죄송하지만, 지금 회의 중이십니다. 메모를 남겨 드릴까요?

Case 2)
A: 안녕하세요? 로페즈 씨랑 통화하고 싶은데요.
B: 죄송하지만, 오늘 안 나오셨는데요.
A: 메시지 좀 전해 주시겠습니까?
B: 물론이죠.
A: 저는 윌 스미스인데 내일 아침에 전화 부탁한다고 전해 주세요.

(3) 전화영어 3

("나중에 연락 주세요."라고 부탁할 때)

4시에 다시 전화 주시겠어요?
스미스 씨가 돌아 오시면 전화 부탁 드립니다.
제가 회의 직후에 곧바로 전화 드릴께요.
다음에 다시 한번 연락 주세요.
존은 다른 전화를 받고 있습니다. 잠시 기다리시겠습니까? 아니면 10분 후에 다시 전화 주실래요?
(상대방의 전화번호를 물어볼 때)
전화 번호가 어떻게 되시죠?
번호를 남기시겠습니까?
번호를 남겨 주시면 연락 드리라고 말씀 드리겠습니다.
제가 어떻게 연락하면 될까요?
지금 자리에 안 계십니다만, 번호를 남겨 드릴까요?

• 관련 대화

A: 존슨 씨와 통화하고 싶습니다.
B: 지금 통화 중이신데요, 한 10분 후에 다시 걸어 주시겠어요?
A: 데이빗 무어에게서 전화 왔었다고 전해 주실래요?
B: 네, 알겠습니다.

(4) 전화영어 4

(같은 모국어(특정 외국어)를 쓰는 사람 또는 전문용어로 대화를 할 경우)
독일어를 하실 수 있는 분과 통화하고 싶습니다.
한국어를 이해하시는 분 아무나 바꿔 주세요.
컴퓨터 프로그램을 아시는 분과 통화하고 싶습니다.
성형수술 전문용어를 아시는 분과 대화하고 싶습니다.
(전화선이 잘 안 들리는 경우)
죄송하지만 잘 안 들리는데요. 좀 더 크게 말씀해 주실래요?
조금 더 크게 말씀해 주세요.
전화선이 좋지 않군요. 다시 한번 말씀해 주실래요?

* **관련 대화**

Case 1)

A: 독일어를 아시는 분과 통화하고 싶습니다.

B: 잠시만 기다리세요.

Case 2)

A: 컴퓨터 프로그램에 대해서 아시는 분과 통화하고 싶어요.

B: (제가 담당입니다.) 말씀하세요. 뭘 도와 드릴까요?

Case 3)

A: 히브루어를 아시는 분과 통화하고 싶습니다.

B: 죄송한데요, 전화선이 고르지 못하네요. 다시 한번 말씀해 주실래요?

4. 국내뉴스

동북아시아 역사기구를 만들자

중국의 한국역사 왜곡을 둘러싼 우려가 커지는 가운데, 한 한국인 학자는 한국, 일본, 그리고 중국의 전문가들로 구성된 역사공동위원회를 설립하자고 화요일 제의했다. "국수주의적인 역사관을 초월하여 동북아의 지역적 정체성을 유지하기 위한 위원회를 설립하는 일은 한국이 앞장을 서야 할 것"이라고 외교안보원구원의 배긍찬 교수가 보고서에서 말했다. "동북아 시대와 한국의 외교적 과제"라는 제목의 분석 보고서에서 배 교수는 한국은 무력으로 이웃나라들을 위협한 적도, 타국을 지배하려고 시도한 적도 없으므로 이러한 프로젝트를 추진하는 데 보다 유리한 위치에 있다고 주장했다. 일본과 중국은 동북아의 지역패권을 잡으려고 치열한 경쟁 속에 있기 때문에, 일본과 중국은 역사의 공동인식을 논의하는 데 주도적인 입장을 취하기가 어려울 것이라고 배 교수는 설명했다. 배 교수는 이 위원회가 연구결과를 만들어 내면 한 · 중 · 일 3국은 궁극적으로 이 결과를 왜곡됨 없이 역사 교과서에 반영해야 할 것이라고 강조했다. 배 교수의 이같은 제의는 역사적 사실을 어설프게 뜯어고치는 중국정부에 대해 한국정부가 대응조치를 취하겠다고 여러 번 선언했기 때문에 특별한 관심을 끌고 있다.

중국 외교부는 자체 홈페이지의 한국의 역사 소개에서 한국의 고대 3국의 하나인 고구려를 2~3개월 전 삭제했다. 그러나 중국정부는 이 홈페이지의 내용을 시정하라는 한국의 요청을 아직도 듣지 않고 있다.

5. Abby

에비 여사에게:

제가 이 여자 친구와 데이트한 지 6개월 되었습니다. 우리는 서로 깊이 사랑하는 아주 가까운 사이입니다. 그런데 그녀가 이번 가을, 대학에 가기 위해 집을 떠나갑니다. 그 학교는 우리 동네에서 2시간 거리에 있습니다. 학기가 시작되면 우리가 어떻게 해야 하는지 그녀와 이야기를 나누었습니다. 그런데 그녀는 우리가 앞으로 자주 만날 수 없으니 헤어지고 싶다는 것입니다. 그러나 저 개인적인 생각으로 멀리 떨어져 있는 것은 문제가 아니라고 생각합니다. 그녀에게 우리가 계속 애인관계를 지속할 수 있다는 것을 어떻게 납득시켜야 합니까? 진정으로 저는 우리가 서로에게 소중한 존재라고 느끼고 있습니다.

―캘리포니아주 호오돈에서 마음에 상처입은 사람이

마음에 상처입은 분에게:

그녀를 앞으로도 계속 만나고 싶다면, 대학에 간 그녀를 독점하려고 압박하지 마세요. 그녀는 대학에 가서 완전히 새로운 사람들을 만나고 싶어 하며 구속받고 싶지 않은 것입니다. 그것은 두 분을 위해서도 바람직한 태도입니다.

사랑하는 연인은 서로에게 자유를 주어야 합니다. 자유를 주지 않는 것은 상대를 자기 맘대로 조정하려는 것입니다. 그러니 상대는 자신을 구속하는 사람에게서 도망치려고 하는 것입니다. 서로에게 그렇게 소중한 존재라면, 그녀가 주말이나 휴일에 집에 왔을 때 만날 수 있을 것입니다. 그녀가 다른 남자와 영화를 보거나 커피를 마셨다 해도 죄책감이 들지 않도록 당신이 마음을 써 준다면 그녀는 훨씬 더 당신과 가까이 지낼 것입니다. 반면에 당신은 그녀가 없는 동안, 인생을 넓힐 수 있는 새로운 방법들을 모색해 보세요. 이때가 바로 두 분 모두가 활기차게 성장할 수 있는 기간인 것입니다.

6. 독해문제

캐나다 주택 시장이 서서히 회복 조짐을 보이고 있다. 거의 9년에 걸친 장기간의 불경기를 겪고 난 후, 주택 시장은 마침내 상당한 성장세를 보이고 있다. '캐나다 주택금융사'에 따르면 주택 할부 대출금리 인하와 주택 가격의 하락으로 올해 11%, 내년에는 9%의 신규 주택건설 부양이 기대된다. 또한 기존 주택물의 매매도 올해 14% 상승할 것으로 예상된다. 이러한 고무적인 수치에도 불구하고 주택시장은 10년 전과 비교할 때 여전히 침체 상황이다. '캐나다 주택금융사'의 경제학자 팻 트렌드씨는 현재의 이러한 현상은 더딘 인구 증가와 높은 실업률, 그리고 실질소득의 감소 등에 따른 것이라고 말하고 있다.

【정답】

(1) ⓐ

(2) ⓓ

(3) ⓐ

(4) ⓓ

7. 유머영어

(1) 정직한 소년

어떤 여자가 사람들로 붐비는 곳에서 크리스마스 쇼핑을 하다가 핸드백을 잃어버렸다. 어떤 착한 소년이 그 핸드백을 찾아 여자에게 돌려주었다. 지갑을 보고 여자가 하는 말, "음… 이상하네. 핸드백을 잃어버렸을 때는 20달러 짜리 지폐 한 장이 들어 있었는데, 지금은 1달러짜리 돈이 20개가 들어 있어." 그러자, 소년이 재빨리 대답하는 말, "맞아요. 지난번에 제가 어떤 여자의 지갑을 찾아주었는데, 그 여자한테 잔돈이 없어서 사례금을 못 받았거든요."

(2) 백만장자가 된다면

"종이와 연필을 꺼내서," 선생님이 말했다, "'내가 만약 백만장자가 된다면'을 주제로 에세이를 써봐요." 모든 학생들이 열심히 쓰기 시작했는데, 유독 필립만이 상체를 (의자) 뒤로 젖히고 팔짱을 낀 채로 있는 것이었다. "뭐가 문제니?" 선생님이 물었다, "왜 쓰지 않는 거야?" "비서를 기다리는 중이거든요"라고 필립이 대답했다.

제13장

1. Warm-up

(1) 용의자가 충분한 증거가 수집되기 전에 도망갈 수도 있기 때문에 유명한 악당을 대할 때는 신중히 행동해야 한다.

(2) 이번 여름휴가가 내 생일, 그리고 다음달에 있을 세 번째 결혼기념일과 똑같다니 재미있군.

(3) 경찰은 용의자의 은신처로 바로 안내했던 사업동료의 밀고를 받기 전까지 그의 소재를 전혀 알지 못했다.

(4) 지구상 모든 국가 출신의 대표단을 포함하고 국제현안을 다루는 토론장을 마련하는 UN은 아주 독특한 조직체이다.

(5) 오늘밤 공연표가 아직 남아 있기는 하지만 5시 이후로는 매진될 것 같으니 그전에 미리 예약하셔야 할 겁니다.

(6) 이 화병은 당신이나 이 박물관이 감당할 수 없는 가치가 나가므로 다룰 때 극도의 주의를 기울여야 합니다 .

(7) 그것은 너무나 뛰어난 보고서였기 때문에 슐츠씨는 보고서가 늦게 제출되었던 점은 눈감아 주었다.

(8) 날씨 때문에 우리는 이번 금요일 회의를 다음주까지 연기하고자 한다.

(9) 재정적 소요액 중 현금 수요액을 충당하기 위하여 적절한 유동성을 유지하고 있다.

(10) 그 젊은 여성은 인터뷰 요청을 받고 너무 흥분하여 자기가 아는 모든 사람에게 그 사실을 말했다.

2. 시사용어

(1) 가신

한편 김사장이 현대건설 사장에서 불명예스럽게 퇴진한 것은 기업 운명이 걸릴 정도로 어려움에 시달리고 있는 현대건설에 새로운 독자 생존의 기회를 제공하게 될 것 같다고 업계 분석가들은 말했다. 게다가 김사장의 퇴진은 정씨일가와 밀접한 관계를 유지하면서 절대권력을 휘둘러온 경영진을 일컫는 이른바 가신시대의 종말을 의미한다고 이들은 밝혔다. 한 업계 분석가는 “이익치 전 현대증권 회장, 김재수 전 현대건설 부사장 등을 포함해 이른바 문제의 가신 3인방이 그룹 주요 경영진에서 완전히 물러나게 되었다"고 말했다.

cf 중국 춘추전국시대에 여러 나라의 대부 밑에서 벼슬한 사람을 지칭하는 용어. 우리나라에서는 부족국가시대 왕이나 대가들이 가신을 두었으며, 특히 고려 무신정권시대에 최충헌이 자기집에서 나라의 정사를 맡아보고 있을 때, 임금의 신하와는 별도로 자기 집안에 부하들을 거느리고 있었던 데서 세력가 밑에서 일하는 사람을 일컫게 되었다. 오늘날에는 언론이 현대그룹처럼 재벌 일가와 더불어 동고동락하면서 그룹의 경영을 사실상 이끌어 온 최측근 인물들을 일컬으면서 널리 알려진 용어이다.

(2) 자이툰

전투 태세 치안 병력을 포함한 3천명의 부대는 미국측의 요청에 따라 키르쿠크 유전 지대 재건을 지원하게 된다. 이들 부대는 현지 배치에 앞서 아랍어 및 문화 등과 같은 문제에 대한 6주간의 교육을 받아야 한다. 아랍어로 올리브를 뜻하는 자이툰이라는 애칭을 가진 이 추가 파병 부대로 우리나라는 미국과 영국에 이어 이라크 파병 규모가 3번째로 크게 된다.

cf 2004년 4월 Iraq Kirkuk에 파견되는 우리나라의 Iraq 평화재건사단 부대의 상징적 명칭임. 샬람(평화), 하맘(비둘기), 휠날(초승달) 등을 물리치고 부대명으로 선정된 Zayitun은 아랍어로 평화의 상징인 Olive를 뜻한다. 비둘기와 함께 평화를 상징하는 Olive는 아랍인들에게 뗄 수 없는 필수품이나 마찬가지다. 아랍 신문들은 cartoon(시사만화)에서 평화를 묘사할 때면 으레 입에 Olive 가지를 문 비둘기를 그린다. 이같은 이유로 평화적 목적으로 Iraq에 파병되는 한국군의 명칭으로 선정된 것이다. 육군과 해병대의 합동 부대로서 사단 사령부와 직할대, 두 개의 민사여단으로 구성된 Zayitun 부대의 깃발에는 태극 마크와 Olive 잎이 함께 그려져 있다. 파병 규모는 월남전 이후 최대이며, 연합군 가운데 3번째로 많은 3600여명으로 알려져 있다. Iraq 북부 유전 지대에 있는 Kirkuk 시를 중심으로 한 지역에서 7000여명의 Iraq 경찰 및 민방위대를 통제하며 함께 민사 작전을 펼치게 된다. 2004년 2월 현재 미국 이외에 Iraq에 파병한 나라는 36개국이며, 이 가운데 Britain(1만1000명)이 가장 많은 병력을 파병했고, 이어 Italy(2700명) Spain(2000명) 순이다. 700여명으로 편성된 서희(건설공병)·제마(의무) 부대를 파병한 한국은 Zayitun사단의 파병으로 Britain에 이어 두 번째로 많은 병력을 보낸 나라가 된다.

3. 실용영어

(1) 여행영어 1 (Julie는 샌프란시스코 행 비행기편을 알아보고 있고 여행사 직원은 여행 일정에 대해 묻고 비행기표 가격에 대한 정보를 주고 있다.)

줄리 여보세요. 샌프란시스코로 가는 비행기편을 알고 싶은데요.
여행사 직원 언제 여행하려고 하시는데요?
줄리 12월 28일에서 1월 10일까지 여행하려고 합니다.
여행사 직원 자리가 있는지 알아볼께요. 몇 명이 함께 여행할 건가요?
줄리 2명이요. 비행기표 가격이 얼마나 되는지도 알려주세요.
여행사 직원 12월 28일 서울을 출발해서 1월 10일에 돌아오는 대한항공편에 좌석이 두 개 있습니다. 2인 비행기표 가격은 2백만원입니다.
줄리 괜찮군요! 예약해도 될까요?
여행사 직원 물론입니다. 성함과 전화번호를 알려 주세요.

(2) 여행영어 2 (비행기표 예약하는 법 ⇒ 여행사 직원(travel agent) A와 고객 B간의 대화)

A: 안녕하세요. 뭘 도와 드릴까요?
B: 방콕 행 비행편을 예약하고 싶습니다.
A: 알겠습니다. 언제 비행기로 예약해 드릴까요?
B: 금요일 아침으로 부탁합니다.
A: 일반석으로 해 드릴까요, 일등석으로 해 드릴까요?
B: 일반석으로 부탁합니다.
A: 좌석 확인해 드리겠습니다.
B: 감사합니다.

(3) 여행영어 3 (비행기표 예약하는 법 ⇒ 여행사 직원(travel agent) A 와 고객 B간의 대화)

A: 죄송하지만, 만원입니다. 오후 비행편은 어떠세요?
B: 몇 시 비행기입니까?
A: 오후 3시 50분 비행기입니다.
B: 좋아요. 그걸로 해주세요.
A: 성함이 어떻게 되시나요?
B: 찰스 바클리입니다.
A: 감사합니다. 잠시만 기다려 주세요.

(4) 여행영어 4 (공항에서)

이민국 직원 안녕하세요, 여권 좀 볼까요?
이 부장 네, 여기 있습니다.
이민국 직원 방문 목적이 무엇입니까?
이 부장 사업차 왔습니다. 기업 박람회에 참석하려구요.
이민국 직원 얼마 동안 체류하실 계획인가요?
이 부장 한 2주 동안 머물 겁니다.
이민국 직원 미국에는 와 보셨나요?
이 부장 네, 이번이 세 번째 방문입니다.
세관원 뭐 신고하실 게 있습니까?
이 부장 아니요, 없습니다.
세관원 가방에 과일이나, 식물, 기타 음식물이 있나요?
이 부장 전혀 없습니다.
세관원 돈은 얼마나 소지하고 계신가요?
이 부장 여행자 수표로 1,000달러 있어요.
세관원 이것들은 뭐지요?
이 부장 아, 그건 제 개인 소지품이에요. 그게 짐의 전부입니다.
세관원 됐습니다. 협조해 주셔서 고맙습니다. 좋은 여행되십시오.
이 부장 고맙습니다.

* **유용한 표현**(여행목적, 짐에 관한 내용, 탑승 시간 등에 관련한 내용)
  관광하러 왔어요.
  사업차 왔습니다.
  수화물 찾는 곳이 어디예요?
  친구를 방문하러 왔어요.
  몇 번 출구로 가야 하나요?
  짐은 어디서 찾나요?
  회의 참석차 왔습니다.
  여기가 대한항공 탑승 수속하는 곳인가요?
  탑승시간이 언제예요?
  사업차 왔습니다.

(5) 여행영어 5

(기내에서)
곧 이륙할 예정입니다.
A: 다른 자리로 바꿀 수 있을까요? 금연석을 달라고 했는데 흡연석을 줘서요.
B: 안 되겠는데요. 비행기 좌석이 꽉 찬 것 같아요. 그리고 곧 이륙할 거니까 안전 벨트를 매주세요.
A: 네, 알겠습니다. 그런데 혹시 빈 좌석이 있으면 좌석을 바꾸고 싶으니까 알려주세요.
B: 네, 알겠습니다.

(교통수단을 이용할 때)
이 버스 공항으로 안 갑니까?
A: 이 버스 공항 안 갑니까?
B: 네, 버스를 잘못 타셨습니다.
A: 어떻게 해야 되죠?
B: 다음 정류장에서 내려서 8번 버스를 타세요.

4. 국내뉴스

경기불황으로 각종 범죄 크게 늘어

실물경제의 침체가 계속되면서 점점 더 많은 사람들이 범죄의 길로 들어

가고 있다. 경찰청이 월요일 발표한 2004년도 경찰백서에 따르면 특히 사기, 횡령 등 경제관련 범죄들이 꾸준히 증가하고 있는 것으로 나타났다. 경제문제로 인해 지난 수 년 동안 사기와 횡령 발생률이 급속하게 증가했을 뿐 아니라, 벌금이나 공공요금을 내지 못하는 사람 수도 증가하고 있다. 백서는 또한 많은 사람들이 정부로부터 실업수당을 받기 위해 실직자인 것처럼 꾸미고 있다고 밝혔다.

경찰청 관계자는 "경제사범의 증가는 IMF 위기 이후에 악화된 경제상황에 기인한다"며 1997년 한국을 휩쓴 금융위기와 그 이듬해 IMF 긴급구제 프로그램에 들어갔던 것을 언급하며 이같이 말했다. "금융위기는 회사들에게 구조조정을 통해서 많은 근로자들을 강제해고하게 했다. 그 이후 신용불량자와 실업자수가 증가했다." 이 관계자는 많은 신용불량자들이 은행 및 타 금융기관 이용을 금지당함에 따라 사기범죄 역시 증가했다고 밝혔다. 이 백서에 따르면, 사기 사건은 2002년 183,327건에서 작년 26.5%가 증가한 231,951건으로 지난 10년 중 최고치를 기록했다. 횡령 사건은 2002년 22,986건에서 2003년 26,702건으로 급증했다. 수표위조 사범은 2002년 14,347건에서 36.5% 증가한 19,582건으로 신고되었다. 절도죄는 2002년 178,457건에서 5% 증가한 187,352건으로 10년 만에 최고치이다. 경제사범 증가로 인해 전반적인 범죄 비율은 2002년 183만건에서 작년 3.4% 오른 189만건을 기록했다. 백서는 1994년 약 130만건의 범죄가 신고되었으며, 범죄율은 지난 10년간 꾸준하게 증가해 왔다고 발표했다. 강도범의 경우도 작년 7,292건으로 23.5% 증가했으며, 살인사건도 2003년에 998건으로 이전해보다 4.3% 증가했다. 사이버 범죄 역시 작년 68,445건으로 1년 전에 비해 14%나 껑충 뛰었다. 경찰백서는 작년에 체포된 여성범죄자 수도 이전해보다 3.1% 증가한 320,859명이라고 했다.

경찰청은 이혼여성이나 독신녀가 늘어남에 따라, 많은 여성들이 스스로 살길을 찾으려 한다고 말했다. 그러나 남성 위주의 사회에서 살길을 찾는데 어려움을 겪는 여성들이 늘어나면서 이들이 범죄에 의존하게 된다고 경찰청은 덧붙였다.

5. Abby

에비 여사에게 :

저는 50대로 심각한 심장병이 있습니다-거의 두 번이나 죽을 뻔했지요-그래서 현재 저는 덤으로 사는 인생이라고 생각합니다. 의사도 알고, 가족들도 알고 있으며, 저도 알고 있습니다. 우리는 이 일에 대해 이야기를 나누었으며 저의 삶의 의지와 장기 기증에 대해서도 이야기했습니다. 또한 우리는 삶의 양에 대한 상대개념으로서 삶의 질에 대한 이야기도 충분히 나누었습니다. 그런데 어떤 사람들은 저를 위해서 제가 아무 일도 하지 않고 가만히 있기를 바라는데 그것은 그릇된 마음씀입니다. 저는 그들에게 저는 아직 살아 있어서 많은 것을 할 수 있다는 것을 일깨워줍니다. 제가 아무것도 하지 않고 가만 있으면 제 생명은 연장될지 몰라도, 그렇게 살아서 무엇합니까? 지금 당장 저는 여행을 할 수 있고 집안 일도 대부분 할 수 있으며 꽃밭을 가꿀 수 있고 남편의 시중도 들 수 있습니다. 저는 손녀를 안아주거나 손녀와 함께 뛰어 놀 수는 없지만, 손녀에게 책을 읽어주거나 설거지를 해 줄 수는 있습니다. 제가 삶의 질과 양에 대해서 사람들에게 설명하려고 하면 사람들은 듣지 않으려고 해서 실망스럽습니다. 그들은 저를 잃게 될까봐 걱정하며 제가 좀더 조심스럽게 생활하기를 바라는 것도 저는 알고 있습니다. 아직은 시간이 있으며 또한 저는 "창조주를 만나러 가려고" 서두르지 않습니다. 하지만 그때가 되면 생명이라는 가장 소중한 선물을 최선을 다해 살았노라고 생각하며 죽고 싶습니다.

에비씨, 당신의 독자들에게 시한부 인생을 살아가는 사람들을 격려하고 그들이 인생을 후회없이 살도록 도와주라고 말해 주세요. 또한 건강으로 축복받은 당신의 독자들에게 건강을 낭비하지 말고 모든 것의 이익을 위하여 생명이란 선물을 사용하라고 일깨워 주세요.

—뉴 햄프셔에서 살아 있는 사람이

살아있는 분에게:

당신의 편지를 게재하게 되어 기쁩니다. 우리는 이 땅에서 영원히 살 수 있는 것이 아닙니다. 그러므로 돈을 투자하듯이 현명하게 우리의 시간들을 보내야 합니다. 당신은 참으로 현실적인 여성이군요. 인생이라는 열매의 주스를 가능한 한 많이 맛보기로 결심하신 것을 보고 감복했습니다. 많이 드십시오!

6. 독해문제

일시적인 소득세 인하정책의 내용을 포함하는 법안이 이번 주에 통과되면 캐나다의 연방 판매세가 7%에서 8%로 인상될 것이다. 판매세 인상을 반대하는 선거공약을 내걸었던 현 집권 보수당의 재선 가능성이 이로 인하여 어두워질 것으로 보인다. 야당은 정부의 이런 움직임은 선거공약을 위반하는 행위라고 재빨리 꼬집었던 것이다.

【정답】

(1) ⓐ
(2) ⓒ
(3) ⓑ
(4) ⓒ

7. 유머영어

(1) 현명한 젊은이

보석상을 찾은 젊은이가 여자친구에게 줄 고가의 로켓 목걸이를 샀다. “받을 사람 이름을 새겨넣지 않을 건가요?”하고 보석상인이 물었다. 청년은 잠시 생각하더니 대답했다. “아닙니다. '하나뿐인 나의 그대에게'라고 새겨 주세요. 그렇게 해 놓으면 우리가 헤어지게 될 경우 여자가 성을 내면서 그걸 나에게 내던져도 다시 쓸 수 있을 것 아닙니까”

(2) 총명한 젊은 사원

고전하고 있는 회사 경영진이 사원들에게 경비절감을 위한 좋은 아이디어를 제시하라면서 가장 좋은 아이디어를 낸 사람에게는 1백달러를 지불하겠다고 했다. 1등상 하나는 총명한 젊은 사원에게로 돌아갔는데 그는 앞으로는 상금 액수를 50달러로 줄이자고 했다.

제14장

1. Warm-up

(1) 비행기에서 내려 주 공항 터미널을 나가기 전에 짐을 챙겨 세관을 통과하세요.
(2) 이 회사의 최고 경영자 중에 가장 훌륭한 최고 경영자가 되기 위해 헌신했던 이 전 회장님을 기념하여 정찬이 있을 것이다.

(3) 시력검사는 이 나라에서 합법적인 운전자로 등록되는 과정의 한 절차 이다.
(4) 이번 회의에 기여한 것에 대한 회사의 감사 표시로 모든 회의 참가자들 에게 간단한 무료 아침식사가 제공될 것입니다.
(5) 일단 담배에 습관을 들이게 되면 끊기는 매우 어렵다.
(6) 전과목 평균 성적이 가장 높은 사람이 장학금을 탄다.
(7) 상당히 많은 수의 사람들이 정부의 이민에 대한 태도에 반대하고 있다.
(8) 다른 회사들로부터 여러 가지 좋은 제의를 받고 제인은 직장을 그만 두기로 결심했다.
(9) 그녀는 좋은 직장을 다니고 있었지만 결혼하면서 그만 두었다.
(10) 차 문을 닫은 후에 나는 차 열쇠를 안에다 두고 나왔다는 생각이 떠올랐다.

2. 시사용어

(1) 프라임 타임

이에 동의하는 공감대가 더욱 확대되고 있다. 예를 들어 우리나라 3대 방송국 가운데 하나인 MBC는 올해 미스코리아 선발대회 주관사인 국내 주요 일간지와의 계약이 만료됨에 따라 내년부터 미인 선발대회의 생방송 중계를 중단할 것이라고 최근 발표하였다. MBC는 12년간 매년 미스코리아대회를 생방송해 왔다. MBC의 김택권씨는 이달초 "우리는 미스코리아선발대회를 프라임타임대의 국내 뉴스처럼 생방송하는 것이 윤리적인 문제를 가져올 수 있다는 데에 동의한다"고 밝혔다.

cf Television 등의 방송에서 하루 중에 시청률이 가장 높은 시간대를 지칭하는 방송 용어임. golden hour, golden time 또는 '황금시간대'라고도 하며 우리나라의 경우 통상 오후 7시에서 9시 사이의 방송시간대를 나타낸다. Prime time대에는 시청자들이 다른 시간대에 비해 월등히 많아 광고 선전의 효과가 상대적으로 크기 때문에 해당 프로그램에 대한 광고주의 광고 요청이 몰리는 현상이 나타난다. 방송국 입장에서는 prime time대의 프로그램이 타 시간대의 것보다 높은 시청률을 올릴 수 있도록 주력하게 되는데 이는 시청률의 높고 낮음이 광고 수익에도 커다란 영향을 미치기 때문이다.

(2) 기업 도시

최대 경제 로비단체인 전국경제인연합회는 어제 고용창출에 기여하고자 "기업 도시"의 건설을 위한 프로젝트를 구상 중이라고 밝혔다. 전경련에 의하면 일자리창출특별위원회는 일자리 창출을 목표로 한 기업 도시를 건설, 기업 투자를 진작하고 평화적인 노사관계를 촉진하며 서비스 산업을 육성하기로 결정했다.

cf 수도권 이외 지역에 1,000만평 규모로 건설과 기업뿐 아니라 주택, 교육 및 의료시설, 생활 편의시설 등을 고루 갖춘 인구 30만명 규모의 자족형 도시를 말함. KFI(전국경제인연합회)가 2004년 2월 제시한 Company town 개발 방안에 의하면 지방 이전을 원하는 일정 규모 이상의 기업이나 기업 컨소시엄이 주체가 돼 시행하고, 개발이익은 지역의 공공시설에 재투자되도록 유도한다. 이같은 제안 배경은 국내 제조업의 경쟁력을 크게 떨어뜨리고 있는 과도한 임금인상의 주요 원인이 되고 있는 근로자들의 주거비 부담을 완화시키겠다는 목적을 두고 있다. Company town은 과거 경제개발 시절 정부가 주도적으로 추진했던 산업단지 배후도시 개발 사례인 울산 신시가지나 반월 신도시 등을 비롯해, bed town 성격의 일산 · 분당 등과 차원이 다른 특징을 가지며, 특히 민간기업이 개발 주체로 적극 참여한다는 게 가장 큰 차이점이다. Company town의 지방 설립은 수도권의 주택 문제 해소는 물론 주택, 공장 등 건설투자에 따른 경기진작 효과를 기대할 수 있으며, 건설 투자로 인한 3만명의 고용효과 창출 및 지역 공공시설과 기반시설 투자 확대 등 파급효과가 경기 전반에 미치게 된다. 그러나 기업의 지방이전 촉진을 위해서는 장기토지이용권 부여, 토지이용계획 변경, 택지매입비용 감면 등 보다 다양한 획기적인 지원과 권한을 부여할 필요성이 있다고 지적되고 있다.

3. 실용영어

(1) 손님 마중 1 (공항으로 가서 손님을 맞이하는 상황)

(마중 나간 분이 누구인지 확실하지 않을 경우)
실례지만, 선샤인 여행사에서 오신 맥나마라 씨 아니십니까?
실례합니다. 토론토 전자회사의 케네디 씨입니까?
안녕하십니까? 남아프리카에서 오신 화이트 씨입니까?
실례합니다만, 콜럼비아 커피 회사에서 오신 산 미구엘 부부 아니십니까?

(아는 분을 마중 나갈 때 쓰는 표현)
안녕하십니까? 핸슨 씨. 당신을 회사까지 모시기 위해 왔습니다.
처음 뵙겠습니다, 영 씨. 브라운 씨의 사무실로 안내하죠.
안녕하십니까, 잭 씨. 저는 씨엘 리서치의 토니 김입니다. 당신을 환영회장으로 모시겠습니다.

• **관련 대화**

A: 실례지만, 미네소타 통상에서 오신 로랜드 양이십니까?
B: 네 그렇습니다. 쿠바 담배 회사의 산티아고 씨 맞으시죠?
A: 네. 처음 뵙겠습니다. 회사까지 모시러 왔습니다.
B: 만나서 반가와요.

(2) 손님 마중 2

(마중 나와 주셔서 감사합니다)
김 선생님, 처음 뵙겠습니다. 환영해 주셔서 감사합니다.
댐스키 씨, 기다려 주셔서 감사합니다.
(손님께 '여행에 관해서' 질문)
Finch 양, 이렇게 만나 뵙게 되어 반갑습니다. 캐나다에서 오는 동안 여행은 어떠셨나요?
안녕하세요, 박 선생님. 뉴욕에서 오시는 동안 힘든 일은 없으셨나요?
알레한드로 씨, 여행은 즐거우셨나요?
메이슨 씨, 처음 뵙겠습니다. 여행은 어떠셨나요? 피곤하시죠?
즐거운 여행이었지요.
여행은 즐거웠지만, 약간 피곤하군요.
여행은 즐거웠지만, 시차에서 오는 피로감이 있군요.

• **관련 대화**

A: 실례지만, 위니펙 스키 리조트에서 오신 잭 양이신가요?
B: 네. 서울 스포츠 장비 회사에서 오셨나요?
A: 네, 그렇습니다. 만나 뵙게 되어 반갑습니다. 여행은 어떠셨나요?
B: 즐거웠습니다. 마중 나와 주셔서 감사합니다.

(3) 손님 마중 3

(우리가 만난 분의 짐을 들어주는 내용)
파슨 양, 가방을 들어 드릴까요?
미구엘 씨, 당신의 짐을 들어 드리겠습니다.
심슨 여사, 여행 가방을 제게 주시죠. 무거워 보이는데요.
(위의 내용에 대해서 정중하게 "괜찮습니다." 또는 "도와 주셔서 감사합니다."라고 말하는 법)
감사합니다, 김 선생님.
아니요, 괜찮습니다. 제가 들고 가겠습니다.
괜찮습니다, 이 선생님. 신경 쓰지 마세요, 제가 들죠.
아뇨, 괜찮습니다. 제가 들죠. 사실 별로 무겁지 않아요.
아뇨, 괜찮습니다. 짐수레 좀 가져다 주실래요?

• 관련 대화

Case 1)
A: 파슨 양, 여행은 어떠셨어요?
B: 좋았어요, 하지만 약간 피곤하군요.
A: 파슨 양, 제가 짐을 들어 드리죠.
B: 감사합니다, 김 선생님. 매우 친절하시군요.

Case 2)
A: 앤더슨 씨, 짐 제게 주세요, 상당히 무거워 보이는군요.
B: 아뇨, 괜찮습니다. 제가 들죠. 사실 별로 무겁지 않아요.
A: 서울 방문은 처음이시죠?
B: 사실 두 번째입니다. 약 10년 전에 한번 관광 왔었죠.

(4) 손님 마중 4

(만난 분과 함께 교통수단을 이용하는 방법)
존슨 양, 여기서 잠시만 기다려 주시겠어요? 제가 택시를 불러오겠습니다.
택시 정류장에 서 있어야 하나요?
스미스 씨, 여기서 잠시만 기다려 주세요. 제가 기사를 불러오겠습니다.
죄송하지만, 어디서 택시를 탈 수 있나요?

공항버스 타는 곳을 알려주시겠습니까?
호텔까지 제가 차로 모시겠습니다.
제가 차를 정문쪽으로 가져 오겠습니다. 이곳에서 잠시만 기다려 주십시오.
Mr. and Mrs. Choi, 호텔 정문에 차를 준비해 두었습니다.
가방을 제게 주세요. 차 트렁크에 싣겠습니다.

*** 관련 대화**

Case 1)
A: 실례지만, 택시를 어디서 탈 수 있나요?
B: 저쪽 택시 승강장에서요.
A: 고맙습니다.

Case 2)
A: Ms. Park, 가방을 제게 주세요. 차 트렁크에 싣겠습니다.
B: 고맙습니다. 하지만 이 서류가방은 제가 들고 가겠습니다. 중요한 서류가 들어 있거든요.

(5) 손님 마중 5 (총복습)

(A는 Nippon통상이 Mr. Tanaka, B는 Hitec에서 온 Ms. Sharif)
A: 실례지만, 하이텍에서 오신 Sharif양입니까?
B: 네. 니폰 통상에서 오신 다나카 씨 맞으시죠?
A: 네, 그렇습니다. 처음 뵙겠습니다. (ma'am은 여자에 대한 '존칭')
B: 만나 뵙게 되어 반갑습니다.
A: 파리에서 오실 때 힘드시지 않으셨나요?
B: 즐거운 여행이었지요. 승무원들의 서비스도 훌륭했구요.
A: 즐거우셨다니 저도 기쁘군요. 나카무라 씨로부터 말씀 많이 들었습니다. 유럽에서 최고의 세일즈맨 중 한 분이라고 칭찬하시더군요.
B: 칭찬해 주셔서 고맙습니다.
A: 피곤하시죠. 가방은 저에게 주시죠. 제가 운반해 드리겠습니다.
B: 아, 고맙지만 됐어요. 카트 (짐수레) 하나 가져다 주시겠어요?
A: 알겠습니다. 여기 있습니다. 제가 차를 가져올 때까지 여기에서 기다리세요.
B: 좋아요.

4. 국제뉴스

원유 가격, 공급 불안으로 21년 내의 최고치 기록

자국 최대 석유회사의 생산 대부분을 중단시키겠다는 러시아 당국의 위협에 시장이 반응하면서 미국 원유가격이 21년 내의 최고치로 뛰어올랐다. 세계 석유의 2%를 생산하는 유코스는 엄청난 미납 세금 때문에 타격을 받아 왔다. 이 회사는 세금 빚을 갚을 현금이 없다고 말했다. 법원 명령에 의해 자산이 동결된 유코스는 수요일 수일 내에 주요 생산설비를 중지시켜야 할지도 모른다고 말함으로써 시장을 불안케 했다.

수요일 거래에서 미국산 경질유 9월 계약분은 뉴욕 상품거래소에서 3% 오른 배럴당 43.05달러로 거래되어 1983년 경질유 계약분을 취급하기 시작한 이래 최고 수준을 기록했다. 런던에선 9월 인도분 브렌트 원유가 국제석유거래소(IPE)에서 배럴당 39.68 달러에 달해, 이전 최고기록, 즉 이라크군이 쿠웨이트를 침공한 당시인 1990년 10월 12일의 39.65 달러를 깨뜨렸다. "유코스 문제가 세계 석유공급에 크게 영향을 끼칠 수 있다"고 런던 소재 도이치뱅크의 유가 전략가 아담 쉬민스키가 말했다.

원유 공급은 이라크의 생산이 파괴 활동가들에 의해 방해받고, 대부분의 생산국들이 할 수 있는 한 최대로 원유를 이미 뽑아올림으로써 이미 극도로 여유가 없는 상태이다. 상당한 잉여 생산능력을 가진 유일한 생산국인 사우디아라비아는 최근 생산을 하루 약 1백만 배럴 가량 추가 생산했으나, 이 추가 생산분 대부분은 아직 소비자들 손에 닿지 않아, 고갈된 재고분을 다시 채워넣지 못하고 있다.

5. Abby

전 공주가 아니랍니다

에비 여사에게:

저는 열 다섯 살의 소녀이고 저희 집은 경제적으로 윤택하지요. 제 가장 친한 친구인 "오드리"는 그렇지 못하답니다. 오드리의 부모님은 이혼을 하셨습니다. 그리고 그녀의 어머니는 가족을 부양하기 위해 하루 종일 일을 하신답니다. 저는 함께 재미있는 무언가를 하자고 제안할 때 항상 망설이는 그 애에게 좀 짜증이 나곤 했지요. 오드리는 결국 그녀가 돈이 없어서 그렇다는 사실을 인정했지요. 전 정말 기분이 안 좋아요. 왜냐하면 전 지금껏 돈 때문에 고생한 적도, 그리고 제 친구들이 돈 때문에 고생할 것이란 생각을 단 한번도 해본 적이 없으니까요. 전 오드리와 같이 노는 것이 정말 재미있답니다. 저는 그녀의 안 좋은 경제 사정 때문에 저희 두 사람 사이의 우정에 금이 가는 것을 원치 않는답니다. 저는 기꺼이 놀이동산이나 영화 또는 다른 행사의 입장권을 대신 내 줄 용의가 있어요. 심지어 함께 쇼핑을 가면 옷도 사주고 싶고요. 문제는 그에게 금전적인 문제에 너무나 민감한 반응을 보인답니다. 그 앤 결코 제 호의를 받아들이지 않습니다. 어떻게 해야 그 애가 동정을 받는 것처럼 느끼지 않고 함께 즐거운 시간을 보낼 수 있을까요?

— 캘리포니아의 패서디나에서 공주가 아닌 사람이

공주가 아닌 분에게:

친구에게 옷을 사 주거나 하진 마세요. 대신 돈이 많이 안 드는 그런 일도 많잖아요. 음악을 듣거나 비디오를 빌려보거나 운동을 하거나, 아니면 숙제를 함께 하는 것이죠. 영화를 보거나 놀이공원에 가는 것 같은 단체활동에 함께 참여하는 것도 좋은 것입니다. 그러나 항상 그녀가 어떤 식으로든 당신에게 답례를 할 수 있도록 해주세요. 그녀의 결정을 존중해 주시고 누군가에게 보답을 해야 한다는 것은 가끔씩 아주 부담스러울 수 있다는 것을 기억하시고 균형을 맞출 수 있도록 하세요.

6. 독해문제

"다른 목소리들: 미국의 이민 여성들"에 채록된 인터뷰들은, 인터뷰 모음에 나타난 바와 같은 민족과 문화의 다양성에도 불구하고 그 주제는 상호 연관되어 있다. 1920년 뉴욕 시에서 보낸 첫 일주일의 생활을 이야기해준 이태리계 할머니에서부터 1989년 미국 공립학교에서의 첫 경험을 들려준 젊은 캄보디아 난민에 이르기까지 모든 여성들은 각자의 이야기거리가 있다. 어떤 얘기들은 미국 도시 생활에서 부딪힌 경제적 궁핍과 인종 편견에 관한 이야기들도 있다. 수집된 인터뷰는 시기적절하게 나온 매우 소중한 구술 사료이다.

【정답】

(1) ⓒ

(2) ⓓ

(3) ⓐ

7. 유머영어

(1) 숙제

어떤 5학년 학생의 얼굴 표정이 시무룩해지자, 담임 선생님이 물었다. "무슨일이니, 캐롤? 또 숙제를 안 했니?" "저, 어, 네" 캐롤이 대답했다. "멍청하게도 숙제한 공책으로 비행기를 접었어요." "캐롤, 네 말대로 잘한 일은 아니구나" 선생님이 말했다. "하지만 이번 한 번만 봐줄 테니까, 접은 비행기를 다시 펴서 숙제한 거 내도록 해." "저, 그런데, 그렇게 할 수 없어요." 얼굴 표정이 더 일그러진 캐롤이 말했다. "사실은 비행기가 납치되었거든요."

(2) 이상한 신혼여행

스코틀랜드 고지 사람들 고유의 복장 타탄 차림의 남자가 더블린의 킹즈브리지 역 플랫홈에 서 있는데 킬트 치마 차림의 또 한 사람의 스코틀랜드 남자가 다가와서 물었다. "어디로 가슈?" "킬러니로 신혼여행가요"라고 그 사람은 대답했다. "신부는 어디 갔어요?" "집에 있어요. 전에 거기 다녀왔다기에 집에 두고 온 겁니다"라고 신랑은 대답했다.

제15장

1. Warm-up

(1) 수 십년 동안의 불경기로 인해 현재는 황폐한 곳이 되었지만, 예전에 화려했던 이 휴양지의 잔상은 아직도 남아 있다.

(2) Micro Software사는 최근에 발생한 시장 수익을 가격인하 덕으로 돌렸다.

(3) 대표자들이 관세를 낮추자는 요청을 만장일치로 지지하는 가운데, 유럽 무역 심의는 결말이 지어졌다.

(4) 성공적인 협상을 위한 처방은 모든 당사자들이 비평 없이 듣는 것을 필요로 한다.

(5) 반대의 내용을 보여주는 증거가 확실한데도 불구하고, 그 매니저는 여전히 나이든 직원 모두가 그들이 할 일을 알고 있는 것으로 가정했다.

(6) 대다수 사람들은 많은 거대 기업들의 국제적인 경영으로 인해 민족적 정체성이 위기에 처해졌다고 믿는다.

(7) 많은 사람들은 법과 질서의 가치를 믿는다. 그러므로 많은 정치인들은 법과 질서를 그들 정책의 중요한 부분으로 삼는다 .

(8) 일반적으로 한 명 이상의 선생님들이 그들 학생들의 성공에 공헌했다고 얘기되어질 수 있다.

(9) 의사가 지시한 때에 맞추어 조제된 약을 먹는다면 더 효과가 있다.

(10) 주(州) 외로부터 누군가를 고용하는 비용이 가장 적게 드는 방법은 고용자가 지원자와 전화상으로 면접하는 것이다.

2. 시사용어

(1) 단체교섭

한국경영자총협회(경총)는 어제 비정규직 근로자들의 동등 대우를 거부할 것을 기업체들에게 권고했다. 배포된 단체교섭에 관한 지침서에서 경총은 또한 주 40시간 근무제가 회원 기업체에서 실시되면 유급 휴가를 축소할 것을 권고했다. 이러한 권고는 노동조합의 요구에 반하는 것으로서, 올해 다가오는 많은 기업체들의 단체교섭에서 사용자와 노조간 대규모 대립이 발생할 수도 있다는 점을 시사한다

cf Labor union(노동조합)이 사용자 또는 사용자의 단체와 조합원의 근로조건의 유지 · 개선 등에 관해서 행하는 교섭을 말함. 근로자 개인의 개별 교섭에 대신하여, 가입 조합원의 이익을 대표하는 조합(조직)이 주체가 되어 사용자와 교섭하고 협정을 맺는다는 의미에서 collective bargaining이라고 한다. 파업이나 사업장 폐쇄를 대신하는 평화적 교섭에 의한 분쟁해결의 방식이라는 뜻도 내포되어 있다. 오늘날에는 Labor Union의 주요 기능으로, 노동조합법에 의거, 근로자의 collective bargaining이 보장되어 있다. 통상적으로 단체협약 개정을 위하여는 정기적인 collective bargaining은 2년에 1회씩 실시하며, 단체협약 유효기간 도중에 보충적 교섭을 갖는 경우에는 유효기간 도중이라도 collective bargaining이 진행될 수 있으며, 임금협상을 위한 collective bargaining은 임금을 1년에 1회 이상 인상하는 것이 통상 관례이기 때문에 1년에 1회 이상 이루어진다. 참고로 단체협약이라 함은 labor union 등 근로자 단체가 사용자 또는 사용자 단체에 대한 단체교섭권을 행사하여 교섭을 하고, 그 결과 교섭의 대상으로 삼은 근로조건에 관한 사항, 기타 labor relations(노동관계)에 관한 사항에 대하여 평화적 · 자주적으로 합의에 도달하여 노사 당사자간에 결정한 내용을 합의 형식으로 체결한 것을 지칭한다.

(2) 얼짱 신드롬

이러한 외모 지상주의는 한국 사회에 새로운 것이 아니다. 많은 여성들은 1990년대 초부터 성형수술을 시도해 왔다. 하지만 "얼짱 신드롬"이라고 불리는 것이 국민적인 단어로 등장하면서 더욱 심각해지고 있는 듯하다. 얼짱은 영어로는 예쁜 얼굴을 의미하는 속어로서 10대들 사이에 가장 먼저 인기를 얻었다.

cf 2003년 이후 Internet을 통해 국내에 유행하고 있는 외모 지상주의를 반영하는 사회적 현상을 말함. 얼짱은 얼굴 짱의 준말로 얼굴이 잘 생긴 것으로 지칭하는 중 · 고등학교 학생들의 은어이자 Internet 신조어이다. Digital camera로 촬영한 사진을 Internet 상에 올려 놓고 일종의 contest를 하다가 netizen 사이에 노출, 확산된 것을 계기로 유행하기 시작한 것으로 알려져 있다. 이는 새로운 것을 즐기려는 netizen들의 욕구를 반영한 대표적인 cyber culture로서 최근에는 Internet뿐 아니라 현실 세계에서도 하나의 신드롬(syndrome)으로 자리잡은 상태이다. 헬스, 성형, 다이어트, 피부미용 등 뷰티사업이 호황을 누리는가 하면 대학가에서도 건강 외모와 관련된 강의가 인기를 모을 정도다. 얼짱 외에도 몸짱, 멋짱 등의 신조어까지 등장한 이같은 사회적 추세로 인해 얼짱의 개념을 확대하면서 스포츠 스타, 정치인, 아나운서 중에도 얼짱이 탄생했다. 심지어 최근에는 현상수배 전단 속 여성도 '강도 얼짱'이란 별명으로 인기를 얻고, 청문회 증인이 '증인 얼짱'으로 인기를 얻기에 이르렀다. 전문가들 사이에는 방송 매체 등이 상업적 목적으로 '얼짱', '몸짱'을 추세로 몰고 간다는 비판적 의견이 많다. 단순히 몸과 얼굴이 예쁘다고 팬 클럽(fan club)이 생기고 스타가 되는 것은 Internet의 선정성과 가벼움이 낳은 병리적 현상이란 지적도 만만치 않다.

3. 실용영어

(1) 초대하기 1 (정식으로 상대방 초대)

존, 회사에 한번 방문해 주시길 기대하겠습니다.
이 선생님의 정년 퇴임 저녁식사에 와 주십시오.

샐리, 제 생일 파티에 와 주시면 감사하겠습니다.
이번 주 토요일에 오셔서 저희와 식사하시지요.
퍼렐 씨 그리고 사모님, 이번 주 금요일 6시에 방문해 주십시오.
클라크 여사, 내일 점심식사에 참석해 주십시오. 제 남편께서도 몹시 기뻐하실 겁니다.
수잔, 제가 내일 7시에 댁으로 모시러 가겠습니다.
12월 28일에 동부인하시길 기대합니다.

*** 관련대화**

Case 1)

A: 이번 주 토요일에 오셔서 함께 식사를 하시겠습니까?
B: 초대해 주셔서 감사합니다.

Case 2)

A: 샐리, 내일 내 생일에 꼭 뵙도록 해요.
B: 미안해요, 선약이 있어요.

Case 3)

A: 이 선생님의 퇴임 저녁식사에 함께 오십시오.
B: 알겠습니다. 언제, 어디서 하나요?

(2) 초대하기 2 (정중하게 손님 초대하기)

내일 시간 있으시면, 동부인하셔서 제 딸의 생일파티에 참석해 주십시오.
모리슨 씨 그리고 사모님, 내일 저녁 초대를 하고 싶습니다. 저희 결혼 기념일이거든요.
짐, 내일 제 진급 축하 파티에 초대하고 싶습니다.
내일은 회사 창립 기념일입니다. 내일 7시에 저녁 초대를 하고 싶습니다.
랠프, 오늘 저녁 함께 해요. 휴의 승진 기념 파티를 할 거에요.
고울든 씨, 오늘 저녁에 혹시 시간 있으세요? 그러시다면, 오늘 저녁 제 아들의 귀향 기념 파티에 초대하고 싶습니다. 막 군 복무를 마쳤거든요.
저희들의 새로운 시설 참관 초대에 와 주시면 영광이겠습니다.

• 관련대화

Case 1)

A: 내일 시간 있으시면, 부인과 함께 제 딸의 생일 파티에 와 주십시오.

B: 물론이죠. 파티는 몇 시에 시작합니까?

Case 2)

A: 내일이 회사 창립 기념일입니다. 7시 저녁 식사에 오시겠습니까?

B: 물론이죠, 초대해 주셔서 감사합니다.

(3) 초대하기 3 (초대에 대한 대답)

몇 시에 당신 사무실에 들릴까요?

클린트 씨, 귀사를 방문하고 싶습니다.

파티에 몇 시에 갈까요?

찰스, 당신 집에 6시 30분쯤 가면 어때요?

피어리 씨 그리고 사모님, 결혼 기념 파티에 초대해 주셔서 감사합니다.

파티에 제 아이들과 함께 가도 되겠습니까?

힐러리 여사, 내일 파티에 초대해 주셔서 감사합니다.

12월 28일의 저녁 만찬에 초대해 주셔서 감사합니다. 저와 남편은 기꺼이 파티에 참석하겠습니다.

• 관련대화

Case 1)

A: 파티에 몇 시까지 가면 되겠습니까?

B: 저녁 식사는 7시에 시작합니다. 그러니 6시 경에 오십시오.

Case 2)

A: 우리 애들을 파티에 데려가도 되나요?

B: 물론이죠!

Case 3)

A: 몇 시에 사무실에 들릴까요?

B: 오전 10:30이면 좋겠는데요.

(4) 초대하기 4 (파티의 host가 되어 직접 손님 맞이하기)

맬로리 씨 그리고 사모님, 이쪽으로 오시죠.
론, 당신 집이라고 생각해요. (편하게 계세요.)
이 선생님, 여기 앉으세요.
숀, 여기 앉으시겠습니까?
린다, 당신을 위해 선물을 준비했습니다.
지금 열어봐도 돼요?
랜더스 씨, 변변치 않지만, 당신 드리려고 일본에서 선물을 준비해 왔습니다.
사모님, 집 구경 시켜 드리겠습니다. 이쪽으로 오시죠.
여러분, 축배의 잔을 듭시다.
윌, 갈비 좀더 드세요.
손을 좀 씻고 싶습니다. (화장실이 어딘가요?)
로스 씨, 좀더 들어요.

• **관련대화**

Case 1)

A: 로스 씨, 좀더 들어요.
B: 많이 먹었습니다

Case 2)

A: 랜더스 씨, 일본에서 작은 선물을 하나 준비해 왔습니다.
B: 정말 아름답군요!

Case 3)

A: 손을 좀 씻고 싶습니다.
B: 이쪽으로 오세요.

4. 국제뉴스

옛 동구권 7개국, 나토 가입

월요일 나토(NATO)는 러시아 국경으로 군사력을 뻗치게 되는 역사적인 회원 확대로 동유럽 7개국과 신규 회원국 서명을 체결함으로써 러시아의 우려를 증가시켰다. 불가리아, 에스토니아, 라트비아, 리투아니아, 루마니아, 슬로바키아 및 슬로베니아의 총리들이 북대서양조약기구, 즉 NATO가 만든 워싱턴 조약에 정식 가입 비준서를 제출, 나토 회원국은 26개국이 되었다.

"이곳에 모인 7개국 정상들과 그 국민들에게 역사상 가장 위대하고 가장 성공적인 동맹 기구에 가입한 것을 환영합니다. 환영합니다,"라고 콜린 파월 미 국무장관이 말했다. 그는 이번 회원국 확대는 발트해로부터 흑해까지 유럽의 자유, 안보 지대를 확대하려는 목적 달성의 하나의 "역사적인 진보"라고 말했다. "나토는 무엇보다 침략 저지를 다짐하고 있다"며 "해방의 범위를 확대하고 평화를 뿌리내리기를 다짐한다"고 파월은 말했다. "오늘날, 우리 동맹체는 새로운 적에 직면하고 있는데, 이 적은 뉴욕에서 마드리드에 이르기까지 무고한 사람들을 죽음으로 몰아가고 있다. 테러리스트들은 이 동맹기구가 지향하는 모든 것을 싫어한다. 그들은 우리의 자유를 경멸하며 우리의 단합을 두려워한다"고 그는 말했다.

5. Annie

친구 왕따 만들기

애니 여사에게:

지금 살고 있는 집으로 이사온 지 1년이 조금 넘었습니다. 이사 오자마자 다섯살짜리 아들 "카일"은 가까이 살고 있는 꼬마 세 명과 곧 친구가 되었습니다. 처음에는 제가 애들과 그 엄마들을 초대해 저희 집에서 놀게 했고, 다음에는 이웃들이 놀이 모임을 가졌습니다. 그런데 몇 달 전에 엄마들 중 한 사람("준"이라고 부르겠습니다)이 놀이 모임에 제 아들을 제외하기 시작했습니다. 우리 집 창문으로 그 집이 보이기 때문에 그녀가 다른 애들을 초대해서 놀고 있는 것이 보이면 카일은 울면서 왜 자기는 부르지 않았냐고 묻습니다.

지난 할로윈 때 준은 이웃에 살고 있는 애들을 모아서 사탕얻기(트릭 오어 트리팅)에 나섰습니다. 카일에게는 함께 가자는 말이 없었습니다. 왜 카일은 뺐는지 준에게 물었더니 그녀는 자기 밴에 자리가 부족해서였다고 대답했습니다. 또 준이 부활절 달걀사냥 놀이에 나섰을 때도 역시 카일을 부르지 않았습니다. 이웃에 사는 아이들 중 유일하게 카일만 함께 가지 못했습니다. 무슨 일이 있는지 이웃들에게 물어 보았지만, 전혀 아는 바가 없다고 했습니다. 카일은 주의력결핍, 과잉행동장애가 있어 가끔 가다 흥분하는 수가 있지만, 제가 항상 따라 다니며 진정시킵니다. 다른 엄마들 말로는 카일이 말썽을 피운 적은 전혀 없다고 합니다.

여사님, 애들은 아주 오랫동안 서로 이웃하며 살아야 할 것입니다. 준은 저를 만날 때면 항상 즐거운 기분입니다. 저희 집에서 놀이 모임을 가질 때면 저는 지금도 그들을 초대하고, 또 그들도 항상 초대에 응합니다. 문제가 있는지를 단도직입적으로 그녀에게 물어야 할까요, 아니면 그냥 그대로 있으면서 잘 되기만을 빌어야 할까요?

–뉴저지에서 가슴 아픈 엄마

뉴저지 분에게:

이제는 물어 보아야 할 것 같습니다. 카일의 행동이 다른 엄마들에게는 문제가 되지 않지만 준에게는 상당히 부담이 되는지도 모릅니다. 또는 그녀의 아들이 카일이 오는 것을 반기지 않는다고 말했을 수도 있습니다. 애들은 종종 다른 아이를 배척하는 단계를 지나곤 합니다. 만약 그게 원인이라면 준은 아들에게 정당함과 친절에 대해 이야기하고 다른 아이에게 상처를 주는 것은 바람직한 행동이 아니라는 것을 설명해 주어야 합니다.

그러는 한편 카일을 이웃 외에도 친구를 사귈 수 있는 활동에 참가시켜 준의 집에서 일어나고 있는 일에 덜 관심을 가지도록 할 때입니다. 공원관리센터나 YMCA 또는 지역자치센터의 프로그램을 알아 보세요.

6. 독해문제

매년 전세계적으로 3백만명 이상의 어린이들이 기아로 사망하는 것으로 추정되고 있습니다. 지난해 아프리카와 중앙아메리카에서만 270만명의 어린이들이 기아로 사망했습니다. 이들은 저개발국가의 희생자들이지만, 여러분들은 이런 비극의 재발을 막는 데 일조할 수 있습니다. 어떻게 돕느냐고요? 여러분이 살고 있는 현지의 "어린이 구호 재단"으로 가능한 금액을 기부하시면 전세계 수백만명의 기아 어린이들에게 음식을 제공하는 데 도움을 줄 수 있습니다. 1달러로 하루 3명의 어린이들에게 음식을 제공할 수 있고, 5달러로 하루 15명의 어린이들을, 10달러로 하루 30명의 어린이들에게 음식을 제공할 수 있습니다. 여러분의 능력에 따라 기부하십시오. 생각해 보십시오–미국의 평균 저녁 식사 값은 30명의 어린이들에게 하루 음식을 제공할 수 있는 비용보다 많습니다. 현지 "어린이 구호 재단"으로 기부하십시오. 자세한 정보와 집에서 가장 가까운 곳의 "어린이 구호 재단"의 위치를 알고 싶으시면 555-KIDS로 전화주십시오. 현금 기부와 함께 통조림

류 식품과 의복의 기부도 가능합니다.

【정답】

(1) ⓑ

(2) ⓒ

(3) ⓓ

(4) ⓐ

7. 유머영어

(1) 집안일

직장을 가진 아내의 휴가는 끝났으나 나는 아직 휴가가 남아 있었다. 혼자 집에서 지내자니 따분했으므로 하루는 설겆이를 하고 먼지를 털며 집안을 깨끗이 정돈하여 아내가 깜짝 놀라게 해 줘야겠다고 마음먹었다. 나는 아내가 돌아와 극구 칭찬해줄 것으로 믿었으나 그녀의 입에서는 아무 소리도 나오지 않았다. 참다 못해 나는 불평했다. "나는 오늘 집안을 말끔히 치웠는데 당신은 본 척도 않는군." 그녀의 대답은 나로 하여금 새로운 것을 깨닫게 했다. "그랬군요. 그건 아무리 해봤자 알아주지 않는 일이란 걸 이제 알겠죠?"

(2) 실수

결혼을 6개월 앞두고 남자는 식구들에게 인사시키기 위해 약혼녀를 집으로 데리고 갔다. 95세의 할머니는 상냥하고 원기 왕성했으나 귀가 어두운 사람들이 대개 그러하듯 말소리가 컸다. 아가씨는 그 집 거실에서 할머님 자손들의 사진을 보고 있었는데 그 때 할머니는 손자를 한 쪽으로 데리고 가서 조심스럽게 말한다는 것이 그만 큰 소리가 나왔다. "걱정할 것 없다. 네가 딴 여자아이랑 찍은 사진들은 내가 죄다 치워버렸다."

시사영어산책

2판 4쇄 발행	2010년 2월 25일
	저 자 이 종 호
	발행인 남 승 우
발행처	**남두도서**
	서울시 동작구 사당로9가길 6(사당동 220-43)
	TEL : (02) 595-1692~4
	FAX : (02) 595-1394
	E-mail : namdoo6@unitel.co.kr
	신고 : 5-76호 (1998. 11. 4)

정가 13,000 원

ISBN 89-5780-071-9 03740